Christians and Muslims

The London Lectures in Contemporary Christianity

This is an annual series of lectures founded in 1974 to promote Christian thought about contemporary issues. Their aim is to expound an aspect of historical biblical Christianity and to relate it to a contemporary issue in the church in the world. They seek to be scholarly in content yet popular enough in appeal and style to attract the educated public; and to present each topic in such a way as to be of interest to the widest possible audience as well as to the Christian public.

Recent lectures:

1995 'The Spirit of the Age', *Roy McCloughry* (published by IVP in 2001 as *Living in the Presence of the Future*)

1996 'The Word on the Box: Christians in the media', *Justin Philips, Graham Mytton, Alan Rogers, Robert McLeish, Tim Dean*

1997 'Matters of Life and Death: Contemporary medical dilemmas in the light of the Christian faith', *Professor John Wyatt* (published by IVP in 1998 as *Matters of Life and Death: Today's healthcare dilemmas in the light of Christian faith*)

1998 'Endless Conflict or Empty Tolerance: The Christian response to a multi-faith world', *Dr Vinoth Ramachandra* (published by IVP in 1999 as *Faiths in Conflict: Christian integrity in a multicultural world*)

(1999 'Justice that Restores', *Charles Colson* [lectures not delivered, but published by IVP in 2000 as *Justice that Restores*])

2000 'The Incomparable Christ: Celebrating his millennial birth', *John Stott* (published by IVP in 2001 as *The Incomparable Christ*)

2001 'Moral Leadership', *Bishop James Jones* (published by IVP in 2002 as *The Moral Leader: For the church and the world*)

2002 'Moving Genes: Evolving Promise or Un-natural Selection?', *John Bryant* (published by IVP in 2004 as *Life in our Hands: A Christian perspective on genetics and cloning*)

2003 'Can Christianity and Islam co-exist in the 21st century?' *Professor Peter G. Riddell* (published by IVP in 2004 as *Christians and Muslims: Pressures and potential in a post-9/11 world*)

The London Lectures Trust

The London Lectures in Contemporary Christianity are organized by the London Lectures Trust, which was established as a charity in 1994. The committee represents several different evangelical organizations.

Peter Riddell

Christians and Muslims
Pressures and potential in a post-9/11 world

The London Lectures in
Contemporary
Christianity

Inter-Varsity Press

INTER-VARSITY PRESS
38 De Montfort Street, Leicester LEI 7GP, England
Email: ivp@uccf.org.uk
Website: www.ivpbooks.com

First published 2004

British Library Cataloguing in Publication Data
A catalogue record for this book is available from the British Library.

ISBN 1-84474-060-9

Set in Adobe Garamond 10/12pt
Typeset in Great Britain by Servis Filmsetting Ltd, Manchester
Printed and bound in Great Britain by Creative Print and Design (Wales), Ebbw Vale

Inter-Varsity Press is the publishing division of the Universities and Colleges Christian Fellowship (formerly the Inter-Varsity Fellowship), a student movement linking Christian Unions in universities and colleges throughout Great Britain, and a member movement of the International Fellowship of Evangelical Students. For more information about local and national activities write to UCCF, 38 De Montfort Street, Leicester LEI 7GP, email us at email@uccf.org.uk, or visit the UCCF website at www.uccf.org.uk.

PRAYER

Sometimes, when I pray,
Not always,
But when I feel
Lost, lonely and afraid,
I humbly kneel
And wait,
Until it seems to me
A Presence stands
Beyond a fragile curtain,
And I know my Lord
Is there

I sense a holy warmth
Enveloping me
And know that he is listening
To my anguished plea
For aid for those in trouble
And for his love and guidance
For myself.

And as I wait,
In my mind, without volition,
I hear the words
'Fear not, my child'
And with them flows
A smiling inner Peace
Which restores my soul
And reassures me
That his love is everlasting.

In my heart
I sometimes long
To pass beyond that fragile curtain
Into his Light,
And know that when I do
He will be there to take my hand
And lead me, without fear,
Away from earthly cares
Into his eternal Peace.

Nancy M. Riddell, 1989

CONTENTS

PREFACE

This work represents the fruit of several areas of activity. First, I have taught a range of subjects connected with Christian–Muslim relations since 1995 in a number of tertiary institutions, and this book represents a synthesis of some of the teaching material I have assembled over the years. Secondly, my on-the-ground involvement in international development work for seven years, first with IDP Education Australia and then with World Vision Australia, was primarily in connection with diverse Muslim communities, and insights gained through this experience have fed into the current volume in various ways. Perhaps most importantly, friendships formed with Muslims over the last three decades have enabled me to crystallize my own perspectives as a Christian on other faiths, particularly on Islam, and these are reflected in this volume, particularly in the later chapters.

I am greatly indebted to a number of organizations and individuals for their role in helping this book to see the light of day. My thanks go to London School of Theology (formerly London Bible College), my home institution, which has provided me with a context for developing most of these materials. I am also grateful to the London Lectures Trust, which provided the platform by way of the 2003 London Lectures series to compile these materials into their present form. I am indebted, too, to Houghton College in the United States of America, which kindly gave me the opportunity to repeat the London Lectures at their campus in February 2004 with funding from the Staley Foundation. Similarly, my thanks are due to St Mark's National Theological Centre in Australia, which employed me to develop and run a course on its undergraduate pro-gramme focusing on Christian–Muslim dialogue, on which these materials have been trialled.

Many individuals have helped in the preparation of this volume in various ways. I am grateful to Mark Greene, Professor Anthony H. Johns, Joel Edwards and Bishop Michael Nazir-Ali for having acted as chairmen for the 2003 London Lectures. My considerable appreciation for commenting on various drafts of these materials goes to Andy Bannister, Peter Cotterell,

Colin Chapman, Eun-ah Hur, Anthony Johns, Anthony O'Mahony, Owen Pidgeon, Radko Popov, Beverly Riddell and Keith Small.

This volume addresses the question why Christians and Muslims need to work on their relationship. It would be appropriate to make a brief comment on this. The fact that Christianity and Islam share so much in terms of their respective theologies should be reason enough for closer relationship. But, in addition, the past history of Christian–Muslim conflict, taken in the context of our present age of growing Christian–Muslim rivalry, provides a compelling reason for Christians and Muslims in wide-ranging contexts to sit and talk, share, form friendships, and listen to each other's faith perspectives.

This volume is primarily written for a Christian audience. Readers wishing to gain a focused Muslim perspective on the issue of Christian–Muslim dialogue are referred to Ataullah Siddiqui's *Christian–Muslim Dialogue in the Twentieth Century* (1997), as well as to other relevant works mentioned in the bibliography. I hope that, in addition to providing tools for Christians to interact with Muslims, this volume's focus on diverse Christian approaches will contribute to building intra-Christian respect and, where appropriate, co-operation. For if we Christians cannot build bridges with Christian denominations other than our own, how can we expect to build bridges with non-Christians?

The book surveys ideological approaches and activities embraced by various expressions of Christianity: liberal, traditionalist and evangelical. At successive stages of volume preparation, reader advisors were sought from all these traditions. Though some readers may feel that my views belong to a particular Christian stream, it is hoped that this will not preclude Christians of wide-ranging positions from finding some benefit in this volume.

The volume is not designed exclusively for an academic setting. On the contrary, it is hoped that it will be accessible to Christians in all the churches. For this reason I have tried not to engage in 'footnote scholarship', as it were, though I have sought to achieve a sufficient measure of scholarly rigour to make the volume credible in academic circles.

Biblical references are drawn from the New International Version. Qur'anic verses are drawn from the Yusuf Ali rendering. References to the Qur'an are given in the form 'Q 9:36' (Qur'an, sura 9, verse 36).

Finally, readers are encouraged to talk to God through prayer in engaging with these materials. Different Christian readers will have different objectives in engaging with Muslims, but all will agree that seeking to further God's purposes in the world should be a valid goal of interfaith contacts. A challenge lies in knowing precisely what God's will is in our respective circumstances, and a good way to address this challenge is through prayer. In the process, Christians will be engaging in an activity that resonates with Muslims, and this can serve as a powerful tool in building interfaith relationships and in dedicating our interfaith efforts to fulfilling the wishes of our Creator, whom we all seek to please.

Peter G. Riddell

ABBREVIATIONS

AMS	Association of Muslim Schools (UK)
CCBI	Council of Churches for Britain and Ireland
IHRC	Islamic Human Rights Commission
ISCA	Islamic Supreme Council of America
LCWE	Lausanne Committee for World Evangelization
MCB	Muslim Council of Britain
MPGB	Muslim Parliament of Great Britain
NEAC	National Evangelical Anglican Congress
OIC	Organization of Islamic Conference
OIRRD	Office on Interreligious Relations and Dialogue (WCC)
PISAI	Pontifical Institute for the Study of Arabic and Islam
RLC	Religious Liberty Commission (WEF/WEA)
UMO	Union of Muslim Organisations
WCC	World Council of Churches
WEA	World Evangelical Alliance
WEF	World Evangelical Fellowship

INTRODUCTION

Defining the constituencies

Both Christianity and Islam are characterized by great diversity, producing debate and revitalization within both constituencies. A user-friendly typology of adherents of both faiths would help us in our journey into Christian–Muslim relations.

Religion and culture are inextricably intertwined. Many Christians and Muslims consider themselves primarily 'cultural' members of their faiths; that is, they identify their faith according to their historical and cultural heritage. For example, a poll in late 2003, commissioned by the Church of England and English Heritage, found that 40% of people in Britain planned to attend a Christmas church service that year,[1] a far higher number than the approximately 9% of the population that regularly attends church services throughout the year. The significance of the cultural Christian phenomenon was even more evident from the 2001 British census, which revealed that 72% of the population identified itself as Christian.

Though the spiritual commitment of cultural Christians and Muslims may be, and often is, not firmly anchored, it is nevertheless important to be aware of the core elements of their faith heritage in any interactions with such people. The elements of belief of the faith may be below the surface of their consciousness, but nevertheless core religious belief usually represents an important element in the cultural worldview of such Christians and Muslims.

For practising Christians and Muslims who regularly engage in an active worship life, core religious belief represents an even more important element in their cultural identity. Many deliberately seek the company of like-minded fellow believers, in order to establish a sub-culture within the broader society in which they find themselves. For them, their faith commitment and practice become inseparable from their cultural identity.

These observations demonstrate the necessity of painting a portrait of the religious communities in question in a way that will identify key streams, trends and sub-groups. This will prevent our falling into the trap of stereotyping.

There are many ways to slice the Christian and Muslim cakes. With regard to the former, the well-established typology within the Anglican Church, based on a differentiation between liberal, traditionalist and evangelical wings, is useful, though the boundary lines are often fuzzy.

A typology of Christians

Christian liberals characteristically use modern context and realities as their starting point in formulating opinion and policy. Their window faces out on to the modern world. Their view may involve a selective use of the biblical materials, which they consider to be texts that emerge from specific historical contexts that may or may not be relevant to modern times. For liberals, no issue is beyond scrutiny, and no authority, be it personal or scriptural, should be regarded as warranting unquestioning obedience.

Christian traditionalists place primary emphasis on accumulated church wisdom as reflected in the writings and thoughts of great Christian minds over the centuries. The biblical materials represent only part of the literary storehouse of the church. The traditionalists' window looks out on the centuries of Christian history and thought. Traditionalists at the grass roots tend to regard policies enunciated by the church leadership as necessarily sound and a model for living.

Christian evangelicals identify the Bible as their focal point in formulating opinion and policy. The biblical materials, seen as God's Word and therefore as propounding a set of ultimate truths, represent a divine yardstick. Nevertheless, there are disagreements among evangelicals as to whether '(every word of) the Bible *is* divine truth' or, rather, whether 'the Bible *contains* (a measure of) divine truth'. Contemporary issues are discussed and policies are formulated according to biblical wisdom. Their window opens on to both the biblical materials and how they inform modern demands and challenges.[2]

A typology of Muslims

In the case of Muslims, a threefold typology is also useful, especially in discussing Muslim reactions to the modern world. Such a threefold categorization is consistent with the views of several prominent British Muslims. Ataullah Siddiqui of the Islamic Foundation in Leicester writes of a threefold split between modernists, traditionalists and revivalists.[3] Ishtiaq Ahmed, scholar of Pakistani politics[4] and chairman of the Bradford Council for Mosques, agrees with this typology, further suggesting a proportional allocation to modernists, traditionalists and revivalists of 15%, 70% and 15% respectively.[5] This threefold typology is similar to that articulated by the Canadian scholar Andrew Rippin,[6] in conjunction with others,[7] who analysed different Muslim responses to the challenges of modernity. So we shall follow such a threefold typology, though we shall slightly adjust the labels.

Muslim modernizers are concerned with defining faith within a contemporary world context. They follow a method of interpreting the Islamic primary texts to fit the modern context. This leads some down a secularizing path, including the 'cultural' Muslims referred to above, and some children of Muslim immigrants born in the West. This approach resonates with liberal Christian approaches to a certain degree. Many, but not all, Muslim modernizers are based in the West.

Muslim traditionalists emphasize the primacy of the scholarly elite, with congregations trained to acknowledge the wisdom of accumulated traditional authority rather than to engage dynamically with the primary sources themselves. In Muslim minority communities in western countries, Muslim traditionalists tend to be the immigrant generation. This echoes certain features of High Church tradition.

Islamists use Islamic scripture as the filter through which all discussion passes. They dream of a past 'golden age', when the Prophet Muhammad was establishing his community in Medina and when God's law, the *shari'a*, held sway. Many Muslim young people born in the West of immigrant parents opt for the Islamist paradigm, because of a sense of alienation from the majority culture. The prioritizing of scripture bears some resemblance to the approach of Christian evangelicalism, though one must be wary of drawing facile parallels. A key distinguishing feature between modern Islamists and Christian evangelicals is the tendency of some of the former to adopt violent methods to achieve their goals. Furthermore, Islamists yearn for the wide-ranging implementation of *shari'a* law in a way that has no parallel among Christian evangelicals.

In the discussion that follows, much attention will be devoted to the nature of engagement between Muslims and Christians, especially in Britain. These communities will be conceived of in their broadest terms, with each community including in its membership those 'cultural' Christians and Muslims referred to earlier. A considerable overlap between Christianity and the West will thus be allowed in our analysis. This reflects the facts that, first, a significant majority of the British population identifies itself as Christian (72% in the 2001 population census) and, secondly, that Muslims usually see Christianity and the West as broadly synonymous. Ataullah Siddiqui alludes to this: 'Now that the United Nations . . . declared year 2001 as the year of Dialogue among Civilizations, the bi-lateral dialogue and its boundaries are now increasingly blurred. There is a lot more overlapping and sometimes it is difficult to differentiate the boundaries between Christian–Muslim dialogue and the Islam and the West dialogue.'[8]

The Bible and other religions

A key feature of this book will be a consideration of Christian attitudes to other faiths. An integral part of the churches' devising of approaches to other faiths down the ages has been reference to the Bible on this issue. It would thus be useful to consider at the outset biblical materials on this point, following the route taken so often by the churches of moving from them to policy and practice.

How does the Bible respond to pluralism, diversity and a multiplicity of religions? Does it take a pluralist line, saying that 'all religions are equally valid variations on a godly theme'? Or does it embrace a more exclusivist position, presenting God's blessing and grace as a restricted gift intended only for a select few? We shall address these questions by examining a selection of representative biblical verses, which point to four overriding themes.[9]

A universal blessing

From the very earliest point in the Bible, we are reminded by God's covenant with Noah (Genesis 9:8–17) and subsequent references that his blessings were intended for all nations and peoples, as is evident in the following passages:

> *Genesis 12:1–3*: The LORD had said to Abram . . .
>
> 'I will make you into a great nation
>   and I will bless you . . .
> and all peoples on earth
>   will be blessed through you.'
>
> *Genesis 18:17–18*: Then the LORD said . . . 'Abraham will surely become a great and powerful nation, and all nations on earth will be blessed through him.'

These verses point to the importance of Abraham as the vessel through whom all nations will be blessed. This theme is refined in other biblical passages that have a more messianic resonance. Nevertheless, though the channel of blessing may be differently identified, the concept of universal blessing is maintained:

> *Psalm 72:1, 17*: Endow the King with your justice, O God,
>   the royal son with your righteousness . . .
> All nations will be blessed through him,
>   and they will call him blessed.

A number of biblical verses further elucidate the message of universal blessing. All people are not only beneficiaries of this blessing, but also recipients of a measure of divine truth through general revelation,[10] and they will be held to account according to their adherence to this truth:

> *Romans 1:20*: For since the creation of the world God's invisible qualities – his eternal power and divine nature – have been clearly seen, being understood from what has been made, so that men are without excuse.

> *Malachi 1:11*: 'My name will be great among the nations, from the rising to the setting of the sun. In every place incense and pure offerings will be brought to my name, because my name will be great among the nations,' says the LORD Almighty.

> *Acts 10:34–35*: Then Peter began to speak: 'I now realise how true it is that God does not show favouritism but accepts men from every nation who fear him and do what is right . . .'

Those who turn away from God

Diverse biblical references, however, record the extent of human rejection of the universal blessing. This takes various forms, whether referring to the rejection by the Jews of their special revelation, by followers of Jesus, who might reject his message, or by others, who might reject the truths of general revelation:

> *Romans 1:21–23*: For although they knew God, they neither glorified him as God nor gave thanks to him, but their thinking became futile and their foolish hearts were darkened. Although they claimed to be wise, they became fools and exchanged the glory of the immortal God for images made to look like mortal man and birds and animals and reptiles.

Further in this vein, the Bible is very critical of certain religious practices:

> *Isaiah 2:6*: [The Israelites] are full of superstitions from the East;
> they practise divination like the Philistines
> and clasp hands with pagans.

> *Matthew 6:7*: 'And when you pray, do not keep on babbling like pagans, for they think they will be heard because of their many words.'

The reference from Isaiah suggests that not all religions are equal. Moreover, not only do certain other faiths include false worship practices, but the nation that had initially been chosen to serve as a model to the nations, the Israelites, was also inclined to adopt such practices. God warned the Israelites in the earliest times against following other faiths, specifying the punishment:

> *Deuteronomy 8:19*: If you ever forget the LORD your God and follow other gods and worship and bow down to them, I testify against you today that you will surely be destroyed.

God later spoke through the prophets to the Israelites, once again warning them against false worship practices, and reminding them of the rewards if they would follow his injunctions:

> *Jeremiah 7:1–2, 6–7, 9–10*: This is the word that came to Jeremiah from the LORD: 'Stand at the gate of the LORD's house and there proclaim this message:
> ' "Hear the word of the LORD, all you people of Judah who come through these gates to worship the LORD . . . if you do not oppress the alien, the fatherless or the widow and do not shed innocent blood in this place, and if you do not follow other gods to your own harm, then I will let you live in this place, in the land I gave your forefathers for ever and ever . . .
> ' "Will you steal and murder, commit adultery and perjury, burn incense to Baal and follow other gods you have not known, and then come and stand before me in this house, which bears my Name, and say, 'We are safe' – safe to do all these detestable things?" '

A similar note of warning is sounded in later New Testament materials, where the faithful are cautioned against turning away from the message of Christ:

> *2 John 7–11*: Many deceivers, who do not acknowledge Jesus Christ as coming in the flesh, have gone out into the world. Any such person is the deceiver and the antichrist. Watch out that you do not lose what you have worked for, but that you may be rewarded fully. Anyone who runs ahead and does not continue in the teaching of Christ does not have God; whoever continues in the teaching has both the Father and the Son. If anyone comes to you and does not bring this teaching, do not take him into your house or welcome him. Anyone who welcomes him shares in his wicked work.

Thus the Bible makes clear that the message of universal blessing is not unconditional. This blessing is intended for all on condition that people do not become embroiled in meaningless rituals, external formulas and misguided religious beliefs.

The centrality of faith

The message of Jesus in the New Testament serves as a corrective in response to this repeated turning away from God by all people. The corrective introduces the concept of faith.

> *Galatians 3:8–9*: The Scripture foresaw that God would justify the Gentiles by faith, and announced the gospel in advance to Abraham: 'All nations will be blessed through you.' So those who have faith are blessed along with Abraham, the man of faith.

Thus faith is the condition necessary in order to benefit from the universal blessing bestowed on all people. On a number of occasions, Jesus pays tribute to individuals who lie outside the normative boundaries of the Jewish faith, yet in fact demonstrate a measure of faith that is exemplary. In the Gospel of Luke, Jesus does not hesitate to point to the profound faith of the Roman centurion.

> *Luke 7:7–9*: 'I did not even consider myself worthy to come to you. But say the word, and my servant will be healed . . . '
> When Jesus heard this, he was amazed at [the centurion], and turning to the crowd following him, he said, 'I tell you, I have not found such great faith even in Israel.'

Similarly, in Matthew 15 Jesus responds compassionately to the Canaanite woman's plea to heal her daughter, pointing to the depth of the woman's faith. Thus possession of faith is not a matter of membership of an established religious group that follows certain codes or laws. Rather, it is a matter of belief, or a state of the mind and heart:

> *Romans 9:30–32*: What then shall we say? That the Gentiles, who did not pursue righteousness, have obtained it, a righteousness that is by faith; but Israel, who pursued a law of righteousness, has not attained it. Why not? Because they pursued it not by faith but as if it were by works. They stumbled over the 'stumbling stone'.

In this, acceptance of the teaching of Jesus is crucial.

> *Romans 10:4*: Christ is the end of the law so that there may be righteousness for everyone who believes.

Thus God's blessing is associated with many biblical personalities who were recognized as people of faith: Abraham when he was put to the test by God;

the Roman centurion; the Canaanite woman. The latter two had faith without being of The (established) Faith. Faith such as that of the centurion and the Canaanite woman is understood as following the teachings of Jesus. They had intuitive, untaught faith in Jesus and his covenant based on faith, not works alone.

Take the message out

Having enunciated the centrality of faith in order to do justice to God's universal blessing, the Bible proceeds to give a series of instructions to people of faith. They are exhorted to preach this new covenant throughout the world:

> *Matthew 28:18–20*: Then Jesus came to them and said, '. . . Go and make disciples of all nations, baptising them in the name of the Father and of the Son and of the Holy Spirit, and teaching them to obey everything I have commanded you.'

Methodological guidance

The message of this new covenant is not one of disrespect, hostility, arrogance or violence. Rather, people of faith are urged to be models of love, respect, compassion and gentleness in preaching the message of this new covenant.

This methodological approach is addressed in 1 Peter 3:8–22, where clear guidance is provided. Several key ideas come out of this text: the importance of living in harmony; the importance of compassion; the need to turn from evil and do good; and the need to seek peace. Verses 15–16 represent the core of this text for our purposes, as they provide us with two critically important lessons:

> *1 Peter 3:15–16*: Always be prepared to give an answer to everyone who asks you to give the reason for the hope that you have. But do this with gentleness and respect, keeping a clear conscience, so that those who speak maliciously against your good behaviour in Christ may be ashamed of their slander.

In other words, the compassionate, harmonious and positive interactions of people of faith with others should not be based on silence. People of faith should speak about their faith, and share the good news of Christ with others in the hope that they will turn to him too. But in sharing the good news, people of faith must be respectful, show interest in the others, be prepared to listen as well as to speak, and be gentle, not aggressive, hostile or insulting.

The apostle Paul reconfirms this methodological approach in the letter to the Colossian church:

> *Colossians 4:5–6*: Be wise in the way you act towards outsiders; make the most of every opportunity. Let your conversation be always full of grace, seasoned with salt, so that you may know how to answer everyone.

In other words, people of faith should be considerate in their interactions with others, not missing opportunities to proclaim the Good News, but conducting themselves with sensitivity and tact.

Acts 17:16–32 also provides a sense of direction in the area of methodology. Paul is addressing the Athenians, and is concerned by their idolatry. He builds upon, rather than demolishes, his audience's culture and belief system. Commencing with a note of affirmation, Paul says, 'I see that in every way you Athenians are very religious.' He quotes from the audience's worldview and poets, so as not to offend. At the same time, he cites from the Athenian materials selectively, so as not to compromise the essence of Christ's message. He engages in diverse ways with different groups – Jews, Gentiles and passers-by in the square – and debates with Epicurean and Stoic teachers. Paul preaches with forthrightness about Jesus and the resurrection. Thus he affirms certain component parts of their belief, but expands them with the truth of the gospel.

It is not only the followers of Jesus who provide methodological guidance. The supreme exemplar, Jesus himself, serves as a model in his own interactions with outsiders. Thus, in John 4, Jesus demonstrates an approach of clarity mixed with sensitivity in his engagement with the Samaritan woman at the well.

It is important to draw together the key ideas emerging from our survey of biblical material. God blesses and makes himself known to all people in various ways. Some people, however, both insiders and outsiders, choose not to observe God's revealed truth, but engage in religious rituals that are meaningless and misguided. Some non-Christian 'outsiders' will have profound faith through God's general revelation, while some Christian 'insiders' will have little or no faith. People of faith[11] are called to preach the Good News of Jesus Christ to others in a forthright, though sensitive and tactful, manner.

This survey of a selection of biblical verses relating to attitudes to other faiths throws up a number of themes. Should the Christian reader give greater weight to verses that emphasize the universality of God's original blessing? Should the primary focus fall rather upon a theme of 'chosenness' of the biblical faiths? How does and should an early twenty-first-century western pluralist context influence our decision in responding to these questions? Christian scholars and practitioners have been greatly divided in recent times over these issues.

PART 1:
ISLAM AND THE WEST

1. THE HOW AND WHY OF CHANGING ATTITUDES

The relationship between Christianity and Islam has attracted increasing attention in recent decades. This fact has been reflected in many ways, including the development of 'Christian–Muslim relations' as a field of study in universities and colleges around the world. This development has been encouraged by many church groups, spanning liberal, traditionalist and evangelical streams, including the World Council of Churches.

Theological colleges and seminaries in the West that establish centres for Christian–Muslim relations are often asked the following question: 'Why would a Christian college want to set up a centre for the study of Islam?' There are a number of variations on this theme, such as 'Why are Christians promoting Islam?' or 'We don't have to look very far to see the evidence of weakening in Christian resolve and commitment among the traditionally Christian countries of the West, so why devote our finite energies to the study of other faiths?'

This questioning points to a sense of concern felt by many Christians about a perceived decline in Christian commitment in the West. But it is important to challenge any assumption that internal problems can be solved by withdrawing into one's shell. A political analogy may be relevant. If a political party loses support, it would be courting disaster if it were to speak to its membership only and ignore the policies of other parties that may have encroached upon its traditional base of support. Rather, political parties that feel that their fortunes are in decline usually respond with forthright and outward-looking efforts to engage with lost supporters and to learn from their competitors.

Christians need to identify appropriate strategies for regaining the ground they feel they have lost and for challenging what appear to be advances made by other ideologies, whether religious faiths or non-religious secularism.[1] Moreover, Christians need to be very clear in their own minds about how they view other faiths that seem to be 'fishing in the same pond'.

All this assumes a sense of *competition* among the various faiths. Yet need this be the only driving force for Christian engagement with other faiths?

Are there possibilities for *partnership* in certain areas, so that competition is not the only starting point for interaction between the faiths? Jacques Waardenburg points to risks resulting from an assumption of competition between communities:

> When we speak about 'Christian' and 'Muslim' minorities as opposed to 'Muslim' and 'Christian' majorities, is this not in fact political terminology that indicates and stresses a power relationship? And when we describe social and human realities in terms of numerical differences and power relationships, do we not in fact neglect the substance of social and human relationship? As long as relationships between a given minority and a given majority were conceived in terms of an opposition between two separated communities, the diversity that exists within both the majority and the minority group was necessarily obscured.[2]

Such issues have presented themselves to all the Christian churches in recent times, especially since the Second World War. Large population movements and migrations in that time have resulted in the creation of genuine multi-faith societies in western countries. These same societies had previously been, if not monolithically Christian, at least structured in such a way that Christianity was seen as being the default, with minority faiths largely pushed out of sight in terms of public policy and discourse.

Thus, in the second half of the twentieth century, the churches of necessity responded by addressing the challenging issue of appropriate Christian attitudes to and methods of engagement with other faiths. In this first chapter we shall consider the context of changing attitudes: the how and the why. This chapter will focus on the macro level, and will make particularly reference to the British context, though many of these observations hold true for other western societies. Subsequent chapters will focus more on the micro level, examining first the British Muslim community and its engagement with non-Muslim majority society. We shall then examine church responses in detail, presenting a range of practical methods used by various Christians in their interactions with Muslims, whatever the nature of those interactions. We shall conclude our study by addressing diverse issues that are of direct relevance to the relationship between Christianity and Islam as the two faiths move into the twenty-first century.

From exclusivism to inclusivism

Christian groups have held a wide spectrum of attitudes towards non-Christian religions. Three key generic points on the spectrum have come to be identified.

First, an *exclusivist* position: this applies to those who believe that Christianity, and only Christianity, possesses divinely revealed truth and offers a path towards salvation. This position tends to regard other religious faiths as either grossly misguided or outrightly satanic.

Secondly, an *inclusivist* position: this holds that certain other faiths may include some specific elements of divinely revealed truth but do not, of themselves, offer a complete path to salvation. In order to offer this, such religions need to embrace Christ. In other words, such religions without Christ represent, at the most, a halfway house.

Thirdly, a *pluralist* approach: adherents of this position tend to lessen the focus upon Christ and increase the primary focus upon God. They allow for other religions to be alternative manifestations of God's truth, offering alternative ways to salvation. From this viewpoint Christianity is merely one of many paths to a knowledge of God and salvation.

Historically, Christian churches have broadly adopted the exclusivist position, especially during the first millennium, the Crusades and the colonial period of the eighteenth and nineteenth centuries. As champions of the Christian faith, Europeans saw it as their duty to spread not only their civilization around the world, but also their faith. The two were often seen as being intertwined. Universal salvation would be denied to non-Christian communities unless they had access to the Christian message. Consider the following statement published in 1792 by William Carey, father of the modern missionary movement:

> Can we as men, or as Christians, hear that a great part of our fellow-creatures, whose souls are as immortal as ours, and who are as capable as ourselves, of adorning the gospel, and contributing by their preachings, writings, or practices to the glory of our Redeemer's name, and the good of his church, are enveloped in ignorance and barbarism? Can we hear that they are without the gospel, without government, without laws, and without arts, and sciences; and not exert ourselves to introduce amongst them the sentiments of men, and of Christians? Would not the spread of the gospel be the most effectual mean of their civilisation? Would not that make them useful members of society? We know that such effects did in a measure follow the afore-mentioned efforts of Eliot, Brainerd, and others amongst the American Indians; and if similar attempts were made in other parts of the world, and succeeded with a divine blessing (which we have every reason to think they would), might we not expect to see able Divines, or read well-conducted treatises in defence of the truth, even amongst those who at present seem to be scarcely human?[3]

Carey's emphasis on a link between Christianity and human advancement and civilization is clear from this quotation. It provides a window into attitudes in his day, a far cry from the British context of the early twenty-first century. His language would arouse some hostility within a postmodern western context because of his use of terms such as 'scarcely human' to refer to non-Christian populations. But such a response might overlook another important element in Carey's words; namely, his enormous confidence in the truth of the Christian message, as presented by the Gospels. It is the kind of confidence that underpins the exclusivist position referred to above, a confidence that has been greatly eroded in the modern West.

We can find examples of the way this confidence in the Christian message survived into the twentieth century. The great Christian scholar of Islamic law, Professor J. N. D. Anderson, wrote during the Second World War:

> Let us summarise the inadequacy of the religion of Islam . . . First, Islam is lacking in any adequate standard of ethical or moral living: the life of the prophet, when placed beside that of Christ, speaks for itself . . . Secondly, the religion of Mohammed provides no adequate or satisfying idea of the character of God . . . Thirdly, the Muslim knows nothing of Redemption . . . Lastly, the Muslim knows nothing of a sanctifying power . . . The Muslim, for all his proud boast of a later revelation, wanders sadly in the darkness.[4]

During the decades since World War II, Christian churches have increasingly devoted their attention and resources to the issue of relations between themselves and non-Christian religions. In drawing up policies and strategies for multifaith relations in the modern world, the churches have examined their contacts with other faiths dating back many centuries and spanning events as significant as the Crusades, the period of European colonial expansion, and the Ottoman Turkish invasions of the countries of Eastern Europe. As the post-colonial era unfolded after the Second World War, some churches felt a need to revise approaches to multifaith contact and to devise new policies and strategies. While some have reaffirmed exclusivist positions, most have made a marked shift from exclusivism towards inclusivism. This has involved moving from Carey's message of taking salvation to others to a consideration of what Christians can learn from others.

This desire to listen to non-Christian perspectives is encapsulated in Roger Hooker's engagement with Hindus, which sounds very different from the statements by Carey and Anderson: 'Hindus deeply resent the Christian claim that salvation is to be found *only* through Christ. This seems insufferably arrogant, the more so when it is made, as it usually is, in total ignorance of what Hindus actually believe and practise.'[5]

There was a time lapse of some 200 years between Carey's and Hooker's statements. This clearly reflects some considerable movement in church thinking towards inclusivism over this period *vis-à-vis* other faiths. In fact, all sections of Christendom have been torn by internal divisions as they have wrestled with one of the most controversial subjects in the modern church.[6] A number of significant factors within broader western society have nurtured and sustained this process of Christian reassessment of views towards other faiths. In the discussion which follows we shall address key factors that have sustained the 'inclusivist train' in recent decades.

The changing religious landscape in Britain

The first main factor driving the Christian reassessment of attitudes towards other faiths over the last half century was changing demography in western countries, which had a direct impact on the religious make-up of countries such as Britain. The surge in immigration to Britain from former colonies following the Second World War was to have a significant impact on religious demography. Numbers of immigrants per year increased from 3,000 in 1953 to 136,400 in 1961,[7] setting a trend for subsequent decades.

Table 1 shows changing patterns in nominal religious adherence in Britain for the period 1975–95.[8] These figures are borne out by the results of the 2001 census of the United Kingdom, where a question concerning religious affiliation was included for the first time. The results are given in Table 2.[9] Thus, for the Christian churches in Britain, no longer were other faiths a distant reality located in far-off lands. British Christians found during the second half of the twentieth century that their neighbourhoods had come to include growing numbers of adherents of non-Christian religions. These new faith communities brought the symbols of their faiths with them, so British towns that had previously been home only to Christian places of worship found increasingly that their skylines were shaped by Muslim

Table 1 Changing patterns in nominal religious adherence, Britain, 1975–95 (in millions)

	1975	1980	1985	1990	1995
Trinitarian churches	38.2	37.9	37.8	37.9	37.6
Hindus	0.1	0.2	0.3	0.3	0.4
Jews	0.4	0.3	0.3	0.3	0.3
Muslims	0.4	0.6	0.9	1.0	1.1
Sikhs	0.2	0.3	0.3	0.5	0.6
% population trinitarian	68	67	67	66	64
% population other	4	5	5	6	7
Total % of nominal adherents	72	72	72	72	71

Table 2 The UK population by religion, April 2001

	Thousands	%
Christian	42,079	71.7
Buddhist	152	0.3
Hindu	559	1.0
Jewish	267	0.5
Muslim	1,591	2.7
Sikh	336	0.6
Other religions	179	0.3
All religions	*45,163*	*76.8*
No religion	9,104	15.5
Not stated	4,289	7.3
All no religion/not stated	*13,626*	*23.2*
Base	*58,789*	*100*

mosques, Hindu temples, Sikh gurdwaras and so forth. This process stimu-lated the churches to reassess their attitudes towards these faiths.

In terms of our particular interest in Christian–Muslim interaction, these statistics suggest a clear comparative trend. The UK Muslim population increased from approximately 400,000 to 1.6 million in the twenty-five-year period between 1975 and 2001, representing an increase of 300%. In the same period the Christian population increased from 38.2 million to just over 42 million, an increase of 9%. Thus, heightened Christian attention to other faiths, including Islam, was inevitable in Britain.

It is important to note, however, that this factor has had an influence well out of proportion to the actual changes in demographics. The 2001 census still showed allegiance to trinitarian Christian groups of almost 72%, compared with barely 5% for other faiths. The concentration of other faiths in urban areas, especially in the capital, has meant that they have had a far greater impact on evolving church attitudes than would be expected of a relatively small minority. The census revealed that, on the one hand, London has the lowest proportion of people born in the United Kingdom (72.9%, compared to 87.4% nationally), and conversely the highest proportion of people from ethnic minority groups (28.8%, compared to 9% nationally).[10]

Furthermore, changing patterns of religious belief across Europe in the postwar period produced a situation where there was high spoken allegiance to state-church structures but low church attendance. When this was com-bined with a flourishing of New Age approaches and the rapid increase in numbers of declared atheists,[11] the increasing diversity of belief within nominal Christian communities provided further fuel for expanding inclusivism.

This factor also holds true for other western countries that are popular destinations for immigrants and asylum-seekers. The United States also witnessed a steady increase in immigration from countries with majority non-Christian populations during the latter half of the twentieth century. It too experienced a particular surge at the beginning of the twenty-first century, with 4.5 million new immigrants reaching the country in the two years following March 2000, of whom almost half were illegal immigrants.[12] In January 2004 it was estimated that a total of 8–10 million illegal immigrants were in the United States; while almost half of these were from Mexico,[13] significant numbers of both legal and illegal immigrants in recent times also came from majority Muslim countries.

Changing social attitudes: guilt in the West

Another factor facilitating reassessment of historical attitudes among Christians relates to the sense of guilt that manifested itself in parts of the West during the latter half of the twentieth century.

This guilt has deep roots. The rise of the middle classes in Europe in the seventeenth and eighteenth centuries had been accompanied by the emergence and flourishing of liberalism as an ideology. Liberalism is a very broad term, encompassing many sub-groups, but all of them sought an ideal society, based on certain core principles: the autonomy of the individual, freedom, reason, justice, toleration.[14]

The key early thinkers who contributed to the surge in liberal thought were John Locke and Adam Smith in England, Thomas Jefferson and Benjamin Franklin in the USA, Voltaire and Jean-Jacques Rousseau in France, and leading members of other European societies. The ideology of liberalism, however, was heavily underpinned by the spirit of Jesus' teachings in the New Testament, which lent themselves readily to ideas of emancipation from oppression.

The nineteenth century heralded the liberal push throughout Europe for mass education and voting rights, especially for men. But it was not only Europeans who benefited from these new winds of change. This new liberal thinking exerted an influence on colonial policy at certain times as well. This is evident in British policy in Malaya, where colonial authorities refrained from direct rule in most Malay states in the late nineteenth and early twentieth centuries, and went to great lengths to avoid intruding in matters relating to the Islamic faith of the Malay population.

Liberalism was also evident in Dutch policies at times in Indonesia, especially in the 'Ethical Policy' of the early twentieth century, which called for advances in education for Indonesians, improvement in living standards and involvement in government. The rise in liberal thought was particularly evident in the policies of the United States of America, a latecomer to colonialism, which began to put in place a programme for eventual independence for the Philippines within a decade of assuming control from the former Spanish colonial masters in 1898.

Liberal attitudes were uncomfortable with the more rapacious approaches to colonialism pursued by European colonial powers in earlier times. These liberal attitudes contributed to the development of a widespread guilt complex both in the colonial period and especially during the post-colonial era among former European colonial powers.

The famous English writer George Orwell served with the Colonial Police Force in Burma from 1922 to 1927. In his *Shooting an Elephant* he writes: 'I had already made up my mind that imperialism was an evil thing and the sooner I chucked up my job and got out of it the better. Theoretically – and secretly, of course – I was all for the Burmese and all against their oppressors, the British.' Further: 'when the white man turns tyrant it is his own freedom that he destroys'.[15]

This developing sense of guilt carried over into the realm of religious faith and mission. Edward Stourton speaks of how he was conditioned to hold a particular view regarding mission in the post-colonial period:

> I had my share of preconceptions about the missionary enterprise, especially in Africa, where it is so closely linked in our minds to colonialism. The image of the missionary as the spiritual arm of European domination and exploitation is difficult to shake, and there is a caricature of missionary history which moves from overweening arrogance in the days of European empire to paralysing self-doubt in the post-colonial era.[16]

The prominent missiologist Lamin Sanneh writes that 'modern historiography has established a tradition that mission was the surrogate of Western colonialism'.[17] This link is regularly asserted by Muslims; in the words of Kate Zebiri:

> The fact of the interrelationship between colonialism and Christian missions has become deeply embedded in the consciousness of most Muslims, and . . . has come to form part of the anti-Western rhetoric. The debate on the degree of collusion between missions and imperialism has become ideologically charged in the era of anti-colonial reaction, and often fails to take into account the haphazard nature of both colonial expansion and missionary activity.[18]

Sanneh writes more specifically of the impact of a guilt complex on the field of Christian mission in Africa in the 1960s:

> When at the age of 18 I approached a Methodist church in the Gambia with a request for baptism, thus signaling my conversion to Christianity from Islam, the resident senior minister, an English missionary, responded by inviting me to reconsider my decision. And, while I was at it, he said, I should also consider joining the Catholic Church. My conversion obviously caused him acute embarrassment, and I was mortified on account of it.[19]

A particular manifestation of the western sense of guilt for the past history of colonialism can be seen in the opposition among many western Christians to the concept of mission. Sanneh identifies diverse reasons for this loss of missionary commitment, including 'genuine . . . remorse, guilt, uncertainty, agnosticism, cultural exclusiveness, fear of criticism, disenchantment.'[20]

The confidence we saw in the statement by William Carey has all but gone from large sections of the church. 'Conversion' has become a dirty word. Sanneh comments:

> I have found Western Christians to be very embarrassed about meeting converts from Asia or Africa . . . Furthermore, when I have pointed out that missionaries actually made comparatively few converts, my Western friends have reacted with obvious relief, though with another part of their minds, they insist that missionaries have regularly used their superior cultural advantage to instill a sense of inferiority in natives.[21]

A further manifestation of the guilt complex in the West is the reluctance to express criticism of certain aspects of non-western cultures. This reluctance takes many forms. Susan Okin relates this to women's issues:

> Liberal guilt about colonialism plays a large role in the 'hands off other cultures' approach, just as anger about colonialism plays a large role in the desire to preserve cultures that are so preoccupied with controlling women. Clearly, colonialism had many very bad effects. But why make things even worse by letting our guilt and anger about colonialism constrict the life prospects of women, under the guise of cultural preservation?[22]

Okin's comments have a direct bearing on a phenomenon of a 'cult of silence', which is addressed later in our discussion.

This guilt complex has played a big part in determining the approach of western societies in general, and the western church in particular, in their interactions with communities and faiths of formerly colonized peoples. With regard to Christian–Muslim relations, this guilt complex has very much impacted on the style of interaction between the western churches and Muslim communities in western countries.

Changing official policy directions
Issues of social advocacy have assumed increasing importance as a direct result of the growing proportion of non-Christian communities in Britain and changing social attitudes. This has triggered the preparation of a number of policy documents related to minority-faith rights. They have in turn played a role in stimulating Christian reassessment of traditional attitudes towards other faiths.

The Runnymede Trust reports
One of the key actors in producing such documents that have influenced official policy has been the Runnymede Trust. This body, a private think-tank funded from various sources, has a long-established reputation for producing influential reports on matters of social concern, which have had a major impact on British Government policy. One of the most influential Trust reports addressed anti-Semitism,[23] and in the late 1990s the Trust produced a further two important reports dealing with Islamophobia and multi-ethnic relations. A brief examination of these reports would provide key insights into the social and political context within which Christian–Muslim relations are currently being moulded.

Islamophobia: A Challenge for Us All was published by the Runnymede Trust in November 1997, and was launched in the House of Commons. The report has ten key chapters and sixty recommendations, with many of the recommendations having been subsequently adopted by the British government at various levels.

The report was prepared by a commission on 'British Muslims and Islamophobia', convened by the Trust. The commission comprised eighteen members, including eight Muslims (academics and one imam), plus several Christians active in the church hierarchy. Thus this activity represents one element in the increasingly rich tapestry of Christian–Muslim dialogue and co-operation in Britain.[24]

The report defined Islamophobia as 'dread or hatred of Islam and of Muslims', and stated that Islamophobia had become more explicit and dangerous in the last two decades of the twentieth century. The report identified eight features of Islamophobia:[25]

1. Islam was seen as being monolithic and static rather than diverse and dynamic

2. Islam was seen as being other and separate rather than as similar and interdependent
3. Islam was seen as being inferior rather than different
4. Islam was seen as being an enemy rather than a partner
5. Muslims are seen as being manipulative rather than sincere
6. Racial discrimination against Muslims is defended rather than challenged
7. Muslim criticisms of the West are rejected, not considered
8. Anti-Muslim discourse is seen as natural rather than problematic

The report highlighted various consequences of Islamophobia, namely exclusion, discrimination, prejudice and violence. A large number of real-life examples of these consequences were presented in the report, citing quotations from the British media, letters received by the commission and other pieces of supporting evidence.

The report listed sixty specific recommendations, covering these general areas:

Legislation on religious discrimination and racial violence
Legislation to ensure participation and inclusion
New education policies: 'citizenship education'
State funding for Muslim schools
Guidance on meeting the pastoral, religious and cultural needs of Muslims
The monitoring of developments, and follow-up action to be taken by the Runnymede Trust

Specific recommendations included the following:

Complaints should be made by the public to the Press Complaints Commission and to the newspapers concerned when encountering anti-Muslim statements in the press
The Press Complaints Commission and National Union of Journalists should review their codes of practice
Muslim organizations should draw up action plans
The Department for Education and Employment should issue guidelines to employers 'on good employment practice on matters affecting Muslim employees'
There should be a question about religion in the 2001 census
'All political parties should take measures to increase the likelihood of Muslim candidates being selected in winnable seats at the next general election'
Muslims should be appointed to the House of Lords

Non-Christian chaplains should be appointed in public organizations, such
as hospitals
'The Public Order Act (1986) should be amended to make incitement to reli-
gious hatred unlawful'
'Discrimination on grounds of religion should be made unlawful'
Muslim schools should be included within the state sector of education and
receive appropriate levels of government funding support
More Muslims should train and be employed as teachers in state schools
The teaching of history in schools should be reviewed, for example, regard-
ing what pupils learn about the Crusades, and about the spread of Islam
over the centuries
There should be more interfaith dialogue
Faiths should co-operate in addressing matters of public concern

There were criticisms that the Runnymede Trust research up to that point
had not sufficiently distinguished between ethnicity and religion, with
the result that legitimate criticisms about Islam could be deemed to be
Islamophobic.[26] So, hard on the heels of its Islamophobia Report, the
Runnymede Trust established a further commission on 'the Future of Multi-
Ethnic Britain' in January 1998. The particular remit of the new commission
was 'to analyse the current state of multi-ethnic Britain and propose ways of
countering racial discrimination and disadvantage and making Britain a
confident and vibrant multicultural society at ease with its rich diversity'.[27]
Professor Bhikhu Parekh was appointed as chair of the Commission. A consultation document was issued in the winter of 1998, and the full report
followed in October 2000.

The formal terms of reference of the commission were:

To consider the political, social and cultural implications of the diversity of
the British people into the twenty-first century
To invite evidence from as wide a range of communities, organizations and
individuals as is consistent with the target date of completion
To make recommendations to policy-makers and opinion leaders

The consultation document included brief forewords by Prime Minister
Tony Blair, endorsing the work of the commission, and by Trevor Phillips,
the chair of the Runnymede Trust, who made the important statement that
'Respect for diversity means giving everyone an equal chance. Just as important is social cohesion.' The presence of the statement by the British Prime
Minister provided official sanction to the work of the commission and
smoothed the way for close attention to its recommendations.

The full report concluded that in order to build and sustain a community of citizens and communities in Britain, a number of measures would be necessary:

1. Rethinking the national story and national identity
2. Understanding that all identities are in a process of transition
3. Developing a balance between cohesion, difference and equality
4. Addressing and eliminating all forms of racism
5. Reducing material inequalities
6. Building a human-rights culture

The final report stated:

> The Rule Britannia mindset, given full-blown expression at the Last Night of the Proms and until recently at the start of programming each day on BBC Radio 4, is a major part of the problem of Britain. In the same way that it continues to fight the Second World War . . . Britain seems incapable of shaking off its imperialist identity. The Brits do appear to believe that 'Britons never, never, never shall be slaves' . . . [But] it is impossible to colonise three-fifths of the world . . . without enslaving oneself. Our problem has been that Britain has never understood itself and has steadfastly refused to see and understand itself through the prism of our experience of it, here and in its coloniser mode.[28]

This statement emphasizes the colonialism theme on three occasions, thereby no doubt connecting with the guilt feelings among many British discussed earlier. Furthermore, the Parekh Report raised the sensitive issue of redefining what it meant to be British, away from past norms towards a more multi-ethnic understanding.

The Runnymede Trust reports are invaluable in providing a window into a particular phenomenon; namely, how documents prepared by or for government can have a major impact on subsequent government policy in the area of inter-religious and inter-ethnic relations. Other documents could equally have demonstrated this phenomenon, and will be referred to in subsequent discussion.[29] At this early point of our study the Runnymede Trust documents are best placed to introduce and demonstrate this issue. We shall also consider in later sections how many of the recommendations by the Trust reports were adopted into government policy.

The emergence of the 'people of faith' notion
A conversation I had with a Muslim acquaintance in 2000 gave me considerable cause for reflection. He expressed anger and hurt at what he described as 'targeting of my people by Christian evangelists'. His view was that the

Muslim community in Britain should not be subjected to the evangelistic efforts of Christians, but should be left alone to develop in their own faith tradition. He saw clear demarcations between communities along faith lines. His 'people' equated with the Muslim community, regardless of sect, ethnicity or other specific characteristic.

How do devout Christians conceive of the notion of 'my people'? It is frequently the case that Christians who engage in regular worship activities are uncomfortable with using census indicators to define religious communities. Many point out that, although around 42 million British residents identified themselves as Christian in the 2001 population census, only around 5–6 million of these regularly attend church, of whom only around one million are Anglicans. One often hears the view among practising Christians that only regular church attenders are true Christians – others are nominal only, and are without faith.

This view has provided sustenance to a rapidly emerging 'people of faith' notion, which is gaining currency in interfaith circles. It is based on the principle that the dividing lines within British society in terms of religion are not between Christians, Muslims, Hindus and others, but rather between those who have faith (observant Christians, Muslims, Hindus, etc.) and those without faith (the nominal Christian majority).

Christians are not the only ones to articulate this viewpoint. The prominent British Muslim writer Yasmin Alibhai-Brown expresses this well in describing a new 'fault-line' in society:

> There is now a new fault-line in this country – and possibly elsewhere too. Once upon a time the fault-line was between, say, a kind of assumed Christianity and all these others: particularly the other faiths that had come in after the Second World War, which did not fit in, which were not part of the Established Church and were not Catholic. They were the others. I think that now the fault-line is a completely different one, and it is very interesting that this should be so. I think now the fault-line is definitely between fundamentalist secularism and liberalism on the one side, and people of faiths on the other, and I find again and again people saying to me, I may be a Jew, I may be a Muslim, I may be a Hindu. But I find that people who have a faith, any faith, understand me better than people with no faith at all.[30]

This notion is not recent. In March 1970 the World Council of Churches sponsored a dialogue event entitled 'Dialogue between Men of Living Faiths', foreshadowing the emergence of a perception of togetherness that cut across traditional faith boundaries. Before long, subtle pressures to embrace this new view emerged within the churches. Writing in the 1980s, David Lochhead described this process: 'One is given the impression that the history of Christian interfaith relations is a simple matter of distinguishing between the "good guys" and the "bad guys". The "good guys" are those who accept people of other traditions as people of faith. The "bad guys" are those who think that people who are outside the Christian Church are ignorant of the truth.'[31]

The notion of people of faith became much more widely used in the 1990s. Prince Charles, the heir to the British throne and thereby future head of the Church of England, made a significant contribution when he stated in 1994 that as monarch he would prefer to be known as 'Defender of Faith' rather than 'Defender of the Faith'.[32] This statement generated considerable controversy.

Many groups and events picked up on this theme. The Faith and Society dialogue conference of October 1998, discussed in detail later in this study, was entitled 'People of Faith in Britain Today and Tomorrow'. In the opening comments to the 2003 conference held by the same group, the chairman encapsulated a key objective of the gathering for the Christians and Muslims present: 'We are citizens of this country. We are also people of faith . . . How do we belong together and interact with one another?'

This notion has emerged gradually and almost imperceptibly and is playing a significant role in fueling 'the inclusivist train' discussed earlier. Advocates of the 'people of faith' notion argue that it serves to build bridges across faith lines, which is especially necessary in times of tension, such as in the early twenty-first century. They argue that widespread Islamophobia among the British community, and indeed among western communities generally, means that special efforts are needed to combat this anti-Muslim feeling. The developing 'people of faith' notion goes some way to bridging the widening gulf between Christians and Muslims, say the supporters of this notion.

Christians, however, should engage with this notion consciously, measuring these benefits against associated risks of allowing a gulf to develop between practising Christians and vast numbers of the broader Christian flock whose practice of the faith is no longer regular. This issue will be discussed further in the final chapter.

Challenges at the turn of the twenty-first century

We have seen how historical Christian attitudes of exclusiveness towards other faiths have been changing in recent decades. There has been a new approach of openness towards other faiths among western churches, including a developing notion of people of faith, nourished by factors such as reassessment of the West's colonial past, demographic changes leading to the emergence of genuinely multifaith western societies, and documents reflecting official multicultural policies that have stimulated the emerging interfaith openness.

The changing attitudes over the last fifty years, however, have been greatly impacted in recent years. The inclusivist train that has been bringing Christians and Muslims together has been set back by various developments, especially around the turn of the twenty-first century. We shall now proceed to address these in turn.

Terrorism and responses

A key factor contributing to a deterioration in Christian–Muslims relations, in Britain and beyond, was the rise in terrorism in the last decade of the twentieth century, culminating in the attacks on US targets on 11 September 2001,[33] the ensuing military campaigns and further terrorist strikes.

Such terrorism has deep roots, and we shall not engage in a detailed analysis of these here.[34] We shall limit ourselves to identifying several key stages on the journey towards worsening relations between Islam and the West at the turn of the twenty-first century.

The bin Laden declarations of war against the United States

In August 1996, Osama bin Laden, the Saudi Arabian leader of the international Islamist group al-Qa'ida, issued his first public declaration of war against the USA.[35] This was followed in February 1998 by a *fatwa* calling for *jihad* against Americans:

> We issue the following fatwa to all Muslims: The ruling to kill the Americans and their allies – civilians and military – is an individual duty for every Muslim who can do it in any country in which it is possible to do it, in order to liberate the al-Aqsa Mosque and the holy mosque from their grip, and in order for their armies to move out of all the lands of Islam, defeated and unable to threaten any Muslim. This is in accordance with the words of Almighty God, '*and fight the pagans all together as they fight you all together,*'[36] and '*fight them until there is no more tumult or oppression, and there prevail justice and faith in God.*'[37] . . .
> We – with God's help – call on every Muslim who believes in God and wishes to be rewarded to comply with God's order to kill the Americans and plunder their money wherever and whenever they find it. We also call on Muslim ulema, leaders, youths, and soldiers to launch the raid on Satan's U.S. troops and the devil's supporters allying with them, and to displace those who are behind them so that they may learn a lesson.[38]

The language of both these declarations, and of bin Laden's multiple other public statements, was heavily couched in Islamic terminology, with copious references to Islamic sacred scripture.

The significance of 11 September 2001
The statement of intent from the al-Qa'ida leader did not initially capture the attention of western societies at the popular level. A series of dramatic events were ultimately to change this initial apathy; they were to contribute to increased suspicion of Islam in the largely non-Muslim West.

On 7 August 1998, bin Laden's al-Qa'ida network struck a major blow in its campaign against the United States with the destruction of the American embassies in Kenya and Tanzania, killing 224 people and wounding more than 5,000 others. This event captured headlines for a period, but in general the western media, public and governments did not connect these terrorist actions with the earlier declarations of bin Laden or with al-Qa'ida's planning for the future. British Foreign Secretary Jack Straw was to argue later that the lack of international action after the previous al-Qa'ida strikes 'emboldened' the terrorist network in the run-up to the attacks of 11 September 2001: 'What the international community should have done is to heed the earlier warnings about the nature of al Qaeda and to have taken earlier action to deal with al Qaeda and the failing state which was harbouring it, which was Afghanistan. Had we done that, we might have avoided September 11 and everything that has followed.'[39]

The 9/11 terrorist attacks, however, opened the eyes of the public, and of western governments, to the scale of the threat from al-Qa'ida. Perceived institutional backing for such terrorist operations from certain regimes increased the level of threat felt by American and other western governments. The events of 9/11 led to an urgent reappraisal of policy by the US government, and to a decision to move from a reactive to a more proactive confrontation of terrorist threats to US citizens and interests.

The emphasis on Islamic rhetoric and the dependence on quotations from the Islamic sacred texts in the bin Laden discourse led to a widespread suspicion of Islam *per se* among western populations. Statements were forthcoming from more moderate Muslim voices who distanced themselves from the bin Laden jihadist rhetoric. This internal debate among Muslims, and declarations by moderate Muslims that 'true Islam' was different, however, was not convincing to many non-Muslims in the West. In this context, the contribution of bin Laden's statements and actions to deteriorating relations between the western and Islamic worlds has been considerable.

Western responses: Afghanistan (2001) and Iraq (2003)
The US and several other western governments considered that the al-Qa'ida threat could be more easily dealt with if that group could no longer call on support from certain regimes. The Taliban regime in Afghanistan and Saddam Hussein's regime in Iraq were seen by some western authorities as particular threats.

By 2001 there were some fifty-five terrorist training camps run by al-Qa'ida in Afghanistan, an estimated 20,000 fighters having passed through these camps since they were established after Osama bin Laden's arrival in that country in 1996.[40] These camps were not only used to train terrorists in military techniques, but were also centres of research into the construction of weapons of mass destruction.[41] In this latter context, the Iraqi regime of Saddam Hussein was also identified by some western governments as part of the broader threat. It had pursued an extensive production programme of such weapons in the 1970s and 1980s and had used them against Kurdish Iraqis and Iranian troops, and there was speculation about loose linkages between that regime and al-Qa'ida.[42]

Hence Afghanistan and Iraq were identified as priority targets for American military action in the aftermath of the 9/11 attacks, and the campaigns of 2001 and 2003 respectively succeeded in expelling the Taliban and Saddam Hussein regimes from power. But these campaigns attracted widespread opposition and criticism from Muslim minorities in the West, as well as from Muslim majority communities in the world.[43]

While opposition to the Afghanistan campaign from the public at large in western countries was not extensive, the case was different with the Iraq War, where millions in western cities marched against the action. The American and British governments were accused by such opponents of duplicity, with claims ranging from the assertion that the chief motivation was a lust for Iraqi oil to the charge that Britain and America had armed Iraq and kept Saddam Hussein in power, though this latter charge had been shown to be baseless by a 1998 report on the Iraqi military, published by the Centre for Strategic and International Studies.[44]

Church groups were heavily involved in the opposition to the Iraq War, a fact noted by the Muslim Council of Britain.[45] Nevertheless, this did not prevent the campaigns from being widely seen among Muslims as attacks against Islam. They therefore had a significant impact on worsening relations between Islam and the West, and – given the common Muslim perception of Christianity as being synonymous with the West – posed severe challenges to Christian–Muslim relations worldwide.

Further terrorist action

As western military interventions in Afghanistan and Iraq unfolded, further terrorist strikes took place in various parts of the world, carried out by groups directly or loosely affiliated with al-Qa'ida. Locations chosen varied, and included Bali (2002), Casablanca (2003), Istanbul (2003, 2004) and Madrid (2004). A key hallmark of these strikes was the indiscriminate nature of the targeting, the aim being to kill large numbers of civilians. The most effective in this regard were the bombings in Bali and Madrid, when around 200 people were killed in each case.

With each of these further terrorist strikes, pretexts given by the groups claiming responsibility included the need to respond to western military incursions into Muslim lands. Other statements by al-Qa'ida, however, suggested that radical motivations were connected with a much bigger agenda. A statement by Osama bin Laden shows that he and his supporters saw the conflict as being between the West and Islam: 'Under no circumstances should we forget this enmity between us and the infidels. For, the enmity is based on creed. God says: "Never will the Jews or the Christians be satisfied with thee unless thou follow their form of religion." It is a question of faith, not a war against terrorism, as Bush and Blair try to depict it.'[46]

Issues related to political correctness

While the issue of international terrorism is driven by a range of factors largely external to Britain and other western societies, there is another key issue that is very much internal to thinking in the postmodern West and is having an increasing impact on relations between the West and Islam. That is the issue of political correctness.

The term 'political correctness' emerged during the 1990s and has gained considerable currency in certain circles. An Australian Muslim writer, Amir Butler, addresses this concept, and says in challenging it that it undermines the very goals it sets itself:

> While multiculturalism has expanded the range of foods on offer, it has also expanded the range of challenges. As a society made up of different races, professing different creeds, and adhering to different cultures, how can we possibly form a cohesive society that doesn't descend into conflict when pressured? The answer, according to many, is political correctness – the idea that multiculturalism can only work if certain types of speech are deemed too dangerous and banned from public utterance, with its speaker shamed and punished. But far from aiding multiculturalism and the minority groups it purports to protect, political correctness represents one of the most serious threats to minorities and social cohesion. When an idea is met with opposition that attempts to silence it, it gains legitimacy, validating and reinforcing its message and encouraging others to rise to its defence.[47]

Butler identifies an important concept of enforced silence. He goes on to unpack this concept in connection with a particular legal case brought against a Christian accused of vilifying Muslims and their faith in Australia. We shall look more closely at that case later. At this point we shall consider how some researchers argue that a cult of silence has developed because of political correctness, preventing discussion of a range of issues and injustices that need to be addressed urgently.

The cult of silence

In June 1995 there was widespread rioting among Muslim youth in the northern English town of Bradford, one of the population centres of the Muslim minority in Britain. In the wake of these disturbances, a public commission was assembled to investigate the causes of the riots. The report from this commission[48] introduced an important new concept into the multicultural arena by referring to a 'cult of silence'. The report pointed to the fact that many issues had been avoided or ignored for some considerable time by local authorities, such as the need for English language teaching for new immigrants, domestic abuse and violence within some immigrant families, and inter-racial friction resulting from changing demographic realities. The reason these issues had not been addressed was that local authorities were striving to avoid being seen to intrude on minority cultures, not wishing to appear as racist in any way. Hence, concern for minority sensitivities had resulted in silence in the face of issues that clearly needed attention. We are reminded of the 'hands off other cultures' mentality referred to by Susan Okin (see above, p. 37).

In an important study, Jenny Taylor documents a case that illustrates the price paid by this cult of silence. It concerns Shazia Shafee, a thirteen-year-old British Pakistani girl who disappeared from her school in Sheffield for twenty months, during which time no action was taken by teachers, social services or the Foreign Office. She was beaten by her father for being too western, sent to Pakistan and married off to a cousin, and lived as a peasant wife in a village hut. Shazia sent desperate letters requesting help to an 'agony aunt' column of a women's magazine; this attracted the attention of a group of activists. As a result she was located and spirited out of her Pakistani village by an employee of *News of the World*, and subsequently lived with a foster family in Sheffield.

Taylor argued that lack of action by British authorities when the child disappeared from school 'is multiculturalism, in its stark postmodern form . . . Personal autonomy – your presumed right to your own liberty – the basis of law and public policy for a generation, breaks down under the writ of "multiculturalism", and silence reigns.'[49] Taylor points out that Shazia was a British citizen; therefore, technically, the family might have been accused of multiple infractions: abduction, transgressing the law regarding compulsory education of children, physical abuse, and facilitating underage sex. In a clarion call for soul-searching on the part of British policy-makers, Taylor asserts that 'respect for difference degenerated into entrapment within homogeneous blocs . . . The cult of silence . . . has led . . . to almost total cultural separatism – in fact, informal apartheid. Neglect would appear to have been government policy.'[50]

Some would argue that the above case relates to matters of culture rather than of religion. The two are closely entangled, however, and can not be so easily separated.[51] What is clear is that the flight of policy-makers from some of the most difficult questions regarding scrutiny of minority communities provides ingredients for a developing cynicism towards multicultural policies. Such cynicism represents a challenge to progress made in the interfaith arena, with parts of the British majority community wondering whether it is appropriate for policy-makers to take a hands-off approach towards cultural practices of minority religious communities.

The incompleteness of reports to government

In this context, some hard questions must be asked of the Runnymede Trust reports described earlier. These reports were groundbreaking in various invaluable ways, principally in challenging aspects of racism among the majority community in Britain. They showed some coyness, however, in subjecting minority communities to the same kind of scrutiny.

The Islamophobia Report and the problem of Westophobia. The Islamophobia Report of 1997 succeeded in bringing the issue of Islamophobia into the public arena, and had quite an impact on British government policy in subsequent years. State funding for several Muslim schools was approved. A question on religion was included in the 2001 census. There was an increase in the numbers of Muslims appointed as chaplains in public institutions. There was official encouragement of interfaith dialogue activities. Political parties also responded to the recommendations of the report, with increased numbers of Muslim candidates being fielded in the 2001 general election, and more Muslims being appointed to the House of Lords.

Little attention, however, was given to a notable omission of the Islamophobia Report. Negative stereotyping is not the preserve of any single community. In multicultural situations, where elements in one community negatively stereotype another, it is probable that the reverse is also true. Moreover, those elements responsible for such negative stereotyping are unlikely to respond to scrutiny if they perceive that only their community is being held to account.

Any examination of anti-Muslim bias in western communities should be accompanied by a study of anti-western bias in Muslim communities. The Islamophobia Report failed to do this. It is not that the Islamophobia Report was inaccurate in what it did. Rather, it was selective and could have benefited from the inclusion of an extra chapter that examined anti-western stereotyping among Muslims. Had it done so, it would have discovered a widespread phenomenon of what has been termed 'Westophobia' in some subsequent research.

The Westophobia Report,[52] produced in 1999, found elements of the Muslim media in Britain guilty of exactly the same type of negative stereo-typings of the West – and Christians – as had been so comprehensively reported in reverse in the Islamophobia Report. A few examples here will suffice.[53] If we were to take the eight features of Islamophobia (see above, pp. 38–39), and replace the word 'Islamophobia' with 'Westophobia', or even 'Churchophobia', some interesting data emerge from an inspection of certain organs of the Muslim press in Britain.

A 1997 newsletter of the Islamic Party of Britain included the statement that 'There is nothing in Western societies . . . that remotely resembles good behaviour. They all walk in haughtiness, vanity and pomp; insolent, arrogant and boastful.'[54] This would seem to parallel features 1–3 of Islamophobia neatly, though in this case what we are observing is Westophobia.

Another example was evident when *Q-News*, arguably the most reputable UK Muslim publication, reported on the death of the Princess of Wales in 1997: 'Diana was killed because "the West fears Islam and was shaken when it realised that Diana was planning to convert." '[55] This particular conspiracy was rampant in the media of Middle Eastern countries. Libyan leader Colonel Qaddafi charged that the British secret service assassinated Princess Diana to prevent a marriage between a prominent member of the British royal family and a Muslim.[56] It is not so easy to place conspiracy theorizing on the eight-point scale, but it would seem to be generally consonant with the fifth feature of Islamophobia, where the other – in this case the West – is seen as manipu-lative, not sincere.

A further example is provided by the statement that 'plotting to equip themselves with excuses comes naturally to the West'.[57]

There is no shortage of statements in the Muslim press in which anti-western discourse is seen as natural, not problematic, which again accords with the eighth feature of Islamophobia. Consider the following in this regard: 'Amongst the western society, there is a lack of questioning as to why corruption such as child abuse, rape and degradation of women is occur-ring.'[58] While many non-Muslims would share the evident concern about moral decay in western societies, to say there is a lack of questioning or debate about these issues would be seen as going too far.

What evidence is there of a sentiment of churchophobia in the British Muslim press? Westophobia often leads on to a kind of churchophobia. Some Muslim writers call the West *An-Nasara* – 'Christendom'. Many Muslims equate the West with Christianity, on the basis of historical factors as well as the fact that the majority of populations in western countries still identify with Christianity in various ways. So anti-western sentiments easily translate to anti-Christian stereotyping.

The September 1997 issue of *Q-News* included a report that carried the headline in large, bold print: 'Christians eat more Muslims'. The report stated that nominally Catholic Dayak tribesmen in Indonesia were engaged in cannibalism against Muslim neighbours, and that this practice may have been legitimized in the minds of the tribesmen in question by the Christian communion rite. In highlighting and circulating such unsubstantiated claims, *Q-News* also is guilty of regarding anti-Christian discourse as natural, not problematic.

In another blatant example of churchophobia, *The Muslim News* of 31 October 1997 reported that Rauf Denktash, President of the breakaway 'Turkish Republic of North Cyprus', stated that the European Union 'has decided to convert Cyprus into a Christian stronghold'. This seems to be a case of feature 4, portraying Christianity as an enemy rather than a partner.

The periodical of Young Muslims UK, *Trends*, resurrected a statement by the nineteenth-century British convert to Islam, Abdullah Quilliam, that 'The fruits of Christianity are . . . drunkenness, gambling and prostitution'.[59] This seems to fall under feature 3; Christianity is being portrayed as inferior rather than different.

Thus we see in the Islamophobia Report further fruits of the cult of silence. A necessary critical scrutiny of majority British society comes easily, perhaps facilitated by the guilt burden relating to Britain's colonial past, described earlier. Policy advisors and makers, however, find it less comfortable to extend the eye of scrutiny to minority cultures and faiths in Britain. A laudable desire for greater inclusiveness has resulted in an imbalance in critique.

There is debate within the British Muslim community about the future direction of Islamophobia research. One anonymous Muslim scholar commented:

> The Islamophobia agenda has to strike a balance between the freedom of expression to criticize religion and its adherents and yet to avoid descending into 'cultural racism' . . . At the same time, British Muslims must retain a sense of moral community, rather than becoming completely ethnicized or politicized in their outlook. That might lead to Islamophobia being used as a sledgehammer to silence criticism or dissent, not just outside *but within the Muslim community.*[60]

Yasmin Alibhai-Brown commented in similar vein: 'It is . . . debilitating to be fighting on both fronts: against Islamophobia and against Muslims who seem to think they can behave as they want because of Islamophobia.'[61]

In terms of our overall assessment, this issue represents a further challenge to the progress made in emerging Christian attitudes to other faiths. For if western Christians feel that they alone are required to undertake a self-critique, when in fact other faiths also engage in negative stereotyping, the likely result is that interfaith barriers will increase, not diminish.

The Multi-Ethnic Report. The research carried out by the Runnymede Trust into Britain's multi-ethnic future also made a valuable contribution to British inter-ethnic and interfaith relations, especially in terms of asking some hard questions of the majority ethnic community in Britain. As with the Islamophobia Report, however, some searching questions need to be asked not only about the final Multi-Ethnic Report but also about the process that produced it. This can be best exemplified by closely examining the consultation document, which clearly laid out the process of research, and which bore evidence of some coyness in asking a range of hard questions about sensitive matters relating to minority communities.

The consultation document identified five key questions that the commission believed needed to be addressed by the British people. They were:

1. Do our democratic institutions belong equally to all citizens?
2. Are we building a culture that facilitates mutual understanding and respect?
3. How can families be supported to provide security and a springboard for the next generation?
4. Do the opportunities and rewards for work recognize that employment dominates our life chances?
5. How can everyone feel safer in their communities, and what is the role of the justice system?

The first question addressed the important issue of whether the democratic institutions of Britain belong equally to all citizens. A related question, which was not asked by the commission, was: 'Do all our citizens come from cultural, ethnic and religious contexts that have equal respect for our democratic institutions?'

In addressing the second question, the document pointed out that over 50% of Pakistani and Bangladeshi women and 20% of Pakistani and Bangladeshi men in Britain cannot speak English fluently, a factor that tends to create rather than to bring down cross-cultural barriers. These percentages provide concrete evidence that some cultures do not prioritize education of their women; there is ingrained discrimination within specific minorities. But here, too, the commission was much more comfortable subjecting the majority community to scrutiny rather than the minority communities mentioned.

Discussion of the document's third question included an assertion that the law intervenes in sensitive issues of private morality such as parental authority over children and relations between men and women, and asked what framework is appropriate in a country of diverse groups. The commission failed to recognize that intervention may be necessary on occasions, as in the case of cultural practices that deserve to be challenged,[62] or cases where Muslim women are stranded in limping marriages (where the state recognizes a divorce but the husband, following Islamic law, may not, thus leaving the wife in a state of limbo).

At several points in both the consultation document and the final report, there were calls for every British citizen to be given an equal chance. The document also underlined the importance of building social cohesion, based on a fair and just society for all.

All too often, however, multicultural policies affirm the fragment at the expense of the whole. In order for social cohesion to be achieved, policy-makers need to closely scrutinize, and to criticize where necessary, social, cultural and political structures pertaining to both the majority community as well as to minority ethnic communities.[63] This was largely missing from the Multi-Ethnic Commission's documentation. The commission's comfort zone lay in focusing on a distant, macro-level view, with the resulting implication (intended or otherwise) that 'society at large' is responsible for multi-ethnic problems. This is further evidence of a 'hands off minority cultures' mindset, which feeds the 'cult of silence' syndrome discussed earlier. In such a climate, inter-ethnic and interfaith relations were bound to be tentative at best.

A more optimistic note, however, should be added here. In April 2004, Trevor Phillips, chairman of the Commission for Racial Equality, stated in interviews with *The Times* and the BBC that there was a need to rethink the whole approach to multiculturalism, which, he asserted, was no longer useful, as it encouraged separateness between communities. 'What we should be talking about is how we reach an integrated society, one in which people are equal under the law, where there are some common values,' said Phillips.[64] This shows that, in a context of increasing inter-ethnic tensions in Britain following the events of 11 September 2001, Britain can no longer afford the luxury of an uncritical approach to multicultural diversity. Other western countries such as the USA and Australia would do well to take note.

The asylum debate

Another factor placing increasing strains on the relationship between majority society and religious and ethnic minorities in Britain in the present day relates to the asylum debate. The number of asylum-seekers in Britain rose steadily from 4,223 in 1982 to 110,700 in 2002.[65] In addition to such new arrivals, an estimated 250,000 asylum-seekers whose applications have been refused by the Home Office stayed on in Britain illegally during the period 1998–2003, disappearing into the community.[66]

Public concern

Whatever one thinks of the asylum issue, the surge in numbers during the 1990s and the early years of the twenty-first century caused considerable concern in different sections of British society. Media reports offer an insight into these concerns:

> Thousands of residents living near the site of a proposed new centre for asylum seekers marched in protest at the Government's plans. Organisers of the protest at Lee-on-the-Solent, Hampshire, said an estimated 8,000 people attended the hour-long march, although police were unable to confirm numbers. The Home Office has announced plans to turn the former naval airbase HMS Daedalus in the seaside village into a centre to hold single male asylum seekers.[67]

Public concern was connected not only with numbers of asylum-seekers, but also with specific stories, as is seen in this report drawn from *The Daily Telegraph*:

> There are serious conclusions to be drawn from the story . . . about the failed asylum seeker from Iraq who has landed an impecunious health trust with a bill for upwards of £440,000. Injured by a crash in a stolen car and left paraplegic, he will need specialist treatment at the cost of £4,000 a week indefinitely . . . Under this Government, we have the largest bureaucracy in our history, but it has proved incapable of one essential function of government, which is regulating entry from overseas . . . The consequences for race relations in this country are grievous . . . public confidence in government's ability to control entry from overseas in an orderly fashion is the key to decent race relations . . . Human nature being what it is, some of the resentment aroused by this administrative incompetence is visited unjustly on the vast majority of ethnic minorities here who have either entered lawfully or, more probably, were born here . . . No amount of toil by quangos and other bodies established to monitor and regulate our race relations can set that in a rosy light.[68]

Some individuals and bodies sought to combat increasing public concern. The BBC announced 23 July 2003 as 'Asylum Day', and broadcast a series of programmes on radio and television airing the asylum debate.

BBC1 broadcast the programme 'Asylum: You Be the Judge'. This programme focused on four case studies of families and individuals applying for asylum, drawn from Zimbabwe, Slovakia, Turkey and Afghanistan. It featured four panels of people in the studio: refugees, professionals, protesters (asylum opponents) and adjudicators (legal authorities formerly involved in making decisions about asylum applications). Each panel was asked to give its views on each case study. The viewing public was invited to phone in and vote on each case study, after which the Home Office decision on each case was given.

The outcome of this process provided further evidence of public concern about the asylum issue. While the Home Office decision was in favour of the applications from Turkey and Afghanistan, and refused those from Zimbabwe and Slovakia, the public vote advocated refusing asylum for each of the case studies without exception and by a significant margin.

The Muslim connection

The above discussion about asylum does not specifically relate to the Muslim minority in Britain. In certain cases, however, the asylum debate assumed a distinctly Islamic flavour. The increase in Muslim numbers in the UK reflected in previous statistics in the 1960s–80s was through immigration. But during the 1990s, refugees from Muslim lands who were seeking asylum had an increasing impact on numbers of Muslims in Britain. Around 37,000 of the 71,365 new asylum-seeker applications to Britain in 2001 were Muslim. Of the 110,700 new asylum-seekers in Britain in 2002, 17.5% were Iraqis, 8% were Afghans, and 7.5% were Somalis, with significant numbers also coming from other Muslim ethnic and national groups.[69]

There was thus a twofold risk. First, any public backlash against the asylum process had the potential for translating itself into a backlash against Muslims, given the high proportion of asylum-seekers who were Muslim by faith. Secondly, increased tensions between the non-Muslim British major-ity community and its Muslim minority in the context of international events had the potential for colouring the public's response to the ongoing asylum debate. Melanie Phillips points to a range of knock-on effects:

> Since most of the mass immigration now convulsing Europe is composed of Muslims, it is therefore hardly surprising that anti-immigrant feeling is largely anti-Muslim feeling. The sheer weight of numbers, plus the refusal to assimilate to western values, makes this an unprecedented crisis for western liberalism. The crisis is forcing it to confront the fundamental questions of what constitutes a country, national identity and the very nature of a liberal society.[70]

This is an issue where, despite its acute sensitivity, it would not be wise to allow a cult of silence to predominate. Yet there are accusations that such a cult of silence has taken over discussion of immigration and asylum, with unfor-tunate consequences. Anthony Browne writes:

> By repeatedly scattering accusations of racism and trying to shame or deny a voice to any individual or group that tries to debate immigration, the pro-immigration lobby has successfully engineered a situation where all

anti-immigration arguments are silenced and no mainstream party can reflect the clear public opinion. This avoidance of honest debate legitimises those on the racist Right who claim there is a conspiracy of silence, and puts them in the politically convenient position of being the only ones that address people's concerns.[71]

A communication I received from a resident of the northern English town of Dewsbury resonates with Browne's observations:

In Yorkshire in a local election in the Calderdale Metropolitan Council . . . the British National Party were the only party that were willing to articulate a clear distinction between racial prejudice and cultural differences; i.e. significant differences between the English and Muslim Asians concerning core cultural attitudes and practices. (The BNP actually praised Hindus and Sikhs for working with and integrating into the majority culture).[72]

To add to this, reports such as the following, which suggested that untidy asylum procedures were being exploited by Islamist radicals, provide further fuel for what Browne terms the 'racist Right':

Two Algerians who entered Britain as illegal immigrants plotted to raise funds to recruit people to Osama bin Laden's al Qaeda terrorist network, a court has been told. The men supported a Jihad, or holy war, against the United States and its allies, a jury at Leicester Crown Court heard. They planned to make money, propaganda material and equipment available to terrorists in support of bin Laden, it was alleged. [The two] were arrested on September 25, 2001, following weeks of surveillance by the security services, the jury heard.[73]

Further:

An Islamic terrorist suspect linked to Al-Qaeda has been arrested after apparently preparing himself for a suicide bombing in Britain. The man, an Algerian asylum seeker, had left suicide notes to his mother and sister warning them that he planned to 'martyr' himself. When he was strip-searched, police discovered he had shaved off all his body hair – a religious obligation often observed by would-be suicide bombers so that they are 'clean' before entering heaven . . . In notes to his sister and mother the man wrote: 'I hope you treat me as a hero and a martyr.' The documents were recovered during a raid on his home, said to be in the north of England.[74]

In another widely publicized case, a group of Muslim activists was arrested and charged after they set up a small factory to produce the poison ricin. They made use of a London flat allocated to one of them, an asylum-seeker, under the asylum support programme.[75]

In a curious twist of circumstances, several former members of the Taliban regime in Afghanistan, which was overthrown by American, British and Afghani opposition forces in late 2001, applied for asylum in Britain subsequently. This media report captures the irony of this situation: 'A Taliban soldier who fought British and American troops in Afghanistan has been granted asylum here because he fears persecution from the new Western-backed government in Kabul. Lawyers representing the 32-year-old fighter have disclosed that the Home Office has given him permission to stay after accepting that his life would be at risk if he returned to Afghanistan.'[76]

A final example is a case that attracted much publicity and concern among the British population. In January 2004 a British soldier was killed by a suicide bomber while on patrol in Afghanistan. Upon investigation, it was found that the bomber was an Algerian-born asylum-seeker who had been given British nationality. Media reports indicated that he had been a worshipper at the Finsbury Park Mosque, where the controversial Abu Hamza al-Masri served as imam.[77]

The British government faces a major dilemma on this particular issue, as do many western governments. The asylum debate is a hot potato, with widespread public concern surrounding what many see as untidy asylum procedures that lead to Britain's reputation as a 'soft touch' in this area. This situation could have significant knock-on effects on inter-ethnic, and especially Christian–Muslim, relations, given the high proportion of current asylum-seekers who are Muslim. The dilemma is compounded by reports of small numbers of radical Muslim asylum-seekers engaged in subversive activity, thereby potentially smearing the reputation of the entire asylum-seeker body. As long as the British government dithers in weeding out such a radical inner circle, as well as in streamlining its asylum processes, and as long as there is pressure to keep this discussion under wraps and to avoid public debate, this issue will continue to pose yet another challenge to the relationship between Muslims and the non-Muslim majority in twenty-first-century Britain.[78]

Political responses
In recognition of public concerns over asylum, the Labour government tightened immigration procedures. Prime Minister Tony Blair announced a plan to halve the number of asylum-seekers coming to Britain within less than one year. Measures taken included the following:

Denying support to immigrants making asylum claims within Britain unless they can explain how they entered the country and why they did not make a claim at the port or airport of their arrival

Requiring asylum-seekers to show they are eligible for benefits, just as British citizens do

Fewer asylum-seekers granted exceptional leave to remain in Britain if their claim for refugee status is rejected[79]

Requiring visas from people carrying refugee travel documents, abandoning a 1959 Council of Europe agreement to allow refugee document-holders to enter the country visa-free.[80]

Introducing language tests for asylum-seekers where doubts were held about their declared country of origin.[81]

The increased use of detention. Some 1,355 asylum seekers were in detention at the end of June 2003, up almost 400 on March.[82]

Imposing a prison term of up to two years for asylum-seekers who 'fail to provide a reasonable explanation for not having the proper documents at immigration control, or . . . fail to co-operate with the authorities issuing replacement documents[83]

Imposing heavy fines on ferry companies that did not take sufficient steps to prevent stowaways entering the country. These steps were to include the use of detection equipment, such as thermal imaging and heartbeat detectors, which was introduced to Belgian ports in late 2003. This equipment reportedly prevented 4,000 would-be illegal immigrants from France reaching Britain in the first six months of 2003.[84]

Presenting a parliamentary bill proposing the introduction of identity cards for British citizens, to reflect established practice in European countries[85]

The Nationality, Immigration and Asylum Act 2002 came into effect on 1 April 2003, embodying the new procedures.[86] They seemed to have had an immediate effect, with new asylum applications dropping to 16,000 in the first three months of 2003, down from 23,000 in the previous quarter. There was a further reduction in the second quarter of 2003, down 34% on the previous quarter.[87] Overall in 2003, there was a 41% reduction in new asylum applications during 2003 over the all-time high of the previous year.[88] Government spokespeople claimed that this reflected the success of tighter restrictions, though only time will tell whether this drop reflects a continuing trend.

Conclusions

This chapter has covered a lot of ground. Many of the issues addressed are highly sensitive and controversial: exclusivism versus inclusivism, political correctness, guilt for colonialism and mission, immigration and asylum. Even to bring them forward for discussion can arouse criticism and hostility. Is there a way to guide Christians in responding to these issues? How can we think through the theological issues raised by this sea change in attitude in church and society?

On the 'exclusivism versus inclusivism' issue, it is important for Christians to strike a balance between William Carey's confidence in the gospel and Paul's debating in the marketplace on the one hand, and acknowledging our shared humanity with Muslims on the other. Genesis 1:27 – 'So God created man in his own image' – applies to all people, Christians, Muslims and others. While we can admire Carey's confidence and, indeed, seek to recapture it in the modern day, we must regard with considerable reservation his reference to some non-Christians as 'scarcely human'.[89]

Nevertheless, our approach to Muslims and other non-Christians needs to take account of a holistic reading of biblical wisdom on this point. The 'inclusivist train' process in the churches, referred to earlier, reflects an increased emphasis on the first of the macro themes encountered in the discussion of biblical context in the Introduction above: the concept of God's universal blessing for all nations and peoples. This is as unbalanced as an extreme exclusivist viewpoint. The four macro themes considered – the universal blessing, those who turn away, the centrality of faith, and taking the message out – should be seen as a package, not as isolated components that can be used individually at our whim to determine approaches to other faiths.

This first chapter has also discussed the 'people of faith' notion. This concept had appeared in the Introduction in the discussion of biblical attitudes to other faiths. But though the labels appear the same, in fact the two uses of the term are different in a significant respect. While the biblical verses we considered in the Introduction affirmed those who had faith in God, especially through Jesus Christ, the 'people of faith' notion currently in vogue in the churches affirms people of faith – virtually any faith – regardless of particular doctrines or beliefs held. Indeed, doctrines might be diametrically opposed, such as the mutually exclusive Christian and Muslim views about the death and resurrection of Christ; but the fact that each holds their respective view sincerely qualifies them both for membership of the category of people of faith. While this may be in tune with twenty-first-century western pluralist norms, it is certainly not in harmony with the concept of people of faith presented in the biblical verses discussed in the Introduction.

In responding to the discussion of immigration and asylum, Christians should consider the exhortations to welcome the alien and stranger that appear regularly in the Bible. The book of Ruth gives us a helpful example. When Ruth, of Moab, marries into the Israelite family of Elimelech and Naomi, she is welcomed as one of them, not marginalized as an alien intruder. Neither should Christians marginalize those strangers who are in their midst.

But when Naomi releases Ruth after the death of her husband, Ruth's response gives us a further model for today. She says to Naomi, 'Entreat me not to leave thee, or to return from following after thee: for whither thou goest I will go; and where thou lodgest I will lodge: thy people shall be my people, and thy God my God' (Ruth 1:16, Authorized Version). This is a model for integration, for joining with the host community rather than for keeping apart. In terms of immigration, the lesson here is that those who pay the host community the compliment of being willing to integrate are contributing to social cohesion rather than to fragmentation.

These themes will recur in different ways in our subsequent discussion. Having considered broad social context and trends over several decades, we shall now examine Muslim concerns and perspectives, and shall listen to Muslim voices in the process.

2. DIVERSE MUSLIM APPROACHES TO BRITISH SOCIETY

In the previous chapter we considered a range of issues that affect the relationship between Christianity and Islam in Britain. The perspective taken was essentially that of a detached observer. In this chapter, I focus more closely on the British Muslim community and try to gain an insight into the diversity of that community. In this way I hope to fulfil the call by the Runnymede Trust Islamophobia Report to combat stereotyping of British Muslims, a tendency highlighted by that report.

How are Muslims in Britain today responding in different ways to the society around them? And what steps are they taking to address the key concerns of their community? Muslims in Britain hold a variety of views about the majority community around them. The Muslim scholar Mohammad Raza speaks of assimilationist, isolationist and integrationist streams,[1] and I shall use his analysis as a jumping-off point in the following portrait of Muslim responses to British society.

Muslims fall into two macro groups in terms of their responses to the majority society in Britain: participatory and separatist. I shall initially consider these differences in general terms, then unpack them in greater detail in relation to a set of key themes.

Option 1: participate

The majority of Muslims in Britain are committed to participating in British society as an integral element in it. They see Britain as their home and their future. Within this macro group, a further division can be made between those who assimilate and those who participate to influence.

Blend in and assimilate

I shall borrow Raza's term of 'assimilationist' for this first sub-group. Very many British Muslims concern themselves on a daily basis with family, jobs, bills, education of children, taxes, sport – the very same things that preoccupy most of the non-Muslim majority community. Many are urbane, westernized and not self-consciously religious, and gradually assimilate to the majority society around them. They are, in essence, typical 'Brits'. This is the group whose Muslim identity may weaken with succeeding generations through intermarriage, secularist influences and conversion to another religion or to no religion.

Participate and influence the society
The second sub-group under the participatory category resembles Raza's 'integrationist' stream. This category evolved during the last quarter of the twentieth century. Initially, such Muslims set themselves ambitious goals, based on participation for the ultimate purpose of establishing an Islamic society. This is encapsulated in *Islamic Movement in the West* by Khurram Murad,[2] former Director of the Islamic Foundation in Leicester: 'the "ultimate objective" of the Islamic movement in the West . . . should be the establishment of a society based on the Qur'an and the Sunnah'.[3] But this key document records the realization by such Muslims that such a goal was unrealistic, at least in the foreseeable future. Murad continues: 'But where does the movement in the West stand in relation to this objective? It is not difficult to find that the vision of a total change and the supremacy of Islam has been more or less abandoned in the local context, if not theoretically, at least for all practical purposes.'[4] Hence, at the turn of the twenty-first century, the 'participate to influence' approach is based on the notion that Muslims in Britain should participate fully in the majority society, but should strengthen their Muslim identity and try to impart Islamic values and views in the process.

The steady growth in numbers of mosques in Britain – from 18 in 1966 to 338 in 1985[5] and to over 1,000 at the turn of the twenty-first century – is a key instrument in facilitating this 'participate to influence' process, especially in view of the decline in numbers of practising Christians, and of church closures. Thus this process does not involve assimilation leading to loss of identity, but rather to a shoring up of the Islamic identity, and to advocacy on behalf of Islam among the majority community.

Certain people and institutions embody this phenomenon. Dr Zaki Badawi, principal of the Muslim College in London and chairman of the Council of Imams and Mosques, is an example. So too is the Muslim Council of Britain (MCB), which is the most representative Muslim umbrella body in the United Kingdom. MCB secretary-general Iqbal Sacranie defines the role of his organization in Britain as being 'to work for a more enlightened appreciation of Islam and Muslims, fostering better community relations and working for the good of society as a whole'.[6] Shagufta Yaqub, editor of the prominent Muslim periodical *Q-News*, also gives a context to this phenomenon: 'I call myself Muslim first and foremost, and because I've grown up in this country I am a British Muslim. I don't see any contradiction in that. Obviously there is one, universal Islam but, being a universal religion, it naturally has to adapt to the society, to the culture, just as Christianity does.'[7]

The particular sub-category probably represents a majority of British Muslims, who are seeking a balance between being Muslim and participating in the majority society around them. Yaqub again is a good example: 'When it comes to global issues I think we can join hands with a lot of other people. We may not agree with all of their beliefs and practices . . . but when it comes to humanitarian issues we should be working together. I mean, Muslims don't have a monopoly on morality and humanity. Those are basic human principles that all good people believe in.'[8]

Further afield, one finds evidence of this same phenomenon among other Muslim minorities in western countries. For example, the Central Council of Muslims in Germany adopted an Islamic Charter in February 2002, which articulated the relationship between the Muslim minority and the German state and society. Section 19 includes the statement: 'The central Council promotes an integration into society of the Muslim population which will not be detrimental to their Islamic identity.'[9]

Option 2: separate

At the macro level, it also needs to be recognized that some Muslims in Britain have a separatist mindset. This can take two forms: separating within Britain, and preparing to leave Britain to live in Muslim majority countries.[10]

'Separate' within Britain

Those Muslims who choose to remain in Britain but strive to cut themselves off from majority society as far as they can form the group Raza refers to as 'isolationist'. The mindset involves a figurative carving out of space within Britain so that Muslims can effectively create a corner of the Muslim world in Britain, shielded from the non-Muslim British majority. This attitude tends to prioritize a loyalty to the worldwide Islamic *umma* (community) over loyalty to the nation state, as reflected in a comment by Kalim Siddiqui: 'Our status as British citizens does not and cannot in any way compromise our global responsibilities as part of the Ummah of Islam.'[11]

In this context, there has been a series of requests for aspects of Islamic *shari'a* law to be formally incorporated into English law. The first effort in this regard was made by the Union of Muslim Organizations (UMO) of the UK and Eire in the 1970s. The UMO represented around 150 different Muslim organizations at the time. The demand was rejected by the governing authorities,[12] in recognition of the potential for clashes between English law and *shari'a*, especially in matters such as marriage ceremonies where the bride and bridegroom are not present, divorce, custody of children, marriages of underage children, and the ban on Muslim women marrying non-Muslim men.[13]

In practice, however, accommodation has been taking place. As Jenny Taylor observes, 'the English legal system turns a blind eye to any ethnic law, so long as it does not actively violate English law'.[14] In family life, the issue of polygamy is a good example. This is specifically forbidden under UK law but sanctioned under Islamic law. A number of polygamous Islamic marriages have occurred and have been publicized in Britain,[15] however, with no action taken, presumably because, as the marriages were Islamic ceremonies, English law does not recognize any marriage ceremony but the first for each couple.

July 1990 saw the launch of the Muslim Manifesto by Islamist groups. This manifesto called for the establishment of a 'non-territorial Islamic state' in Britain, presented as an alternative to more participatory approaches: 'The options of integration and/or assimilation as official policy in Britain must be firmly resisted and rejected and the community should develop their own identity and culture within Britain.'[16] The manifesto launch was followed in January 1992 by the creation of the Muslim Parliament of Great Britain (MPGB). This body consisted of an upper house that included wealthy Muslims who would pay a fee to sit in the chamber, and a lower house that debated and made policy decisions on issues facing Britain's Muslims. The lower house consisted of 200 members from the UK Muslim community, vetted by a specially appointed committee. This body had strong links with the government of Iran. As Anthony McRoy observes: 'Aspects of statehood could be seen in MPGB departments, such as *Bait al-Mal al-Islami* (Islamic treasury), Halal Food Authority, Human Rights Department, and Jihad Fund.'[17]

The MPGB attracted strong support from some sections of the Muslim community. Zaki Badawi, however, described it as 'a pantomime . . . an ego trip . . . a programme of separate existence doesn't make sense at all'.[18] It embodied a mindset of separation within Britain. Although it gradually collapsed following the death of its founder, Kalim Siddiqui, in 1996, the ideology that inspired it lived on in other, more militant, groups.

Another good example of the 'separate within' approach is the radical Islamist group Al-Muhajiroun. Its leader, Omar Bakri Muhammad, seems to talk the language of 'participate to influence' when he says: 'I am working to see Islam implemented in Britain instead of the capitalist ideology which is dominant. Christianity is not in power here. We know some Christians say, 'Leave what is for God to God and what is for Caesar to Caesar', but what if

Caesar does not implement God's commands?' But he is really talking the language of separation within Britain when he expresses his means of achieving this goal by 'inviting people to Islam, to reflect on the commands of God and not to obey man-made law, not to participate in elections or in any action which angers God, such as unlawful sexual or economic transactions'.[19] Al-Muhajiroun admiration for the former Taliban regime in Afghanistan further points to their separatist tendencies: 'Afghanistan's Taliban regime were the closest we have had to an Islamic State . . . The conditions of an Islamic State are for the authority to be in the hands of the Muslim and to implement Islam internally and externally.'[20]

Islamist separatism is a phenomenon found throughout the western world where Muslim minorities exist. The prominent American Sufi leader Muhammad Hisham Kabbani describes the American situation in words that could be equally true of Britain, explaining how radical Islamist groups find support among young Muslims:

> Unfortunately, it is often young adults who are inclined toward radical ideas, and are attracted to extremism. Some hard-line extremist groups, on the pretext of 'looking after the affairs of Muslims', search out such people among worshippers and invite them to private, secret meetings to brainwash them in extremist ideas. They organize small cells of four or five. The people who are recruited into these cells don't know each other but the leaders do know each other. These cells are becoming networks of extremist thinking, and they can become a big problem in America. What I see, travelling around this country, is that places of prayer – mosques – are increasingly turned into places of politics, and extremist politics at that.[21]

Return to the Muslim world

The other sub-group within the separatist mindset is that which seeks to leave Britain for a Muslim-majority country. This aim is encapsulated by Sheikh Abu Hamza al-Masri, the leader of the radical pro-Taliban group Supporters of Shariah. In response to the question 'What is your agenda for Muslims in this country?' Sheikh Abu Hamza replied: 'Not to melt in this society. To take from this society what is good for them and leave it when it is dangerous. Not to plan their future life and death in this country. Treat this country for what it is: a vampire land which is thoroughly anti-Islam and [anti-]Muslims.'[22]

Individual Muslims may swing between the participatory and separatist options. Some may be participatory in their views on education but separatist on issues of public morality. In order to examine these notions more closely, we shall consider several themes of current interest and debate and see how Muslims respond differently to them.

Education: Christian, secular or muslim?

Muslim parents in Britain, like non-Muslim parents, must decide which educational system to use for their children.

Use church or government schools . . .

Many Muslim parents of a participatory mindset opt to send their children to independent church-based schools, preferring the emphasis that such schools reputedly place on discipline, academic achievement and traditional values. Moreover, many Muslim parents are attracted by the attention given to religious faith in church schools, even though the faith in focus is Christianity, not Islam.[23]

Some Muslim parents of a more 'participate to influence' mindset, however, are wary of church-based independent schools for their children, considering that they might lead to assimilation. Thus many of them prefer government schools, as the multicultural and multifaith policies of the government mean that Muslims can exert a significant influence in determining the identity of the schools, especially in areas of high Muslim population.

The Muslim Council of Britain is committed to increasing the Muslim presence within the national education system. In a statement on education the MCB called on the government to 'support and encourage the drive to recruit more Muslim and ethnic minority parent and school governors'. On matters of educational content, the same statement asserted that 'the national curriculum should reflect and celebrate the rich religious, as well as racial, diversity of this country by teaching pupils more about non-European faiths and civilisations'.[24]

In a widely publicized incident that illustrates a struggle for identity within the government school system, a Muslim teacher in an English government school disrupted the Christmas carols the children were singing, objecting to the Christian message of the songs.[25] This action attracted supportive comment from some sectors, with *The Independent* justifying the teacher's behaviour in its editorial by commenting that 'given the ongoing discrimination against Islam in Britain's schools, it is perhaps unsurprising that one fervent Muslim decided he had heard one "Oh Little Town" [*sic*] too many'.[26]

In a letter to *The Times*, a Muslim reader commented: 'I heartily congratulate Mr Israr Khan on speaking out and reminding the Muslim children at the school where he teaches whom they worship . . . with us Muslims, following the truth is the primary essence of our faith and any contamination is strongly shunned . . . this Pagan/Christian festival of Christmas . . . is a continuation of practices of falsehood and lies.'[27]

The incident proved to be highly controversial, with the press also reporting and including a barrage of criticism of Mr Khan. It opens a window into the struggles for identity that go hand in hand with a 'participate to influence' approach among some Muslims.

... or promote the Muslim education system

The Muslim independent school system represents a more separatist approach to education among Muslims.

One of the first Muslim independent schools established in Britain was the Islamia Primary School in London. Speaking in 2003 of its original establishment twenty years before, headteacher Abdullah Trevathan said:

> There were two different motivations shared by two different types of parents; namely parents who were . . . born in this country and who were interested in pioneering a Muslim approach to teaching and viewing the state system education as influencing children in secular and materialist modes of being and thinking and therefore inherently un-spiritual. The other type of parents were those who had emigrated [*sic*] to Britain and were more prone to a protectionist mindset. They felt frightened by their encounter with the west, particularly in relation to their children and the influence of western mores. There is a significant difference between these two perspectives so there was a strange but potent mix of pro-active and reactionary motives behind the initial vision of the school. I think ultimately the former has won out – we are more engaged in creating a British Muslim culture than attempting to preserve a particular culture.[28]

On 14 November 1992, the Association of Muslim Schools (AMS) was established. The Constitution of the AMS lists its objectives as teacher training; curriculum development; resource development; public relations, parental involvement and community awareness; school management training; monitoring and inspection; voluntary-aided and grant-maintained status; new and existing school development; and assessment, evaluation and accreditation. In advertising its wares, the AMS declared that 'Muslim schools can offer pupils the opportunity to gain sound Islamic knowledge, incorporating all aspects of a broad and balanced curriculum'.[29]

The AMS website stated that there were over 110 full-time Muslim schools in the UK at the time of writing. It further boasted that 'Muslim Schools consistently out-perform local non-faith schools in the league tables'.[30] A complete syllabus for primary schools had been published, modelled on that of the Islamia Primary School in London. The AMS gained many ideas and inspiration from fellow Islamic schools networks outside Britain, through attending events such as the sixth International Islamic Education Conference held in Cape Town in 1996.

A breakthrough occurred in 1998 in the wake of the Runnymede Trust Islamophobia Report, with the British government extending grant funding for the first time to two AMS-member Muslim schools: the Islamia Primary School in London and the Al-Furqan Primary School in Birmingham. In 2002 another private Muslim school in London, Balham Preparatory School, received grant funding. Abdullah Trevathan speaks of the impact government funding had on the Islamia Primary School:

> Being connected to the state system has been beneficial for the general development of policies and procedures within an educational institution like ours. We also have more access to general resources than previously – though we still require a significant amount of money from our school community. Voluntary Aided Schools like ours receive 85% funding from the Government and the religious community meets the 15% left. The [Local Education Authority] advises and provides us with the legal and curricular support that they give to all schools under their remit. We have absolutely no interference from them in our teaching of the *deen* [religion]. As a result of its being the first Muslim state funded school we are well known and get many visitors, which is a very natural and effective form of *da'wa* [outreach]. [31]

One feature that attracts Muslim parents to the private Muslim schools is their single-sex education. The Islamic Party of Britain identifies the reason for this:

> The demand for single-sex education at secondary-school level does not only come from Muslim parents. A comparison of league tables shows that pupils (particularly girls) at single-sex schools do generally better in exams than their peers in co-educational schools . . . Most Muslim parents would prefer single-sex schools for their teenage children, but other measures recommended by the teachings of Islam include modesty in dress and behaviour. [32]

The surge in support for the establishment of and attendance at Muslim schools among the Islamic community has the effect, intended or otherwise, of separatism. Many Muslim schools are willing to offer places to non-Muslim students but are unable to do so because of long waiting lists of Muslim applicants. [33] Further expansion of both the Muslim schools system and grant funding from government is on the agenda of many Muslim groups, including the MCB, which states: 'The Government's decision to extend state funding to three Muslim denominational schools is welcomed

. . . We hope similar support will be forthcoming for more Muslim denominational schools in the near future.'[34]

Yet the separatist mindset can in some instances be flexible with regard to the group to which one separates, as seen in the following comment by a Muslim parent in a web-based discussion forum:

> My own experience is that 'Religious' schools help in inculcating a sense of responsibility, respect and dignity along with an intellectual rigour. My children go to a so-called Muslim School. If this option was not available, I would have opted for a Church of England/Catholic or similar School. In so-called 'normal schools' the value goal posts are constantly moving, teachers are not really the 'budding examples' they once were and unfortunately the children come out not knowing right from wrong.[35]

Others call for the independent Muslim schools network to be expanded in a *de facto* way as state schools with high proportions of Muslim students are taken over by Muslim trusts. This call was expressed by a Muslim in a web-based discussion forum, responding to an 'honour killing' that received much media attention in October 2003:

> A Muslim was jailed for life for slitting his daughter's throat in an 'honour killing' after she embraced western culture and began dating a Christian . . . The tragedy could have been avoided if the poor girl was educated in a Muslim school by Muslim teachers. She is a product of de-education by state school . . . This tragedy is an eye opener for all those Muslim parents who send their children to state schools where they are exposed to teachers who have no respect for Islamic faith and Muslim community . . . The silent majority of Muslim parents would like to send their children to Muslim schools but there are not enough schools to go by. The only alternative left is either British Government should introduce voucher system for parents to choose the school of their choice or designate all those state schools as Muslim community schools where Muslim pupils are in majority. There are hundreds of state schools where Muslims are in majority. Such schools may be handed over to Muslim educational Trusts or charities for their management.[36]

In addition to Muslim educational establishments at primary and secondary levels, a group of some twenty-five specialized Islamic seminaries, defined as '*ulama*[scholar]-led educational institutions training students in the traditional Islamic sciences',[37] existed throughout Britain and prepared their students to take up positions as religious specialists and imams in mosques and other Islamic institutions.

Electoral participation

Another area where varying approaches to participation and separation are evident within the British Muslim community is that of electoral participation.

To vote . . .

Prior to the June 2001 general elections, the Muslim Council of Britain was proactive in giving advice to the Muslim community. It urged Muslims to vote, declaring that 'if we accept that the Muslim community has important needs that require government action . . . there are precious few alternatives to the ballot box'.[38] The MCB argued forcefully that non-voting would lead to further marginalization of the Muslim community.

In order to facilitate the task of voting for its constituency, the MCB set up a dedicated website[39] to provide assistance to British Muslims in making their choices. The advice given was not party-specific, but attributed a ranking to candidates in constituencies with a heavy Muslim population according to their attitudes on issues of key concern to Muslims: Palestine, the Terrorism Act, Iraq, Kashmir, Kosovo, gay marriages, and so forth.[40]

The Islamic Party of Britain also urged Muslims to vote, as would be expected of a party contesting the elections. Nevertheless, it pointed to per-ceived imperfections of the electoral system, expressing a clear 'participate to influence' mindset:

> Muslim participation in politics . . . must put forward meaningful alternatives which are viable for society at large, Muslims and non-Muslims alike, and improve the situation of both. It is the old task of *Dawah* by appropriating people's concerns and showing them a way out of the disastrous consequences of abiding with a system built on falsehood, oppression and ignorance.[41]

. . . or not to vote

Some Muslim groups, however, advocated against electoral participation, taking a more separatist approach. In this they are influenced by the Islamist writer of the Muslim Brotherhood, Sayyid Qutb (d. 1966), who opposed 'any notion of popular sovereignty and man-made laws as a form of apostasy, rejecting the sovereignty of God and His law'.[42]

Thus Omar Bakri Muhammad, head of Al-Muhajiroun, in his capacity as judge of the Shari'ah Court of the UK, issued a *fatwa* opposing voting:

> 3. Any Muslim who votes for a person knowing that the Parliament is a body of legislating law is an apostate.

4. Any Muslim who participates in elections to become an MP knowing the reality of Parliament as a legislative House is an apostate.

5. Any Muslim who does not know the reality of Parliament and he votes is sinful because he did not seek the divine ruling for his action before committing it, since the Juristic Principle is that every action, verbal or physical, must be based on an Islamic ruling which is derived solely from the Qur'an and Sunnah.[43]

The very tone of this *fatwa* is intimidatory. In similar vein, a radical preacher who preached at Finsbury Park Mosque, Abdullah El-Faisal, told his followers that the way forward was 'the bullet, not the ballot' and urged them to train for a holy war: '"It is Islam versus democracy. It is Allah versus Satan. It is Muslims versus unbelievers," he told audiences around the country in lectures which were tape-recorded and sold in bookshops.'[44]

Social participation

Divisions exist among Muslims in Britain regarding the nature and degree of social participation within majority society.

Lobby for influence . . .

The MCB leads the way in developing strategies for improving the profile of Islam in the British community. An MCB news release reporting a meeting of imams and *ulama* (scholars) on 29 September 2001, in the wake of the 9/11 terrorist attacks, encapsulated MCB strategy: 'The best way to protect the Muslim community is to inform and explain the teachings of Islam and the Qur'an to the wider public.' It went on to argue that Muslims should aim to create 'a positive milieu' among the leaders of opinion in the West; that mosques should become centres of dialogue and discussion with the wider public; that more attention and resources should be dedicated to visiting schools and to meeting staff and students; and that there was a need to tackle racism and 'Islamophobia' at both individual and institutional levels.[45]

One of the key campaigns pursued by the 'participate to influence' group concerned the request for anti-religious-discrimination legislation. As we saw earlier, the 1997 Runnymede Trust report on Islamophobia called for legislation to outlaw religious discrimination. It argued that, while Jews and Sikhs are protected under race discrimination laws, because Muslims are multiracial, existing anti-discrimination legislation concerned with race protects Muslims only against being targeted for their ethnicity, not against being targeted for their faith.

The Islamophobia Report highlighted cases of religious discrimination against Muslims. Furthermore, surveys conducted by the Islamic Human Rights Commission (IHRC) in 1998–9 and 1999–2000 found that 45% of those surveyed reported having experienced discrimination on the basis of their religion.[46] In 2000 the IHRC produced a detailed report on Islamophobia,[47] adding weight to the campaign for anti-religious-discrimination legislation.

In 1999 the Muslim peer Lord Ahmed of Rotherham led a debate in the House of Lords on extending existing laws about racial discrimination to cover religion.[48] He called for the adoption of a similar law as exists in Northern Ireland, where for the previous twenty years religious equality had been enshrined in the province's Fair Employment Acts. Similarly, the Muslim Council of Britain has been very vocal on this issue: 'Government cannot ignore the real fears of its Muslim citizens. Legislation banning all forms of religious discrimination, harassment, and incitement to hatred must be urgently enacted.'[49]

The MCB website incorporated a facility that enabled visitors to log incidences of religious discrimination they had experienced. An anti-religious-discrimination bill was almost passed by the British Parliament in the wake of the 9/11 terrorist attacks, but was rejected at the last minute. In December 2003 a narrower law specifying regulations for employment relating to religious discrimination came into effect. No doubt much more will be heard on this subject in the future.

. . . or attack the system

A movement towards segregation within Islamic ghettos is clearly discernible in some British towns and cities. This can best be seen in connection with riots in the English north in the summer of 2001.

Riots in northern towns and cities

The borough of Oldham had a total population of around 219,000 at the time, of whom 24,600 were of Asian ethnic origin. Of this latter number there were 14,000 Pakistanis, 9,000 Bangladeshis and 1,600 Indians; thus the vast majority of Oldham's Asian was Muslim. The borough was divided geographically into mainly white, Pakistani or Bangladeshi areas.

Oldham was a powder-keg, with inter-community resentment simmering below the surface. According to police sources, during the twelve months up to June 2001, 572 racist attacks were recorded in Oldham. These attacks were not only white on Asian; in fact, 60% of those recorded by the police were perpetrated by Asians on whites.

All communities were dissatisfied with measures taken by the authorities to address the situation. Muslims complained that their reports of racial harassment and attacks were not acted upon swiftly or taken seriously. One Muslim said, 'National Front members come on weekends and trouble and tease Asian taxi-drivers.'[50] Whites pointed to racially motivated attacks by Asians, as well as to the reported creation by Asian youth of no-go areas for whites. Furthermore, Oldham served as the site of the UK headquarters of several radical Islamist groups that supported the Afghan Taliban and Kashmir resistance groups.[51]

Other northern English urban areas, such as Burnley and Bradford, also faced similar inter-racial tensions. Bradford's population included 12,000 Hindus and 80,000 Muslim Pakistanis, adding a further dimension to inter-religious tension.

From May to June of 2001 gangs of white and Asian youth clashed in the streets of these three northern locations. There were widespread arrests, as the authorities struggled to restore order and inter-racial stability. A number of reports on the riots were produced by both government and Islamic bodies. The official government report on the Bradford riots, by Lord Ouseley, described the city divided along racial, ethnic and religious lines, and called for greater integration within the schools in heavily mixed communities such as Bradford.[52] An IHRC report on the riots of June 2001 called for an independent inquiry into institutionalized Islamophobia in the police, judiciary and other bodies.[53]

Conscious creation of ghettos through intimidation of non-Muslims
Evidence emerged of the separatist tendency referred to earlier. In the wake of the summer 2001 riots, there were media reports of Muslim activists using intimidatory tactics to try to drive non-Muslim residents from certain neighbourhoods so as to consolidate the distinct Islamic identity of these neighbourhoods. There were many reports that young Muslim militants were setting up no-go areas for whites in Oldham as well as intimidating non-Muslims of various ethnic backgrounds. One letter from an Asian Christian to *The Guardian* ran: 'During the past three years, a mini ethnic cleansing, largely encouraged by mullahs from mosques, has been taking place in Oldham. Young Muslims have been encouraged to attack Hindu homes and shops . . . The most terrifying incident was in 1999 when the Diwali celebration lights in a Hindu enclave were torn down and destroyed by Muslim thugs.'[54]

It also emerged that a number of Christian churches in Burnley had often been vandalized. The Full Gospel Mission in Brierfield, Burnley, had become a frequent target. In April 2000 the church's wooden hall was fire-bombed. The pastor's car was petrol-bombed and the church's evangelism caravan was overturned in the street by Asian Muslim youths. Simultaneously, a leaflet had been distributed in the area 'urging worship of Allah' and warning

Christians to leave the area. Members of this church argued that this represented pressure on the church from local Muslims who had previously
approached the church to buy a vacant plot of land on which to build a
mosque, and had been refused.[55]

Some of the clearest cases of a separatist tendency occurred in the city of
Bradford. After the Bradford riots of 2001, the local police denied the existence of no-go areas. But there were increasing reports that young Islamists
were using intimidatory tactics to stake out territory and push non-Muslims
from specific neighbourhoods. The priest at St Cuthbert's Roman Catholic
Church was threatened by Muslim youths that he would be targeted if he
did not close the church. St Clement's Church was fire-bombed twice in
October and November 2001, following 'an unsuccessful approach by the
neighbouring mosque to purchase the building'.[56]

Such tactics have attracted severe criticism from some Muslim organizations and individuals. The Bradford Council of Mosques condemned these
attacks but said it was powerless to stop them. The Muslim journalist Yasmin
Alibhai-Brown picked up on reports in the religious press by Anthony
McRoy and wrote in *The Independent*:

> Churches have been firebombed, sexual threats have been made against the
> wives of preachers, a church caretaker's dog was hanged and a group of
> Brownies was chased, pelted with eggs and stones by a crowd yelling 'Christian
> bitch'. Black Pentecostal churchgoers are also threatened, as are Ahmadiyyas, a
> Muslim sect, for not being 'proper' Muslims . . . Why have Muslim leaders not
> condemned properly the anti-Christian terror mounted in Bradford by some
> young men who claim to be Muslim? Where are the grand protests by the
> Muslim peers or MPs or local councillors?[57]

The interfaith advisor to the Bishop of Bradford, Dr Philip Lewis,
commented that 'the attacks suggest that the young men who perpetrate
such are signalling that this is our territory and those deemed outsiders are
unwelcome'.[58]

The media

Many Muslim commentators lament the reported ignorance about Islam
among the British masses. A YouGov poll commissioned by the Islamic
Society of Britain in November 2002 on attitudes towards British Muslims
reflected this widespread ignorance. It found that 73% of Britons admitted
to knowing either nothing or very little about Britain's Muslim community,
while 82% agreed that 'members of Britain's Muslim minority often keep too

much to themselves, when they should be trying to mix in more with non-Muslims'.[59] In other words, there is a widespread perception among the non-Muslim majority population that British Muslims tend towards a separatist mindset.

Many Muslims consider an engagement with diverse media essential in addressing this situation. Shagufta Yaqub of *Q-News* stresses this: 'I think [British Muslims] need to not only integrate but be seen to integrate, and that's being a bit more media-aware in the way we do things.'[60] Muslims in Britain do not necessarily agree among themselves, however, about the best means of connecting with the media.

Embrace the system to get the message out . . .

The YouGov poll of November 2002 was commissioned for Islam Awareness Week, an annual event since 1994, which defines as its aim 'to invite all Muslims to work together during the week in sharing Islam with the public at large, providing information regarding its message and way of life, and removing misunderstandings in the process'.

Islam Awareness Week for 2003 fell in November, with a feature to include the launching of a virtual classroom by the Secretary of State for Education and Skills. The press release announcing this development unpacks the goals:

> Using the latest techniques of information technology the virtual classroom is offered to schools across Britain as a new resource to fill a gap in conventional history books . . . The virtual classroom has been set up because most British people are more familiar with the history of conflict and tension between Europe and the Muslim World than the positive connections . . . that made life better for everyone. It's the constructive story that doesn't make it into history books used in schools. But it's the kind of thing children who live in an increasingly globalised world need to know about the history of their classmates and fellow citizens.[61]

Another interesting example of Muslims of a 'participate to influence' mindset who engage with the media is seen in the 'BBC Islam season' held in the summer of 2001. For this series the BBC consulted with and was advised by various British Muslim bodies in determining programme content and focus. The series included an assortment of films on history, contemporary social issues, theology and doctrine. A number of characteristics of these programmes were striking.

First, the Islamic programmes sought to debunk negative stereotypes of Islam among the majority non-Muslim community. In this they were trying to fulfil one part of the advice offered by the Runnymede Trust's

Islamophobia Report. Initially, interviews with non-Muslims in the street were presented, highlighting negative popular views of Islam.[62] Then a sympathetic focus on women's rights in marriage and divorce was included in one programme.[63] Moreover, the programmes portrayed Islamic radical groups such as the Taliban as being driven by nationalist concerns rather than by Islamic teaching.[64]

Secondly, the programmes placed a heavy emphasis upon white British converts to Islam, thus seeking to appeal to a non-Muslim audience in Britain.[65] One white convert interviewed declared: 'Hopefully this is the future of England . . . Islam has taken root here and it is growing, and *insh allah* [if Allah wills] it will spread and people will come to know what it is.'[66]

Thirdly, those interviewees and situations selected often seem to have been chosen to appeal to, and to be identifiable by, the ordinary masses among the viewing audience. For example, one young woman convert to Islam adopted a speaking style that was interspersed with exclamations such as 'Oh my God!' and 'Damn it!', thus striking chords with many young non-Muslim British viewers who frequently blaspheme and curse.[67] Lord Ahmed of Rotherman was portrayed as a self-made man and a former worker in a fish-and-chip shop, and described himself as the 'peer of the people'.[68] Prince Naseem, a sporting icon, was chosen as the focus of one programme in order to attract widespread interest. He commented that, 'although I've made my name as a boxer, what really matters to me is my faith. Islam is the cause of my confidence and my strength.'[69]

Fourthly, programmes addressing history adopted Muslim perspectives in a range of ways. This was consistent with one of the Runnymede Trust recommendations, which proposed that the teaching of history in British schools should be reviewed, for example regarding what pupils learn about the Crusades and about the spread of Islam over the centuries.

Both Muslim and non-Muslim scholars were consulted in preparing these programmes, thus creating an impression of balance. Nevertheless, Islamic perspectives on historical events were themselves not subject to scrutiny, being presented as historical accounts rather than as statements of faith. For example, one programme included the assertion that, at the end of the pilgrimage, animals are sacrificed 'to commemorate Prophet Ibrahim who was asked to sacrifice his son Isma'il'. No recognition was offered of the alternative view, found within both the biblical materials and in many classical commentaries on the Qur'an, that the attempted sacrifice by Abraham was of Isaac, not of Ishmael.[70] Furthermore, a programme on Islamic history painted Muslims as supremely tolerant of other faiths. This idealized view was not challenged with reference to the status of *dhimmi* (non-Muslims living in a Muslim society) or to the discrimination against and persecution of minorities that occurred during certain periods of Islamic imperial history.[71] The same programme presented a very negative portrayal of the Christian Crusades and associated massacres, but no mention was made of Muslim territorial expansion and massacres of non-Muslims.

Fifthly, frequent comparative comments were made regarding Islam and Christianity. All favoured Islam and included thinly veiled criticisms of Christianity. For example, a middle-aged white female convert presented her Christian upbringing as irrelevant to the real world.[72] A spokesman from the Birmingham Mosque commented that, 'if Islam is relegated to rituals, then it will become a kind of religious ghetto . . . a religious zoo'. This statement was made in a way that suggested that churches and temples appear in this very manner.[73] Furthermore, references to miracles experienced by Muslims in the modern day[74] stressed the extraordinary spiritual claims of Islam in a British society that was increasingly rejecting its own spiritual heritage.

The final key characteristic of the season of Islamic programmes was that discussion of Islamophobia made no reference to the existence of similar phobias among Muslims towards the West and Christianity, such as were discussed in the previous chapter.

. . . or lambaste the system

Not all British Muslims saw the 2001 BBC season on Islam in positive terms. Those of a more separatist mindset were cynical about it, with the radical fringe of the Muslim community lambasting the BBC series.

In a press statement, the radical group Al-Muhajiroun saw it as 'another attempt by the BBC, the mouthpiece of the British Government which is run by pro-Israeli Jews, to cajole the Muslim masses into believing that Islam is in harmony with Western Civilization and that countries such as Britain are at the forefront of allowing Muslims to practice [*sic*] their religion'. It added that 'those presenting the pure and uncorrupted version of Islam were either not approached by the BBC team at all or had any interview shot left on the cutting-room floor, such as Sheikh Omar Bakri Muhammad . . . and Mr Anjem Choudary'.[75]

9/11 and the war on terror

The most influential factor in setting the tone for Christian–Muslim relations in Britain and beyond in the early twenty-first century relates to the terrorist attacks of 11 September 2001, and the ensuing War on Terror declared by the American President George W. Bush. The military campaigns in Afghanistan in October 2001 and in Iraq in March–April 2003 were seen by the US administration as the key stages in this War on Terror.

The negative impact of these events on Christian–Muslim relations were discussed in the previous chapter.

British Muslim responses to this series of events have again shown some diversity, though perhaps not as much as in the case of certain other themes considered in this book.

Engage and seek to influence . . .

Those British Muslims of a 'participate to influence' mindset spoke out loudly about 9/11 and the War on Terror campaigns.

Responses to 9/11

In the wake of the 9/11 attacks, Dr Zaki Badawi spoke on BBC Radio 4's 'Thought for the Day'. He issued a powerful condemnation of the terrorist attacks: 'Those who plan and carry out such acts are condemned by Islam, and the massacres of thousands, whoever perpetrated it, is a crime against God as well as against humanity.'[76] A Muslim Council of Britain news release of 13 September 2001 declared that 'the values, principles and precepts of Islam stand absolutely against wanton acts of terror'.[77] The leading British Muslim periodical *Q-News* commented:

> The name of Islam . . . has been dishonoured. That is one of the crimes of the terrorists . . . these people are committing a shari'a offence by bringing the religion into disrepute . . . Terrorism has no place in the vocabulary of Islamic law . . . the Muslim world now needs to become more stern with extremists . . . The terrorists are therefore the extreme of an extreme . . . We need to tell the world that Islam is guiltless, and that terrorism is carried out by members of an aberrant cult, called Kharijism, which borrows some Islamic forms but is in fact a separate religion.[78]

Continuing the idea that the 9/11 terrorists had nothing to do with true Islam, Dr Manazir Ahsan, director of the Leicester-based Islamic Foundation, said: 'Such an attack has been called an attack on civilisation; I would also add that it was an attack on Islamic values that one billion Muslims around the world treasure and that we hope to share in some small measure with the government and people of the USA.'[79]

Prominent UK Muslim academic and writer Ziauddin Sardar wrote in the *Sunday Observer* of 23 September 2001:

> To Muslims everywhere I issue this fatwa: any Muslim involved in the planning, financing, training, recruiting, support or harbouring of those who commit acts of indiscriminate violence against persons or the apparatus or infrastructure of states is guilty of terror and no part of the Ummah. It is the duty of every

Muslim to spare no effort in hunting down, apprehending and bringing such criminals to justice.

All these statements were thus of one voice in expressing a clear condemnation of the 9/11 attacks, as well as a determination to divorce those attacks from Islam in the minds of the non-Muslim majority community in Britain. To all intents and purposes, the above statements all set out to excommunicate the radical groups involved in 9/11 from the Islamic fold.

Responding to action against Afghanistan
The 'participate to influence' group, however, was somewhat divided regarding the ensuing Afghanistan War, launched by the USA and Britain to overthrow the radical Taliban regime, which had hosted Osama bin Laden and his al-Qa'ida group.

Some Muslim voices spoke out in favour of the campaign. Hesham El-Essawy, president of the Islamic Society for the Promotion of Religious Tolerance in Britain, said he believed that the allied attacks on the Taliban were 'fully justified'. 'Everyone can understand it, even if not everyone can applaud it,' he said. He asserted that he would support military action 'to the end', as there was no other option for dealing with the Taliban. 'These people [the Taliban] are doing everything that is un-Islamic . . . They're harming Muslims more than they're harming non-Muslims. In some ways you could see this [war] as an action for Islam, not against it.' [80]

Similarly, the director of the Manchester Council for Community Relations, Khan Moghal, believed that the campaign was justified: 'They want to destroy the al-Qaeda network which has been responsible for a lot of problems, not just in America but in the rest of the Muslim world as well.'[81] In a similar vein, Masood Akhdal, the imam of Luton's Central Mosque, said, 'I do not agree that this is a war against Islam. This is a war against terrorism.'[82]

The influential Muslim Council of Britain, however, took a clear stance in opposition to the military campaign in Afghanistan before it started, suggesting that the interests of justice would not be served: 'The world powers must not respond with military action; that will only add to the tally of innocent lives lost . . . We can only demand justice for all innocents who suffer worldwide if we do what is right and just without hesitation or equivocation.'[83]

Once the campaign was under way, the MCB raised the stakes in speaking out against it. Yousuf Bhailok, MCB secretary-general, said: 'British Muslims want justice to be done for the horrifying events of 11 September. These day and night strikes, which are already leading to innocent civilians' deaths amongst the long-suffering Afghan population, will not achieve this purpose.'[84]

Tariq Ali, the prominent British Muslim writer, took a similar stance in opposing British military action in Afghanistan, suggesting that the real motives were different from those expressed by the British government:

> Was there ever an alternative to the bombing? If the real intention was not a crude war of revenge, but to seriously weaken and eliminate terrorism and bring to trial those who ordered the crimes committed on 11 September, then the answer is yes . . . A lesson could have been learnt from Israel's patient stalking, capture and trial of Adolf Eichmann who was accused of a far more serious crime . . . If the real aim is simply an old-fashioned imperialist one, i.e. to topple the Taliban regime and replace it with a protectorate considered closer to 'Western values' (as the Taliban once was), then and only then does the bombing make sense.[85]

The Islamic Society of Britain warned of negative results that would follow the military campaign against the Taliban:

> Stop the attacks against Afghanistan, because: 1. These attacks will not solve the problem of terrorism. Rather it may lead to an increase in terrorist acts as people become more radicalised. 2. We still have not seen any evidence that would stand up in court. 3. These attacks may create further backlash against US and the alliance, as many will perceive this as an attack against Islam and Muslims. This could drive more people into the hands of extremist groups. 4. The inevitable humanitarian catastrophe is unthinkable. 5. The past record of US and allied attacks shows how accurate so-called 'precision bombing' really is.[86]

Responding to action against Iraq

If there was some diversity of viewpoints among British Muslims of a participatory mindset regarding the Afghanistan War, this was far less the case regarding the Iraq War in 2003, where there was almost total British Muslim opposition to the British government decision to join the US-led invasion.

In this case the position taken by the Muslim Council of Britain was generally representative of British Muslim opinion. Before the military campaign began, the MCB lobbied to persuade the British government to avoid participating in it. An MCB news release in January 2003 had a tone of cynicism and a prediction of dire economic consequences:

> While the military occupation of Iraq may help secure increased supplies of cheap oil and create trillions of dollars worth of reconstruction contracts, the human costs and lasting damage this would cause to US relations with the Muslim world would be incalculable. The MCB was loath to contemplate what

this would also do to Britain's economic and bi-lateral relations with the Muslim world.[87]

On the eve of war, the MCB made its position patently clear to the British government, claiming to speak for all British Muslims in the process: 'The MCB's position on the war is in TOTAL solidarity with the millions and millions of people who have marched and continue to march, in this country and across the globe, to voice their rejection of a war which is seen as an undisguised attempt to impose a neo-colonialist world order and occupy the lives and resources of the earth.'[88]

As the war was launched, the MCB expressed great cynicism about the motives of those governments taking part, seeing a link with the perceived bogey of Zionism: 'this war appears to be part of a plan to redraw the map of the Middle East in accordance with the agenda of Zionists and American neo-Conservatives'.[89] Following the rapid collapse of the Iraqi regime after the US/British military invasion, the MCB continued its campaign of opposition to British government policy, further raising the spectre of Zionist conspiracy: 'We do not want to see Britain being viewed in the Muslim world and beyond as an accomplice to this neo-Conservative-Zionist design for a post-Saddam Middle East . . . We call upon the international community to give this tragedy their urgent attention and we also call upon the US/UK governments to withdraw their troops from Iraqi soil immediately.'[90]

. . . or separate or emigrate

Those of a separatist mindset responded to 9/11 and the subsequent Afghanistan and Iraq wars in militant terms. Support for the radicals responsible for the 9/11 attacks was evident in the comments of groups such as Al-Muhajiroun, which issued a press statement on 16 September 2001 that included a call to arms:

> O Muslims, stand together and unite our Ummah to fight against the enemies of Allah (SWT [*subhanahu wa ta'ala*, 'glorified be he']) and his Messenger Muhammad in this time of need. The Book of Allah calls you, the Ummah cries for your help and Paradise awaits you. Verily, Allah (SWT) orders you in the Qur'an: '*Go and fight, young or old and sacrifice your wealth and life in order to get paradise*'[91] and '*Fight the Mushriks all together the way they fight you all together*.'[92]

In the face of the imminent American and British military campaign in Afghanistan there were calls for Muslim solidarity. Once the war started, calls for *jihad* increased in intensity, as seen in the Al-Muhajiroun press release of 7 November 2001: 'Muslims will proclaim that the only solution to the atrocities being committed against them in Palestine, Kashmir, Chechnya or Afghanistan is Jihad; an obligation to engage in physically upon those nearest and an obligation upon the Muslims around the world to support verbally, financially and physically.'[93] The Al-Muhajiroun website also proclaimed a *fatwa* against Muslims in the British army: 'Warning to Muslims in the British & US Army not to engage in attacking our Muslim brothers in Afghanistan. It is an act of apostasy [*sic*] under Islam. Those who do must fear God (Allah) and pay severe punishment.'[94]

Demonstrating a pronounced separatist minset, Al-Muhajiroun also issued a web-based 'Islamic Verdict. A Call for Muslims in Britain to give up their Citizenship before they go to Afghanistan, as Islam forbids us to commit treason. Calling Muslims that hold citizenship to go to Afghanistan.'[95] The Al-Muhajiroun leadership was quite open about its militant ideology. Sheikh Omar Bakri Muhammad of Al-Muhajiroun said provocatively: 'Do we recruit [young British Muslims for overseas *jihad*]? There is no need. Do I encourage them to go? Of course.'[96]

There was no shortage of evidence that separatist-minded British Muslims were willing to engage in the jihadist cause. One twenty-six-year-old British Islamic activist, Abu Yahya, who received military training in Afghanistan and Pakistan, said in interview: 'There is an obligation on Muslims to defend other Muslims. I would also ask people to fulfil their divine obligations . . . I would say to the youth: "If you can fulfil your divine obligation then by all means go and fight on the frontline." We will do whatever we can to change the world order to an Islamic world order.'[97]

Accusations emerged of links between British-based militants and the al-Qa'ida group responsible for the 9/11 attacks. Khalid Al-Fawwaz, aged thirty-eight, a London-based Saudi businessman, was accused of finalizing and editing Osama bin Laden's declaration of *jihad* against the US and of playing a part in the 'ongoing and sustained conspiracy' to murder Americans. Al-Fawwaz was accused of establishing the Advice and Reformation Committee in north London as the British link in the al-Qa'ida network, and of procuring a satellite phone that was reputedly intended to communicate with bin Laden.[98]

The separatist groups among the British Muslims set about converting the 9/11 attacks from atrocity to idealized legend. At an Al-Muhajiroun conference at the Finsbury Park Mosque on 11 September 2002, entitled 'September 11: A Towering Day in History', topics of discussion included 'the positive outcomes of the attacks'. At this event supporters were seen to hang banners from the mosque building, calling for Britain to be turned into an Islamic state. Dr Muhammad Al-Mass'ari, secretary-general of the Commission for the Defence of Legitimate Rights, said that the 11 September attacks may not have been 'the wisest thing' but they were 'legitimate'. He described Osama bin Laden as 'a fighter and fighting according to his beliefs. Anyone who fights according to his beliefs is a hero.'[99]

One member of al-Muhajiroun, Abdul Rehman Saleem, later expressed in even more laudatory terms the admiration radical Islamists feel for Osama bin Laden:

> I believe Shaykh Osama Bin Laden has earned his leadership around the world. I believe a vast majority of the Muslims follow, and revere and respect this great man called Shaykh Osama Bin Laden. I believe there's not a man on this earth that is like Shaykh Osama. I believe he is from one of the citizens of heaven, from one of the citizens of *jannah* [paradise], and I believe he has been sent by God to revive the Muslims. I believe he is the best of the best of the best.[100]

The British authorities monitored such separatist groups with increasing attention in the wake of the 9/11 attacks, and in connection with the Terrorism Act. In July 2003 there were police raids on the homes of Omar Bakri Muhammad and Anjem Choudary, the two leading lights of Al-Muhajiroun. The response of the organization in a press statement expressed grievances and a sense of separateness, as well as thinly veiled threats:

> With the worst housing, the highest unemployment, the largest number of race murders in Europe, a whole range of draconian laws tailored to intimidate the Muslim community, the Blair regime is today sitting on a box of dynamite and have only themselves to blame if after attacking the Islamic movements and the Islamic scholars, it all blows up in their face.[101]

Radical clerics in other western countries similarly acted as voices of incitement from time to time. The most senior Islamic religious figure in Australia, Sheikh Taj al-Din al-Hilali, was reported as saying during a visit to Lebanon that 'whoever carries out a martyrdom (operation) is a pure shahid (martyr) and one of the men of Paradise. Moreover, he stands at the head of the shahids.'[102]

Support for different viewpoints

Consideration of differences among the British Muslim community inevitably raises the question of what proportion of Muslim hold the varying views described. Some surveys have been held, which can assist in this regard.

Following the Afghanistan War of October 2001, *Q-News* polled over 1,000 of its readers, and published the results in its November 2001 issue.[103] This survey showed that 79% were not convinced that bin Laden and al-Qa'ida were responsible for the 9/11 attacks, and 23% said that they would go to Afghanistan as *jihad* fighters alongside the Taliban and bin Laden. A further 54% felt that the participationist-inclined Muslim Council of Britain did not represent them.

Around the same time the BBC commissioned a poll of 500 British Muslims.[104] The results were strikingly similar to those of the *Q-News* poll. Some 80% opposed the military action by the US and UK in Afghanistan, while 25% said they were in favour of fighting alongside the Taliban. A total of 57% said they believed that the war was directed against Islam, not just against terrorism (as was claimed by Prime Minister Tony Blair). Some 15% said the terrorist attacks of 9/11 were justified or somewhat justified, and 67% were unwilling to accept that bin Laden was responsible for 9/11.

Further support for these findings was provided by a *Sunday Times* survey, the first large-scale poll of the Muslim community after the commencement of the bombing campaign against Afghanistan.[105] Some 1,170 British Muslims were interviewed outside mosques across Britain. Around 40% considered that bin Laden had cause to wage war against America, and 11% believed there was some justification for the attacks on the World Trade Center and the Pentagon. Around 40% said British Muslims who chose to fight alongside the Taliban were right to do so. When asked if it was more important for them to be Muslim or to be British, 68% said their faith identity took priority.

In the lead-up to the Iraq War, a further BBC poll of 500 British Muslims was taken in December 2002. It found that over half still believed that Osama bin Laden and his al-Qa'ida terrorist network should not have been blamed for the 9/11 attacks.[106] Some 11% held that further attacks on America by al-Qa'ida would be justified, and 8% said that such an attack on Britain would be justified. A significant majority of 84% wanted the British government to have the approval of the United Nations and Parliament before taking any action against Iraq.

The Research and Documentation Committee of the MCB carried out a special survey of over 120 Muslim bodies as military preparations for the Iraq War intensified. It reported that 'the vast majority of British Muslims were opposed to any military strike against Iraq'.[107] This was borne out by a survey taken by *Q-News* via email from mid-March to mid-April 2003. This survey showed opposition to the war at 97%; only 3% were in favour of the American and British invasion, mainly believing it necessary in order to remove Saddam Hussein from power. Those surveyed were mostly living in Britain (70%), with smaller numbers resident in the USA (10%), Netherlands (6%), Turkey (5%), Pakistan (3%), Canada (2%), Indonesia (2%), and the United Arab Emirates (2%). *Q-News* summed up the results of this survey: 'The results showed a range of views and reactions in one respect, but in another, something very strange for the global Muslim community; that of being homogeneous and having a united instinct.'[108]

Internal tensions and self-criticism

While these figures show overwhelming opposition among British Muslims to the military campaigns in Afghanistan and Iraq, it is also evident that the community is not monolithic in regard to these issues. Even though Muslim opposition to the Iraq campaign was considerable, there were Muslim voices who spoke in support of the campaign. Chief among these were British Kurds, though their opinions received short shrift from the MCB in its various statements.

What is evident is that, while a clear majority of British Muslims fall into the participatory mindset described earlier, there has been a rise in militant ideology among British Muslims, especially among the youth. In 1996 Zaki Badawi could confidently dismiss the influence of extremist groups, saying that 'the vast majority of Muslims want to live as full members of the British community and participate in the whole life of the society'.[109] Shagufta Yaqub considers radical groups to be marginalized and irrelevant, saying that Muslim extremists 'have a very narrow understanding of Islam and, to some extent, a distorted one which most British Muslims cannot relate to'.[110]

The struggle between participatory and separatist mindsets is, however, still very much alive. In 1997 *Q-News* cited a new book that suggested that 'a whole generation of aspiring [Islamic] youth disillusioned by social and economic marginalisation is in danger of falling under the spell of the false prophet of Islamic extremism'.[111]

The militant groups carry their struggle into the very faces of their Muslim opponents. A protester from Al-Muhajiroun who was picketing the launch of the MCB in November of that year said: 'The name itself is unIslamic. There is no such thing as British Muslims. [It is better to say] a Muslim living in Britain . . . Every problem that exists in Muslim countries is my problem as well. With this mentality of being a British Muslim, if problems exist outside Britain, it's not your problem – and that is contrary to what Islam says.'[112]

Anjem Choudary of Al-Muhajiroun carried the criticism of MCB much further:

> We don't think that the Muslim Council of Britain represents Islam. What they are trying to do is they're trying to go to the Government with their begging bowls to ask them for hospitals, for schools, for changes to the law. Hospitals, schools and mosques – building of these things is not going to bring about a revolution. You're not going to change society and make them embrace Islam as an ideology, as a way of life.'[113]

The antagonism between the MCB and radical groups reached a head in early 2004. When more than a dozen young radical British Muslims were arrested and charged with planning a terrorist attack in Britain, the MCB sent a letter to heads of mosques and Islamic organizations in Britain, calling for vigilance within the community in the face of such activities by radicals and for liaison with and reporting to police if any terrorist activity was detected within the community.[114] Lord Ahmed of Rotherham, a Muslim peer in the House of Lords, issued a similar statement.

Radical groups responded quickly, with Shaykh Omar Bakri Muhammad issuing a *fatwa* against Lord Ahmed. Iqbal Sacranie, head of the MCB, condemned this response, saying, 'This so-called *fatwa* that is issued is clearly incitement to murder.'[115] But even more moderate elements among the British Muslim community were uncomfortable with the suggestion of co-operating with the authorities. In a somewhat less vitriolic response, Fareena Alam, managing editor of *Q-News*, described as 'deeply offensive and parochial' such a call for Muslims to report their co-religionists to the police, adding: 'if we were to turn in "suspicious" people or the militant few, we would be turning them over to a police force that detains without charge, a justice system that can bypass due process and a media that is [*sic*] ruthless'.[116]

Sahib Mustaqim Bleher of the Islamic Party of Britain addressed the 'participate v. separate' dilemma, and lambasted the approaches of militant Muslim groups as well as of the MCB:

What should Muslims do? Withdraw, participate, infiltrate? The discussion goes on forever. There is the idea that we could run a separate system parallel to the dominant one, Muslim Parliament style, for example. It is as exciting as the illusion in the head of the little child whom the captain of a large ship lets hold the steering wheel for a few moments and he imagines he is solely responsible for the voyage of the vessel through the sea. It is idealistic and illusionary, but certainly not mature. Neither is the fanatical everything-is-haram[sacred territory]-until-we-have-a-caliph approach of Hizb-ut-Tahrir or Al-Muhajirun. On the other side of the spectrum are those who, like the Muslim Council of Britain, attempt to get concessions by flirting with the powerful. But are two, three Muslim schools and a recognition of Eid as a public holiday going to make a substantial difference to the lives of two to three million Muslims in Britain? Are they going to make them feel less insecure economically, socially and vis-à-vis rising levels of prejudice and racism? And what about the rest of the population? Do we have no responsibility towards them whatsoever?[117]

The last word could be usefully left to Sarah Joseph of the Islamic Society of Britain, who casts a theological spin on Muslim diversity in

Britain: 'There are divisions within every religious and political group, and diversity and variation is [*sic*] a sign of the creating and creative forces of God . . . Why as human beings do we seek to have homogeneity? That is not the purpose of Islam, and one of the greatest aspects or . . . real strengths of Islam is its incorporation of diversity.[118]

Conclusions

The preceding discussion raises many issues for Christians. From a certain angle one can discern much that is alien. For example, the refusal to participate in the electoral process because it is seen as promoting human sovereignty over that of the divine is not likely to attract much support from Christians. Violent confrontation with a British social system seen as alien is difficult to reconcile with mainstream Christian doctrine and teaching.

Yet in other ways certain Muslim perspectives as presented in this chapter are not so far away from those held by Christians. The motivations that drive Muslim parents to choose a particular education system for their children are often similar to those driving Christian parents. A desire to provide a good education within a sound moral and ethical context, where an overt recognition of God is present, is shared across faith boundaries.

Furthermore, one could argue for a sense of kinship with Muslims in their struggle to retain a pure faith in a hostile environment. There are parallels with the Christian's desire to be 'in the world but not of it', a discussion that forms the basis for many a Sunday church sermon across denominations. Many Christians and Muslims share the experience of living in a foreign land. And both Christians and Muslims would see themselves as functioning as 'the salt of the earth' (Matthew 5:13), although they would not see each other in this role.

Christians and Muslims often fail to appreciate that they have these concerns in common. It is all too easy to focus on the difference and overlook the similar perspectives. Yet it is these very similarities that can provide bridges across faith boundaries. We shall return to this theme in later discussion.

3. INTERNATIONAL ISLAMIC PERSPECTIVES ON GLOBALIZATION

There has been a marked increase in attention within the Islamic world to the challenges of globalization in recent years. Discussion of this phenomenon has increased in quantity in line with the worldwide resurgence of Islamic identity in the last quarter of the twentieth century.

This Muslim consideration of the impact of globalization has resulted in the holding of a steadily increasing number of events connected with the issue at various locations in the Muslim world. One such event was the fifth International Conference on Islamic Economics and Finance, held at the University of Bahrain on 6–8 January 2003, which included a section on Islam and globalization. This event was jointly sponsored by the Islamic Research and Training Institute of the Islamic Development Bank (Jeddah), the University of Bahrain, and the International Association for Islamic Economics (UK). Conference documentation posed the following question to participants:

> What is the stand of Islam with respect to the integration of mankind through various means, including the free movement of goods, services, capital and manpower, and the conditions that have been laid down by Islam and Muslim scholars for this purpose? A critical evaluation of the present globalization movement, and in particular, the effort of the WTO [World Trade Organization] and the IMF [International Monetary Fund] to liberalize trade and capital movements. What can the Muslim countries do to promote the beneficial characteristics of globalization and to strip it of its undesirable characteristics and effects?

Southeast Asian Muslims have also been active in addressing the globalization issue, giving particular attention to it in Malaysia. For example, the International Institute of Public Policy and Management (INPUMA) of the University of Malaya held a seminar on 'Islam, Globalization and the Knowledge Economy: Issues and Challenges' on 26 March 2002 at Concorde Hotel, Shah Alam.[1] The three papers presented were devoted to

'Globalization, ICT [information and communications technology] and Islam after September 11: A Brief Commentary', 'The Encounter between Islam and the West: Changing Relationships in Knowledge and Power, with Special Reference to the History of Science' and 'Globalization and Islamisation: from Clash to Dialogue'.

The World Conference of Islamic Scholars, held in Putrajaya, Malaysia, on 10–12 July 2003, focused on the theme 'Islam in the Era of Globalization'.[2] Almost 900 participants, including ninety foreign scholars, attended the conference. Papers presented included: 'Faith in the True Religion in the Era of Globalization', 'Prudent Management of National Wealth Resources for Muslims in Confronting Global Competitions: Malaysia's Experience', and 'Problems of Muslim Women in the Era of Globalization'.

These events and the discussion surrounding them highlight the concern that many Muslims feel about the phenomenon of globalization as they perceive it. As Prince Hassan of Jordan says, 'Globalisation (*'awlamah*) in our part of the world is held in deep suspicion.'[3]

This chapter surveys a number of different Muslim perspectives on globalization, and provides some context to feelings of concern felt by Muslims, as well as solutions that they propose to its challenges. In order to avoid the trap of stereotyping Muslim views, I shall make reference to the three-way typology of Muslim approaches to the modern world presented in the Introduction above, distinguishing between modernizers, traditionalists and Islamists, as this typology is relevant in considering Muslim perspectives on globalization.

Muslim diagnoses of contemporary aspects of globalization

What is globalization?

The prominent western scholar Professor Fred Halliday of the London School of Economics neatly encapsulates the various aspects of globalization: 'Globalization . . . encompasses . . . the breaking down of barriers between societies, economies and political systems and the greatly increased volume of exchanges they enjoy, be they in terms of trade, finance, people or ideas.'[4]

This multidimensional nature of globalization is also emphasized by Professor Ali Mazrui, whom we could consider a Muslim modernizer. He is a leading Muslim authority on globalization, and Director of the Institute of Global Cultural Studies at the State University of New York. He suggests that globalization has acquired three distinct meanings. The first relates to information, and is best exemplified by the information superhighway. The second is economic, related to 'forces which are transforming the global market and creating new economic interdependencies across vast distances'. The third usage is composite in nature, represented by the coming together of forces that act together as 'major engines of globalization: religion, technology, economy and empire'.[5] Mazrui suggests that the combination of these four forces have created globalization processes to such an extent that by the end of the twentieth century the world had become gradually and culturally homogenized as well as hegemonized. Mazrui argues that this process has been reinforced by the policies of the International Monetary Fund and the World Bank.[6]

A. S. Gammal supplies an Islamist perspective on globalization. He sees it as essentially trade-driven:

> Globalization is essentially an economic process that begins in America and eventually involves its trilateral partners in Europe and Japan. Taking the ideology of neo-liberalism as its rhetorical fuel, globalization seeks to create a world economy that benefits American corporations, first and foremost, and other transnational companies that operate by American-defined rules.

Like many fellow Islamists, Gamal sees conspiracy at work. He considers that the global media are agents in this process of globalization: 'The global news media uniformly trumpet the virtues of "globalization" . . . But these media are merely an arm of the process they claim to report as news, and they have vested interest in convincing humanity that there is no choice but to globalize.'[7] Rahhalah Haqq writes in similar terms: 'Globalization is a euphemism for Westernization (more specifically, Americanization), and . . . the Western corporate media have already convinced most of the world that globalization is inevitable and that everyone will have to accept it and adjust to it.'[8]

In southeast Asia, arguably the most outspoken critic of globalization is former Malaysian Prime Minister Mahathir Mohamad, who is particularly concerned about the impact of globalization on the Islamic world. Though he would be best described as a modernizer, Mahathir agrees with Islamists in seeing globalization as an instrument for re-establishing western colonial control over the developing world:

> Recolonization has begun, and it is recolonization by the same people . . . This is what globalization may be about . . . [Developing] countries are faced with globalization, a single world in which they know they will have little say, their voices drowned, and their interest ignored in the pursuit of global interest and objectives as defined by others.[9]

In summary, the Muslim writers considered thus far see multiple dimensions to globalization, with trade as the primary driving force; and America is held to be ultimately responsible. We shall now look at a more detailed Islamic analysis of these various dimensions of globalization.

Economic globalization

Most Muslim writers on globalization draw on statistics to make a case for a serious imbalance in the distribution of the world's wealth. One such writer points out that the West has only 22% of the world's population but consumes 70% of total world resources.[10]

Dr Mahathir Mohamad sees globalization primarily in economic terms: 'Globalisation is presently concerned only with opening up existing markets and maximising profits.'[11] And he sees conspiracy driving economic globalization:

> It is clear that the developed countries wish to use the [World Trade Organization] to impose conditions on the developing countries which will result, not in improving human rights or labour practices or greater care for the environment, but in stunting their growth and consequently the suffering for their people . . . Already, the developed West has shown they are not interested in these matters in themselves, but are interested in these only in those countries which pose a threat to the West. If these countries are absolutely poor and producing nothing that constitutes a threat to the developed countries of the West, the plight of their people in terms of human rights or labour practices or environment matter not at all. But if these countries are competing with the West in any way then their records are scrutinized and threats issued. The net effect is to prevent the development of these countries and their emergence as newly industrializing economies.[12]

Mahathir goes on to explain how economic globalization will swamp small-business enterprise in the developing world:

> The effect of economic globalization would be the demise of the small companies based in the developing countries. Large international corporations originating in the developed countries will take over everything . . . The manufacturing, trading and telecommunications companies together with the banks will grow and merge, controlled and run by the huge core companies of the developed world. The little players from the small countries would be absorbed and would disappear. Their shareholders, big players when they were in the small companies, will wield insignificant authority in the huge conglomerates. And so will their CEOs and other executives, reduced to mere names on the payroll.[13]

His comments on globalization can be seen as part of his strongly anti-western rhetoric.

President Husni Mubarak of Egypt expressed concern with economic globalizing tendencies at a summit of the D8 group of the eight most populous Muslim nations, held in February 2001: 'Open markets in today's world are basically accessible for the products of advanced countries, while our exports . . . are faced every day with new protectionist procedures, overt or covert, that impede their access to the advanced countries' markets.'[14]

The D8 members (Bangladesh, Egypt, Iran, Indonesia, Malaysia, Nigeria, Pakistan and Turkey) have a combined population of 800 million, representing about 17% of the world's population, but only a 4% share in world trade. The formation of this group represents in part a response to globalization.

While modernizing politicians such as Mahathir and Mubarak offer a sophisticated analysis of economic factors and trends in the globalization discussion, Islamist voices focus more on popular responses to international economic factors. A. S. Gammal warmly endorses the 'People's Movement' against globalization, which has been increasingly active through demonstrations in Seattle, various parts of Europe, Australia and other locations in recent years. Gammal writes:

> Beginning in the 1970s, the anti-globalization citizens' movement is presently centered around four well-organized and active international campaigns that work on opposing the World Trade Organization, supporting Third World debt-cancellation, reforming international financial organizations (e.g. the World Bank and the International Monetary Fund), and countering global financial markets by way of a tax on all financial transactions.[15]

Many Muslim writers such as Gammal are happy to endorse such campaigns, but the thrust of their rhetoric is not that Muslims should join such existing campaigns, but rather that they should seek Islamic alternatives.

Globalization and regionalization in the world economy, and relative marginalization of the Muslim states from this trend, are certainly fuelling the resurgence of political Islam and of activist groups. But other factors are at work too, especially in the area of social and cultural globalization.

Other globalizations
Social and cultural globalization
When restrictions on the formation of political parties were lifted in Indonesia after the fall of former President Suharto in May 1998, Muhammad Anis Matta became General Secretary of the new Islamist Partai Keadilan (Justice Party) at the tender age of thirty. This party described itself as 'one of the many parties which are based on the Islamic masses . . . Our party, which supports the concept of a united Indonesia, rejects Pancasila as the ideological foundation of the party.'[16] In rejecting the Indonesian state philosophy of Pancasila ('Five principles'), the Justice Party was placing itself

firmly in opposition to the multifaith pluralist policies that had characterized Indonesia up to that point.[17]

Anis Matta is particularly cautious towards cultural globalization. One of his public lectures reflects an Islamist critique of this form of globalization. He argues that in the modern world it is inevitable that different nations will be in contact with one another, with a consequent impact on identity, both personal and cultural. Anis Matta expresses great concern about the globalizing impact of American culture, which he sees as spread by various means: tourism, Hollywood films and fast food.[18]

These themes are repeatedly articulated by Islamist writers. Zafar Bangash[19] similarly sees cultural globalization in terms of Americanization:

> Globalization means not merely uniformity but also conformity to the dominant, primarily American culture. This applies as much to food as it does to music and clothes. People around the world are expected to eat greasy McDonald hamburgers, drink Pepsi or Coke, wear Levi jeans and gyrate to Michael Jackson music. If they have any spare time left, then the ubiquitous CNN is there to occupy it.[20]

Bangash laments how this cultural influence overflows in negative ways in the moral sector: 'Culture is not value-free. It brings with it such other baggage as feminist rhetoric, concern about environmental issues, drugs, the "freedom" to indulge in homosexuality and lesbianism, the "right" to have an abortion and to have children out of wedlock.'[21]

Bangash sees the presence of westernized 'political and business elites' in non-western societies as serving as a fifth column for the American globalization of culture. Furthermore, Bangash speaks of 'another, more sinister agenda that is wreaking havoc in non-western societies'; namely, feminism and select environmental and human-rights concerns: 'The problems non-western women face are not related to the right to earn equal wages with men or to be "free" to sleep with as many partners as possible. They have more basic concerns: how to feed their children, get safe drinking water, clothe and shelter them and to be able to give them medicine to prevent their premature death from preventable diseases.'[22]

Such a critique is not just expressed by Islamist individuals such as Anis Matta and Bangash. The militant Jamaat-e-Islami party of Pakistan echoes these sentiments, finding in their arguments justification for Islamic resurgence:

> Movements of Islamic resurgence are not allergic to modernity. They stand for modernisation and progress but they want to achieve modernisation and progress in the context of their own culture and values. What they disapprove of

is imposition of Western culture and values through overt and covert means over a people who have their own distinct culture and civilisation.[23]

Furthermore, it is not only Islamist writers who are concerned with social and cultural globalization. Dr Mahathir Mohamad laments the effects of globalization on local culture:

> Globalization will result in all societies being exposed to the global culture . . . Today violence and sex already dominate the screens. Attempts to reduce this unwholesome fare have met with little success. The appeal of thrill and sensuality are too great and too effective for the profit-oriented companies to eschew these themes. With globalization the effect of the 24-hour thousand channel TV would be to standardize world culture as promoted by the broadcasting giants of the world. They are not likely to be conservative and responsible. They are going to ensure that their companies outbid each other in terms of profits. Today's youth already wear the same uniforms – the jeans. They keep their hair long and as untidy as possible. They only care for the pleasures of life. They have little regard for traditional values, for age and the family and institutions such as marriage and family.[24]

Again, in this statement we see that economic globalization forms the primary driving force behind other manifestations of the globalizing phenomenon.

Political globalization

American President George Bush Sr came out in early 1990 with a fresh call for a new world order. The collapse of the Soviet Union and the Gulf War victory were key catalysts for such a declaration. Bush's vision was based on six principles:

> It was claimed that 'no aggressor would in the future be allowed to go unpunished', that 'occupation by force would not be tolerated', that 'international boundaries would not be allowed to be changed arbitrarily', that 'human rights would have to be respected by all', that 'it would be ensured that any violence of human rights is brought to an end' without the constraint of national boundaries, and that 'the United Nations would play a new role as the peace-keeper of the world'.[25]

Though President Bush no doubt genuinely foresaw new possibilities of global political stability, many Muslim commentators considered that this call was motivated by an American desire for greater political hegemony.

Dr Ahmed Kamal Aboulmagd,[26] a prominent Egyptian Muslim modernizer, points to the change in the world political order over the last thirty years as a key factor in stimulating the contemporary march of globalization. The collapse of the former eastern bloc is seen to enforce the notion that there is 'only one way . . . and that way is capitalism', according to Aboulmagd. He asks how Islamic society can contribute to the 'march of humanity' without losing its individuality, because 'to lose your individuality is to become irrelevant'.[27]

The Islamist Jamaat-e-Islami of Pakistan characteristically expressed its opinions in more conspiratorial terms. It was not persuaded that the USA as the sole military and political superpower would create utopian conditions in the world: 'Pax Americana is as revolting as Pax Britainica or Pax Espania. All talk about [a] unipolar world and only one supreme power gives rise to newer fears and apprehensions. This is seen as the beginning of a new imperial order. A just world order cannot be produced through hegemonistic encounters.'[28] The Bush statements stressed the spread of democratic values and human rights as central to principles of the new world order. The Jamaat responded cynically:

> Democracy at the philosophic level, which affirms the principle of sovereignty of man and denies existence of eternal and absolute religious and moral values, is at variance with the Islamic concept of world and society. Islam affirms the sovereignty of God and believes that man needs divine guidance. By definition the Muslim is one who accepts the divine law as the source of guidance for his individual and collective behaviour.[29]

Muslim remedies: Islamic globalization

Having examined the diagnosis of a range of Muslim writers, let us now turn our attention to the remedies proposed by Muslim writers on the much discussed topic of globalization.

Professor Ibrahim Abu-Rabi, a modernizing writer on Islam and globalization, says: 'Most thinkers in the Muslim world, from the radical to the most conservative, assume globalisation is an "inevitable phenomenon".'[30] He concludes that the globalization process by the West will effectively recolonize the Islamic world. Similarly, Ali Mazrui, the modernizing academic considered earlier, sees an inevitability about the ongoing challenge of globalization, predicting that the Muslim world will become 'a battle ground' of the forces of globalization in the twenty-first century.[31]

Dr Mahathir Mohamad diagnoses the cause of the Muslim world's ills in the context of globalization in terms that have been regularly heard through-out Muslim history, especially at times of weakness:

> We must ask ourselves why the Muslims have to endure this humiliation presently; why we have become so weak and incapable of standing up for our rights. What has changed which has made the great Muslim civilisation fall to such a low level? Is it because Islam is a backward religion; is it what Allah has ordained for us, or takdir [fate] or is it that we, the Muslims have wrongly understood our religion and not practised it correctly? . . . The only conclusion that we can make for the sad fate of the Muslims is that they are not practising the true teachings of Islam, that the Islam that they now practise is wrongly interpreted.[32]

This diagnosis resembles that provided at many points in past Muslim history when Islam was weak. Examples can be found in the writings of Ibn Taymiyya, writing in the thirteenth century when the Arab world was recovering from the devastations of the Mongol invastions, as well as the writings of Muhammad Ibn Abd al-Wahhab during the reformist revolution in Arabia in the late eighteenth century. Unlike some of his reformist predecessors, however, Mahathir eschews violence in identifying a remedy: 'Our salvation will not be achieved by blindly killing innocent people [as occurred in the 9/11 attacks]. Rather we should plan and execute a long-term development plan and to excel in all fields. Our rehabilitation will take a long time. We have to be patient.'[33]

How is such a development plan to be laid out? What specific remedies are proposed by our Islamic writers, thinkers and leaders to address what they see as the destructive effects of Americanization/globalization?

It is crucial to note that the solutions proposed are not built on an opposition to globalization *per se*. As Miasami observes: 'Islam is not against the process of globalization per se, but rather . . . the tension is due to the process of Westernization.'[34] Solutions are based on harnessing the forces of globalization for different ends. In other words, globalization itself is not necessarily bad as an idea, providing that it is the right kind of globalization.

This is articulated in the final resolution of the World Conference of Islamic Scholars, held in Malaysia on 10–12 July 2003, which focused on the theme 'Islam in the Era of Globalization'. It succinctly proposed Islamic globalization as the remedy for existing forms of globalization in identifying future objectives:

> Striving to create awareness among the Muslim community on the dangers of globalisation whose concept is designed by the superpowers which are the new

colonialists (neo-imperialists) in the field of politics, economics and culture, and to enhance efforts to explain the type of globalisation enjoined by Islam as a system which brings mercy to the universe.[35]

But such high-sounding ideals need to be unpacked to be of much use. Prince Hassan of Jordan suggests interfaith dialogue, mutually agreed codes of conduct, and a recognition of a necessary balance between rights and responsibilities, or rights and obligations.[36]

Dr Mahathir Mohamad calls for 'globalization in the service of mankind. Globalisation must serve us and not we humankind serve globalisation.'[37] He calls for globalization to be planned carefully, and for the planning to be carried out by people from all parts of the globe, not just by rich westerners. He argues for an Islamic dimension to globalization if it is to be desirable.

Islamic economic globalization

The 'Cairo Declaration', issued after the summit of D8 leaders in February 2001, voiced concern that developing countries were unable to get a fair share of the benefits of globalization, and stressed the private sector's role in development. In a vote for Islamic unity, the D8 leaders decided to 'negotiate as a bloc with developed countries during the next meeting of World Trade Organization economy ministers'.[38]

This sense of greater solidarity, and the recognition of the need for Muslim nations to act in the face of economic globalization, were reflected in the final resolution of the World Conference of Islamic Scholars held in Putrajaya in July 2003, which included calls for concerted action:

> Efforts must be carried out to enhance the economy of the ummah by managing its wealth and resources systematically, effectively and competitively; and by establishing a resilient economy network and strong cooperation among Islamic countries, besides establishing smart cooperation with countries across the world in order to create an economic balance among the international community.[39]

Muslim nations, groups and individuals are thereby exhorted to take such a general statement of intent and translate it into concrete suggestions. Malaysian leaders have been prominent in moving ahead with these proposals.

Dr Mahathir unpacks his ideas in interesting ways. He points out that there is a significant volume of business and trade between Malaysia on one side and Europe and America on the other. He proposes that a way out of this dependence on the West would be afforded by greater Islamic solidarity in trade: 'Much of this business and trade can be redirected to the Islamic world

...We have asked Petronas, the national petroleum company of Malaysia, to invest in transportation, oil and gas exploration projects in Sudan.'[40]

In fact, the oil reserves of Muslim nations are a key factor in this altern-ative Islamic economic globalization. This idea is developed by Datuk Ishak Iman Abas, director of finance of Petronas, who proposes that income from the oil of Muslim nations is the 'Basic Economic Strength of the Ummah'. He states that lack of economic productivity in Muslim nations 'is simply because of the gross inadequacy of capital resource'. He puts forward a spe-cific proposal:

> As a long-term measure to effectively address the capital resource inadequacy, it is necessary that [Islamic Development Bank] Member countries establish a capital formation mechanism with the sole objective of accumulating and building capital resource to fund investments on productive capacities within IDB Member countries. For the capital formation initiative it is suggested that IDB Member countries incorporate an Investment Corporation. The Corporation is funded by way of contributions by oil-producing IDB Member countries. The contribution be set at 1.5% of the value of oil produced and that the contribution be made monthly or quarterly. The contribution should be classified as Capital Fund and not loan or grant. Profit made by the Corporation is distributable as dividend to the contributors of the Capital Fund.[41]

Mahathir goes so far as to propose that a unified currency for the Muslim world may be worth considering:

> The gold dinar was the single currency of the Muslim world until the collapse of the Ottoman Empire in 1924. Trade flourished and a prosperous Muslim rule was established based on knowledge, a strong economy and global conquests. Through trade, Islam also spread to the farthest corners of the earth. In recent years, however, Islamic currencies have become tools of speculation and manipulation . . . I . . . suggested that the gold dinar be adopted in trade deals among Islamic countries to cushion them from foreign currency risks and protect the sovereignty and wealth of Islamic nations from the ravages of globalisation.[42]

Specific matters of trade co-operation and currency-sharing could fall within a broad-based Islamic economic and financial system, according to Mahathir:

> The [Islamic Financial Services Board] was suggested some time ago but its creation became very important after 11 September [2001]. It is aimed at reinforcing the stability of the Islamic banking system and making it a global

force in the face of conventional Western markets . . . if we persist and act rationally, we will be able to build a sound and strong Islamic financial system.[43]

A key factor in resisting the trend for Muslim economies to follow western models is the rapidly developing Islamic banking system. Malaysia is at the forefront of innovations in Islamic banking principles and practice.[44] In the two decades following the establishment of the country's first Islamic bank, Bank Islam Malaysia Berhad, in 1983, Malaysia's Islamic financial institutions increased to thirty-six in number, comprising fourteen commercial banks (of which four are foreign), ten finance companies, five merchant banks, and seven discount houses.[45] Indeed, the Bank Negara Malaysia has claimed that the country's innovations in Islamic banking are 'recognised by many Islamic countries as the model of the future', though that model has attracted criticism from some quarters within the Muslim world.[46] Nevertheless, the impact on the southeast Asian region is unquestioned, as indicated in a *Q-News* report: 'The Malaysian experience of Islamic banking has had a tremendous impact on neighboring countries. Indonesia established its first Islamic bank in 1992, followed by Brunei Darussalam in 1993. Thailand has also announced the creation of its first Islamic bank.'[47]

Malaysia wishes to promote itself as the hub of the rapidly developing market for Islamic investments, especially bonds. HSBC Holdings estimates the global market for Islamic investment products as worth more than $200 billion. Malaysia made a significant entry into this market in 2002 when it issued $600 million in five-year Islamic bonds denominated in dollars.[48]

Other Islamic globalizations
Social and cultural globalization

Key instruments for promoting an Islamic form of social and cultural globalization are the media in their various forms. The Islamist writer Rahhalah Haqq proposes an engagement with modern technologies:

> The time is ripe for Muslims to launch their own media conglomerates, with independent satellites and broadcasting. There is certainly ample wealth and talent in the ummah for this, and colonization and fear are the only real obstacles. This needs to be done not only for *da'wah* or providing information about Islam for public-relations purposes, but in order to provide an alternative perspective – in this case Islamic – on how the world works, why it got that way, and where it might be heading.[49]

Haqq emphasizes the important role to be played by Islamic sacred scripture in this process: 'By mining the Qur'an, Seerah, and other sources of Islamic wisdom and insight, Muslims can contribute to an emerging "third way" and leave the West to its own devices, to implode or self-destruct, or simply fade away.'[50]

Anis Matta emphasizes the importance of education for Muslims. He argues that if Indonesians are not strong in knowledge (i.e. education), then Indonesian culture will not be strong. He stresses that the new generation of Muslims must be educated in both Islamic and secular knowledge if they are to compete with the globalizing American culture.[51]

Ali Mazrui provides evidence of the 'counter-penetration of Islam and Muslims at large in the Western world. The evidence of significant Islamist presence in the Western world may reverse the wheel of cultural homegenisation,' he concludes.[52] Echoing this, the prominent Christian scholar Yvonne Yazbeck Haddad writes of 'The Globalization of Islam: The Return of Muslims to the West'.[53]

There are various other instruments for achieving a kind of Islamic globalization in social and cultural spheres. These include the increased prevalence of wearing head-covering by women throughout the Muslim world, in addition to the growth of this phenomenon among Muslim minority communities in the West. Also noticeable is the increased adoption of the Islamic calendar alongside the western calendar in Islamic societies, more Islamic television and radio programming in majority Muslim countries,[54] and the promotion of both the study of Arabic language and the use of Arabic script for local languages in countries such as Malaysia and Indonesia.

Political globalization

The key instrument for achieving a kind of Islamic political globalization is the concept of the *umma*, or the worldwide Islamic community. This concept embodies a push for identity that transcends family, tribal, clan, ethnic or national identities, and dates back to the covenant drawn up at Medina between Muhammad and the various tribes of Medina in AD 622. This concept is prioritized in the rhetoric of Islamist groups, such as Pakistan's Jamaat-e-Islami. Commenting on the ubiquitous nation-state structure, the Jamaat states:

> We can accept the nation state as a starting point, although it is not the Muslim ideal. It constitutes the present day reality and we do not want to dismantle political systems in an arbitrary manner. We want to bring about a greater sense of unity in the Islamic ummah, greater cooperation and increasing integration between the different Muslim states. Under Islamic idealism, every nation state would gradually become an ideological state and these would go to make up the commonwealth of Islam.[55]

Islamist groups have been increasingly prominent in recent decades as part of the worldwide Islamic resurgence. The 1990s, the first decade since the collapse of one of the world's two superpowers, witnessed the burgeoning of Islamic activist organizations with worldwide connections, often referred to as 'the Islamic movement'. Many of these organizations established their headquarters in Britain, benefiting from Britain's long tradition of liberalism in providing sanctuary for groups in exile from hostile home governments.

Many such Islamist groups have increasingly called for the resurrection of the *khilafa* (caliphate), arguing that the institution of caliph, which headed the worldwide Sunni community and was abolished by Kemal Attaturk's secularist government in Turkey in 1924, should be re-established so that God's blueprint for the world has an earthly structure that can oversee its implementation. These groups see this restoration as a key step in their overall goal of strengthening Islam's place in the world and, in effect, empowering a process of Islamic political globalization. The Jamaat-e-Islam of Pakistan embodies this approach: 'Islam has also propounded the principle of human vicegerency (Khilafat). This Khilafat is a popular Khilafat and is not confined to any group of people or class. Divine law provides the framework.'[56] The last sentence is crucial, indicating the central role of Islamic *shari'a* in achieving the worldwide Islamic society considered as ideal, especially by Islamists. The growing influence of Islamic law in various Muslim societies at the turn of the twenty-first century – such as Nigeria, Pakistan, Malaysia and Indonesia – is testimony to the slow but steady advance of this form of Islamic globalization.

Modernizing Muslim writers do not place such emphasis on the re-establishment of the caliphate or on the full implementation of *shari'a* in their support for the concept of *umma*. They prefer instead to stress international Islamic co-operative bodies, such as the Organization of Islamic Conference (OIC), an association of fifty-six Islamic states. The OIC charter aims to strengthen

- Islamic solidarity among Member States;
- Cooperation in the political, economic, social, cultural and scientific fields;
- The struggle of all Muslim people to safeguard their dignity, independence and national rights.[57]

In order to increase the political power of Muslim nations, the World Conference of Islamic Scholars, meeting in Malaysia in July 2003, indicated in its final resolution that enhancing military co-operation among Muslim states was a desirable objective:

> Striving to build a military force which is not dependent on foreign powers, by intensifying research and development (R&D), intelligence and training

activities, mastering military technologies, and inculcating the spirit of jihad. This is achieved through continuous and solid cooperation among the Islamic countries in the field of research, military equipment manufacturing and marketing.[58]

A Sufi perspective

So far we have considered the views of modernizers and Islamists on the various dimensions of globalisation. What of the Sufis, the mystics of Islam, who could be regarded as expressing a traditionalist, far less politicized approach to their faith? We shall consider the thinking of a local Sufi notable in Java, Muhammad Zuhri, who is attracting a following in his region of central Java.

In one of his writings,[59] Zuhri cites the famous medieval Sufi scholar Jalaluddin Rumi:

> Come, come, whatever you are
> It doesn't matter
> Whatever you are
> An infidel, an idolater, or a fireworshipper
> Come
> Our convent is not a place of despair
> Come
> Even if you violated your oath
> A hundred times
> Come again.

These verses embody a pluralist dimension usually lacking in Islamist writings. Zuhri suggests that Rumi had a globalizing mindset centuries before the term 'globalization' was coined. Zuhri writes:

> Seven hundred years ago before mankind had ever dreamed whether the thought of globalisation could occur to humanity or not, Maulana Jalaluddin Rumi (born 30 September 1207 in Balkh, Afghanistan) called to all people, whether infidels, idolaters or fire worshippers to approach him so that he could whisper in their ears that God's earth is not a place of despair and that their being was eternal.[60]

Zuhri argues that Sufism, not a modern understanding of globalization, is the default position. He insists that one should question, not whether the Sufi path is still relevant in the era of globalization, but rather whether the modern understanding of globalization is relevant. Zuhri goes on: 'A concept which has been established as clear and final does not need to be made an issue [for investigation], but rather should be either chosen as a way of life or not. Sufism, the path for the individual person to Godliness, is actualised through servanthood to all mankind for life.'[61]

Zuhri argues that, in contrast with Sufism, globalization is a term that has only recently been coined and is only in the process of being accepted by society. He insists that it is the 'newcomer' that should be made to justify its existence as a term, rather than Sufism, which is frequently subjected to challenge by Islamist as well as modernizing writers. In fact, says Zuhri, globalization has been around in the form of Sufism for centuries: ' "Globalization" can be seen as nothing new except for its name.'[62]

Zuhri's writing, though localized in impact, nevertheless reminds us that we need to exercise caution in uncritically accepting either modernizing or Islamist opinions as representative of all Muslim viewpoints. Clearly Zuhri and his followers look to Sufism as illuminating the path ahead.

Conclusions

Our survey of Islamic writers has shown us that Muslims of various types hold deep-seated reservations about globalization as it is most commonly perceived today; namely, as a western-driven set of forces impacting upon the political, economic, social and cultural fabric of Islamic societies. The prominent Malaysian scholar Farish Noor, of the Institute for Strategic and International Studies, speaks of 'the predicament of a Muslim world that feels itself increasingly threatened and marginalised by the forces of globalisation, leading to the defensive posture being adopted by many Muslim leaders themselves'.[63]

Modernizing Muslims tend to focus on the economic and political dimensions of globalization. Islamists, by contrast, express grave concerns about the impact of western globalization upon Muslim societies and cultures, and their response is typically defined in much more combative and rather more backward-looking terms.

Muslim criticism of western-driven globalization does not advocate its replacement by greater regionalism and localization. Indeed, Muslim writers, whether modernizing, Islamist or indeed Sufi, look to the inner resources of Islam for solutions to the challenges of globalization. Islam itself offers a number of different angles on an alternative globalization, be it in the political, economic, social or cultural sphere. Many of these paths of alternative globalization are already being trodden, as part of the worldwide resurgence of Islam. The World Conference of Islamic Scholars in Malaysia in July 2003 drew up plans to set in place structures to work towards objectives agreed at the gathering, with Malaysia to play a central role:

> In order to foster continuous cooperation and interaction among Islamic scholars and intellects across the world, it is crucial to establish a permanent secretariat based in Kuala Lumpur whose function is to act as a catalyst to build and produce sound and constructive ideas in order to enhance the status of the ummah and contribute towards the development of the Muslim world.[64]

These sentiments were echoed in the statements issued by the tenth session of the OIC Islamic summit conference held at Putrajaya, Malaysia, on 11–18 October 2003, which called for

> coordinated, focussed and regular interactions and exchange of views and ideas among Muslim scholars, businessmen, entrepreneurs, industrialists and policy makers on important issues of concern to the Muslim Ummah in the fields of economics, business, research and development, particularly in the context of the rapid process of globalisation and liberalisation.[65]

Yet from another angle Christians can identify with some Muslim responses to globalization. A concern with what is perceived as capitalist exploitation is felt equally strongly by many Christians, as is distaste for the impact on society of globalizing forces of an amoral nature. But such responses, while bearing similarities across faith lines, also potentially lead to rivalry, since the Christian message is no less global in its call than the Islamic. Christian mission is as much an alternative globalization as is Islamic *da'wa* (outreach).

To borrow and adapt a phrase from Samuel Huntington, we may well be on the threshold of a clash of globalizations, with Islamic globalization in its multiple forms posing an increasing challenge to the western-driven form of globalization that has dominated world trends for several generations. In turn, Christian global outreach will add another element to a potentially three-way rivalry.

PART 2

THE CHURCH RESPONDS

4. EVOLVING APPROACHES TO OTHER FAITHS AMONG THE CHURCHES

In chapter 1 we considered the move from exclusivism to inclusivism within both the church and society in the West over the last two centuries, and identified a range of contextual factors at work in driving this change in recent years, with particular relation to Christian–Muslim relations. We then proceeded to focus more closely on the Muslim community in Britain and its engagement with British society, and considered Muslim diversity in terms of specific issues. This was supplemented by an examination of international Islamic responses to western-driven globalization.

In the next two chapters, we shall undertake a comparative study of the Christian world, especially as it relates to Britain, and identify diverse Christian approaches to the question of right responses to other faiths, especially Islam. We shall examine three macro-level umbrella groups of Christians: the World Council of Churches, the World Evangelical Alliance, and the Roman Catholic Church.

The ecumenical approach and the World Council of Churches

The World Council of Churches (WCC) dates back to 1937, when church leaders agreed to establish a world council to strengthen Christian unity. This initiative was delayed by the onset of the Second World War, but the proposal was presented soon after the war concluded. The WCC was established on 23 August 1948 at its first General Assembly in Amsterdam.

At the beginning of the twenty-first century, the WCC includes almost all principal Christian denominations (over 330 denominations, and fellowships). It covers over 400 million Christians in over 100 countries. The notable absentee from the WCC is the Roman Catholic Church. However, Catholic–WCC contacts are regular. The Vatican sends observers to WCC Assemblies, Central Committee meetings and conferences. The Pontifical Council for Promoting Christian Unity also co-operates with the WCC in preparing materials.

The WCC has witnessed a remarkable change in the relative make-up of participation churches. At the time of its establishment, almost two-thirds of the founding churches came from Europe and North America. By the turn of the twenty-first century, almost two-thirds of the member churches came from the Caribbean, Latin America, the Middle East, Asia and the Pacific. This reflects a notable shift in the centre of gravity of world Christianity from Europe and North America to the Third World.

At its third Assembly at New Delhi in 1961, the WCC finalized its organizational basis, as part of the WCC Constitution. The basis serves as a mission statement. It simply states: 'The World Council of Churches is a fellowship of churches which confess the Lord Jesus Christ as God and Saviour according to the scriptures, and therefore seek to fulfill together their common calling to the glory of the one God, Father, Son and Holy Spirit.' This basis comprehensively addresses both key theological positions and the possibilities of fellowship and working together. A sense of Christian partnership has driven the WCC since its establishment. Indeed, the WCC has sought closer contact with other Protestant groups outside its umbrella, but progress has been slow, as indicated by a statement made after fifty years of activity:

> The fellowship of the WCC is limited by the absence of other churches which, for various reasons, have not sought membership. For example, unjustifiable barriers have arisen between the WCC and some Evangelical and Pentecostal churches because of tendencies on both sides to caricature or remain indifferent to each other. Some of these barriers have begun to break down through the development of ongoing contacts between the WCC and other bodies, such as the World Evangelical Fellowship. These efforts should be sustained by the search for new forms of relationships at all levels between WCC member churches, other churches and other ecumenical organizations.[1]

The World Council of Churches and other faiths

In 1961 the WCC Commission on World Mission and Evangelism was established to articulate and co-ordinate WCC activities in an area of major traditional church activity. The commission held its first meeting in 1963 in Mexico City and three years later convened a consultation in Lebanon. The consultation was attended mostly by Christian representatives based in Muslim countries, and it was agreed to initiate meetings with Muslims. This was a significant event, as it set in train a series of developments that were to crystallize the approach by the WCC to other faiths over coming decades.

From this point on events moved rapidly. In March 1967 a consultation was held in Kandy, Sri Lanka, where a significant statement was issued: 'Dialogue implies a readiness to be changed as well as to influence others . . . The outcome of dialogue is the work of the Spirit.'[2]

Two years later, a Muslim–Christian dialogue under the auspices of the WCC was convened in Cartigny, Switzerland. Three principal aims of dialogue were set down for the future:

- to achieve greater mutual respect and better understanding
- to raise questions which lead to deepening and renewal of spirituality
- to lead Christians and Muslims to accept and fulfill common practical responsibilities[3]

A note of caution was expressed in the statements emerging from the Cartigny meeting: 'The aim of dialogue cannot consist in arriving at artificial agreement. The encounter must not succumb to either syncretism or relativism. Dialogue must open the way for the two religions, on the basis of both their common ground and what is distinctive to each, to meet and ask each other the true questions.'[4]

In 1971, in recognition of the importance of the dialogue initiatives of the previous decade, the twenty-fourth meeting of the WCC Central Committee at Addis Ababa established a new unit, called 'Dialogue with People of Living Faiths and Ideologies', known simply as the Dialogue Unit.

In a watershed meeting in 1977 in Chiang Mai, Thailand, 'Guidelines on Dialogue' were drawn up.[5] The WCC itself states: 'These guidelines serve as the basis of interreligious dialogue sponsored by the WCC and many churches around the world.'[6] Indeed, various local guidelines have been subsequently drawn up by groups as diverse as the Episcopal Church of Canada[7] and the Presbyterian Church (USA),[8] but they closely reflect the 1977 Guidelines of the WCC.

In discussing the effectiveness of the early dialogue activities, Ataullah Siddiqui of the Islamic Foundation in Britain observes that 'at the international level [dialogue] with Muslims did not seem to take the path WCC wanted . . . Initially the Muslims invited by the WCC's Dialogue Unit were, broadly speaking, those whose views were not widely endorsed within the Muslim community itself, e.g. Hassan Askari.'[9]

The hesitancy to engage in dialogue among Muslims related in part to a problem of representation, with governments not being seen as appropriate speakers on religious issues and many Muslim religious scholars unwilling to participate. This left West-based Muslim liberals as the main Muslim contributors to dialogue activities.[10] This situation caused much suspicion towards dialogue among Muslims, as seen in the response of

the London-based Muslim periodical *Impact International* to the WCC
meeting between Christians and Muslims in Broumana, Lebanon, in 1972:

> Unless Muslim scholars make Islam comprehensible in a new terminology and,
> at the same time, see that nothing of the letter or essence of Islam is lost in the
> process, they will be cut off from the Muslim community, and any dialogue that
> Christians may choose to have with them as representatives of Muslim religion
> and culture will be no less and no more than a fiction, a make believe.[11]

During the 1980s, the WCC gradually changed its focus from the international to the regional level for promoting dialogue activities. In the early
1990s, however, the Dialogue Unit was closed because of financial con-
straints. Its functions did not cease altogether. Rather, it was restructured to
become a sub-unit of the WCC Secretariat called the Office on Interreligious
Relations and Dialogue (OIRRD).

The WCC dialogue staff, whether associated with the former Dialogue
Unit or the OIRRD, have issued several significant publications in the field.
The monograph *My Neighbour's Faith – and Mine* serves as a practical
manual that groups at the grass-roots level can use as the basis of local
dialogue activities. It has seen various editions since 1986. The periodical
Current Dialogue, a twice-yearly journal, reports on dialogue activities held
under WCC auspices around the globe, and also addresses strategic issues
relevant to multifaith relations.

In September 1997 the WCC issued a document called *Towards a
Common Understanding and Vision of the World Council of Churches*, which
addressed the role of the WCC in a religiously plural world. It commented:

> The inseparable connection between work for the unity of the church and
> work for the healing and wholeness of all creation will often bring the Council
> into dialogue and collaboration with persons, groups and organisations that are
> not identified by a specific Christian purpose or commitment. This includes in
> particular representative organisations of other faith communities or
> inter-religious bodies . . . they are indispensable partners for the WCC in its
> effort to foster dialogue and co-operation with people of other faiths in
> order to build viable human communities.

It was from this perspective that the WCC decided to invite fifteen guests of
other faiths to the 1998 Assembly[12] in Harare. Furthermore, the Assembly
asked the OIRRD to give visibility to 'dialogue and co-operation with people
of other faiths'. Thus the WCC has been one of the pioneers in emphasizing
the importance of interfaith dialogue in building bridges between the faiths.[13]

Fundamentally the WCC has identified dialogue, rather than traditional mission, as the central plank of its multifaith policy.[14]

The Four Principles of interfaith dialogue of the Council of Churches for Britain and Ireland

Hard on the heels of the WCC Guidelines on Dialogue, the British Council of Churches published *Relations with People of Other Faiths: Guidelines on Dialogue in Britain* (1981). This document introduced the Four Principles for dialogue developed by the WCC. In 1991 the Four Principles were revisited and discussion was carried forward in a document entitled *In Good Faith: The Four Principles of Interfaith Dialogue: A Brief Guide for the Churches*, published by the renamed Council of Churches for Britain and Ireland (CCBI). The work of the CCBI in this area was carried out by the Churches' Commission for Inter-Faith Relations. These Four Principles were endorsed by diverse British Protestant churches: the Church of England, the United Reformed Church, the Methodist Church of Great Britain, the Scottish Episcopal Church, and the Joppa Group of the Baptist Church.

The Four Principles, with explanation, are as follows.

1. *Dialogue begins when people meet each other.* Christians are encouraged to focus on individuals, not on systems, in this regard. In other words, when meeting a Hindu or a Muslim, Christians should not assume that they match stereotypes of the system of Hinduism or Islam. The CCBI documentation points out that often the individuals concerned know as little about their own faith as nominal Christians do in Britain.

2. *Dialogue depends upon mutual understanding and mutual trust.* On this point, the CCBI documentation stresses that partners in dialogue should be free to define themselves, in their own terms. Christians should seek to clear away misconceptions held by others about what Christians believe and teach.

3. *Dialogue makes it possible to share in service to the community.* It is pointed out that community depends on the co-operation of all its parts. When the parts consist of people with differing religious faiths, dialogue offers a way towards harmony.

4. *Dialogue becomes the medium of authentic witness.* This principle holds that dialogue based on trust provides opportunities for all to witness to their faith. It requires that each person be prepared to listen as well as to speak. The CCBI documentation adds: 'Dialogue assumes the freedom of a person of any faith including the Christian to be convinced by the faith of another.'[15]

Anglican perspectives on Christian–Muslim dialogue

At the level of the individual denominations that are members of the WCC, there has also been a noticeable shift in attitudes to other faiths, both reflecting and reinforcing WCC policy directions. The Anglican Church shows this trend clearly, and we shall examine it by considering several key Anglican perspectives on Christian–Muslim relations.

Kenneth Cragg: a new approach

The preface to the 1959 book *Sandals at the Mosque* by the well-known Anglican evangelical bishop Kenneth Cragg[16] highlighted a significant challenge that faced Christians in the post-war period. This challenge was based around three main concerns.[17]

First was the need to redefine Christianity so that it was no longer seen as being synonymous with the West in the context of a deteriorating reputation of the West among the newly emerging states that were formerly colonized by European powers. Second was the importance for the Christian church of presenting the gospel in a way that was inclusive of developing world societies. Third was the need to co-exist with other religions in a way that would not lead to a betrayal of the gospel.

This redefining of fundamental approaches, pioneered in the 1950s, relates closely to the issue of the guilt burden borne by the West for its colonial past (discussed earlier in this study). This new approach has been widely articulated within the Anglican Church since then. The church has moved to take decisive action and so to reflect this new approach. It has worked to embrace positively a Christianity that has an external profile very different from that which went before, and to approach other faiths with 'a spirit of expectancy to find how God has been speaking to [that faith] and what new understandings of the grace and love of God we may ourselves discover in this encounter'.[18] Here Bishop Cragg gives voice to the notion encountered in chapter 1, that Christians should seek to learn from other faiths, a far cry from William Carey's call to take the truth out to others. Cragg himself embraced this principle in his first book,[19] in which he calls on Christians to listen to what Islam has to say and to appreciate Islam at its best, before engaging in specific Christian responses to the Islamic message. In a later volume,[20] Cragg compiled an anthology of Christian and Muslim devotional writings, illustrating his belief that much of what Christians hold dear in the expression of their own faith finds echoes in Muslim writings.

Prince Charles: learning from Islam

Such calls for a new approach to other faiths within the Anglican Church had made a profound impact on the church at the highest levels by the turn of the twenty-first century. For example, during the 1990s HRH Prince Charles, future British monarch and thereby future head of the Church of England, was devoting increasing attention to religion in the United Kingdom, with particular reference to multifaith issues.

In a television interview with Jonathan Dimbleby,[21] in what was reported as 'the most watched and talked about documentary of 1994',[22] the Prince said that as monarch he would prefer to be known as 'Defender of Faith' rather than 'Defender of the Faith'. This reflects a response to the increasingly pluralist society around him, and it generated a considerable degree of controversy. There were calls for the coronation of Prince Charles to be a multifaith event, rather than a Christian coronation with its thousand years of tradition.[23]

The Oxford speech, 27 October 1993.[24] On Christian–Muslim relations, Prince Charles has delivered several key speeches. The first was given on 27 October 1993 at the Oxford Centre for Islamic Studies. This institution, of which Prince Charles is patron, received substantial funding support for its establishment from several overseas Muslim sources, principally the Sultan of Brunei and the royal families of Saudi Arabia and Kuwait. Its plans to build a 33-metre (108 ft) minaret in the centre of Oxford drew strong opposition from colleges of Oxford University and the public at large, though Prince Charles gave support to the plan.[25]

In his 1993 speech, which was interspersed with Arab proverbs, the prince pointed out that 'the degree of misunderstanding between the Islamic and Western worlds remains dangerously high'. He was critical of the West because of the history of European imperialism, as well as because it perpetuates superficial attitudes towards, and stereotypes of, the Muslim world. He reminded his audience of 'the debt our own culture and civilisation owe to the Islamic world', and declared that 'medieval Islam was a religion of remarkable tolerance for its time, allowing Jews and Christians the right to practise their inherited beliefs'. He concluded that 'Islam is part of our [European] past and our present, in all fields of human endeavour. It has helped to create modern Europe. It is part of our own inheritance, not a thing apart.' Addressing the future, Prince Charles called for the West to learn from Islam in the modern era, admiring 'its preservation of an integral view of the Universe', and observing that 'Christianity itself is poorer for having lost' this integrated view.

The Wilton Park speech, 13 December 1996.[26] In Prince Charles's second speech, given three years later on 13 December 1996, he developed the themes of the first presentation. He began by observing that 'Islamic civilisation at its best . . . has an important message for the West in the way it has retained a more integrated and integral view of the sanctity of the world around us'. The Prince observed that Christianity also once had this integral view, but, 'during the last three centuries, in the Western world at least . . . Science has tried to assume a monopoly – even a tyranny – over our understanding'. Interspersing the second speech with quotations from the Qur'an and Hadith, the Prince called for efforts 'to encourage understanding between the Islamic and the Western worlds'. Offering a specific suggestion, he said, 'Perhaps, for instance, we could begin by having more Muslim teachers in British schools.'

Prince Charles's two speeches generated widespread and passionate discussion within religious circles and the press. *Q-News* commented that for many the first 'oration was a public affirmation of the Prince's genuine affinity with Islam, an inevitable, almost logical step in his long and arduous quest for truth'. In contrast, an article in *The Guardian* on the second speech set out multiple quotations from the Qur'an that offered a different perspective from that of those cited by the Prince, claiming that they demonstrated the oppressive side of Islam regarding the place of women, punishment for extramarital sex and punishment for unbelievers.[27] The article pointed out that Prince Charles's anti-materialism tirade in his speeches was at variance with his own lifestyle, and speculated that his second speech was connected with his forthcoming trade promotional tour on behalf of the British Foreign Office to Kuwait, Bahrain, Qatar, Bangladesh and Saudi Arabia. In a similar vein, an article in *The Daily Telegraph* commented that Muslim teachers in schools might seek to undermine the foundations of British society and argued that it was unfair to compare the worst of the West with the best of Islam.[28]

The East London Mosque speech, 23 November 2001.[29] Prince Charles's two key speeches in the 1990s served clearly to state his perspectives on multifaith issues, especially with regard to the relationship between Islam and the West. The Prince has continued to address these issues since the 1996 speech, especially at times of increased tension between Islam and the West.

In the wake of the 11 September 2001 terrorist attacks on American targets, Prince Charles used the occasion of the launch of the London Muslim Centre Project at the East London Mosque to return to the topic of Islam's contribution to the West. In this speech the Prince pointed to the commitment of the British Muslim community, saying, 'I was extremely impressed to learn that the funds to buy the land were put together from the modest contributions of thousands of people who believed in the project's importance.'

He went on to address the spiritual points shared across faiths: 'The Christian, Jew and Muslim shares [*sic*] on an inner religious plane many of the same spiritual beliefs – in one divine God, in the transience of our earthly life, in our accountability before God for our actions, and in the assurance of life to come.' The points in common are not restricted to spiritual values, said the Prince, but included social values: 'We also share many key social values – compassion, tolerance, respect for family and the community, belief in justice and the search for greater wisdom and understanding.' In the context of the heightened tensions felt at the time, Prince Charles called for a focus upon elements that united across faiths, rather than divided:

> In fact, there is, I believe, far more that unites than divides the different faiths in this country, if only people would spend the time to investigate. Nobody has a monopoly on the truth. To recognise that is, I believe, a first step to real wisdom,

and a vital blow against the suspicion and misunderstanding that too often characterises [*sic*] the public relationships between different faiths.

The Islamic Foundation speech, 24 January 2003.[30] This further speech, of significance for our discussion, was made at the opening of the Leicester-based Islamic Foundation's Markfield Institute of Higher Education. In this speech, Prince Charles emphasized the wide-ranging debt of Europeans to Muslims:

> The legacy of Muslim scholarship is vast, ranging from mathematics to astrology, science, medicine, geography and the arts . . . Generations of school children have Muhammad Al-Khwarizmi to thank for introducing Europe to the joys of Algebra . . . It might even be questioned whether Columbus would ever have found his New World without the experience and skills of his Muslim navigators.

But the Prince went beyond expressing a debt of gratitude to Muslims as outsiders. Rather, he stressed that Islam in Britain is not a recent arrival, but has deep roots: 'As Muslims began to make this island their home, we saw the establishment in the early nineteenth century of "Mahomed's Baths and Shampooing Establishment" in once-fashionable Brighton.' Indeed, early converts to Islam meant that the faith could stake a claim for a measure of indigeneity: 'Liverpool solicitor and noted traveller William Henry Quilliam established the country's first Muslim school and orphanage in his home city, as well as a mosque and Islamic library . . . [there were] Muslim convert Lord Stanley of Adderley [and] Lord Headley, who announced his conversion to the faith of Islam in 1913.' Even the Royal family owes a debt to Islam, according to the Prince: 'My own family benefited from Islamic wisdom too – Queen Victoria, my great, great, great grandmother, was taught Hindustani using Persian script by Hafez Abdul Karim, one of several Indian staff in her household.'

Thus Prince Charles's speeches can be seen as developing a theme of much greater openness to other faiths, especially Islam, from the highest levels of British society. There is an overriding sense of inclusiveness in these speeches, even to the point of seeming at times to affirm Islam at the expense of Christianity, especially in regard to the integration of the temporal and the spiritual.

Clinton Bennett: outsiders becoming insiders

Growing numbers of Anglican clergy have become specialists in the study of Islam and Christian–Muslim relations. This has resulted in an increasing supply of scholarly studies by Anglicans in this field. One such scholar-priest is Clinton Bennett, author of two important historical studies, *Victorian Images of Islam* and *In Search of Muhammad.*[31]

The latter work is particularly useful in providing an insight into evolving Anglican approaches. In this work, Bennett presents Muhammad as a prophet from the outset. Furthermore, Bennett begins by defining his motto (following Wilfred Cantwell Smith): 'The aim of an outside scholar writing about Islam is to elicit Muslim approval.'[32] He adds: 'To pursue this study, I have tried to become a virtual Muslim.'[33] His tone tends to be apologetic, but is inclined towards an Islamic apologetic. For example, when Bennett addresses the occasion when Khalif Walid destroyed churches and forced Christians to use Arabic in place of Greek, he adds his own comment: 'Positively, this meant that Christians were subsequently able to play a fuller part in the intellectual life of the 'Abbassid Khalifate.'[34]

Towards the end of this study, Bennett addresses the traditional choice offered by scholars and missionaries between Christ and Muhammad. He asks, 'Is there any possibility that we are faced not with a choice between rivals but with complementary exemplars, both rooted in divine self-disclosure?'[35] He adds, crucially, 'I do not know *how* the Qur'an was communicated by God through Muhammad, but I can accept that it was.'[36] Bennett summarizes his position as follows: 'My ... preferred option is therefore for Christians and Muslims to accept that whilst on the one hand our theological formulations do not lack "truthfulness", on the other hand they do not exhaust the mystery of God.'[37]

These Anglican voices have demonstrated a marked shift in position away from a traditional exclusivist view of Islam. Bennett is approaching a pluralist position, while the views of Cragg and Prince Charles might be placed somewhere within the inclusivist spectrum of views.

Anglican evangelical voices
The new mood of greater openness towards other faiths in the period following the Second World War was to make itself evident gradually in the Anglican Church, with Anglican evangelicals playing a key role. A pioneering figure in this regard was E. C. Dewick, an educational missionary in India and Ceylon for twenty-six years and later a theological-college lecturer in Britain. Writing just after the war, Dewick applied his experience and knowledge to a reappraisal of Christian attitudes to other faiths, and concluded:

> Christ's message definitely condemns some elements in all the non-Christian religions. But it is of no less (perhaps indeed of greater) importance to recognize that in most of the great world-religions, and in some of the lesser and more primitive ones, there are features of belief and practice which are endorsed by the Christian Gospel. And if Truth is One, and God is Truth, we must welcome these as gifts from God, and as channels by which He has revealed Himself to man.[38]

Anglican evangelicalism was soon to face a major decision regarding its identity, which affected both internal and external policies. The inaugural National Evangelical Anglican Congress (NEAC 1), held at the University of Keele in April 1967, proved to be a significant turning point in the history of Anglicanism.[39] This event was attended by a thousand people, split equally between clergy and lay people. J. N. D. Anderson, then professor of Islamic law at the University of London, called for the conscious involvement of evangelicals in the world, rather than a separatist withdrawal into evangelical ghettos. After lengthy debate NEAC took the decision to continue to work within Anglican structures rather than to withdraw from the Church of England.

Another key figure at this congress, John Stott, called for greater openness to other Christian traditions, echoing Anderson's call for involvement rather than separation, and reflecting developments within other church contexts. Stott's call opened the way for increased inter-religious dialogue, which NEAC 1 described in paragraph 83 of its congress declaration as 'a conversation in which each party is serious in his approach both to the subject and to the other person, and desires to listen and learn as well as to speak and instruct'.[40]

This congress mirrored the rapid growth in evangelicalism in the Anglican Church in post-war Britain.[41] In the early 1950s fewer than 10% of new ordinands identified with evangelicalism. By 1969, however, 31.2% of those training for Anglican ministry chose evangelical Anglican training colleges, and by 1986 this figure had risen to over 50%.[42] Many others chose interdenominational evangelical colleges, such as London Bible College (now the London School of Theology), for their training in theology.

In part this growth reflected the powerful impact of the Billy Graham crusades in the 1950s and 1960s. Meanwhile, there was a corresponding decline in liberal training colleges, with the period 1960–76 witnessing the closure of seven Anglican training colleges in England, all at the liberal end of the spectrum.

This new evangelical upsurge was to have a significant impact on Anglican views of other faiths. In 1992 the Anglican Evangelical Assembly issued a paper that called for a new approach. But, like the Dewick statement of almost fifty years before, it mixed a sense of greater openness with an affirmation of the uniqueness of the Christian message:

> It is important to distinguish between recognising that we as Christians have something to learn from people of other faiths, and thinking that God's revelation and salvation itself needs to be corrected or supplemented by other faiths. We should be humble enough to be challenged in many ways by other religions, but at the same time convinced and confident in the adequacy and finality of the biblical witness to God and Christ.[43]

This is a 'yes, but' kind of statement. It suggests a willingness to explore a more inclusivist approach, while at the same time affirming that there are certain red lines that must not be crossed.

Lesslie Newbigin. A key evangelical writer in the Church of England in the latter part of the twentieth century was the late Bishop Lesslie Newbigin. A prolific writer, he devoted his literary and research efforts in later years to his 'Gospel as Public Truth' project, which tackled the pluralist society around him.[44] In his writing, Newbigin continued to call on the church to rediscover its own distinctive vision of public truth, rather than retreating into a privatistic accommodation to pluralistic modern western society. Newbigin argued that, in withdrawing into the private sphere, Christians have limited the public claim of the lordship of Christ over all things.

For Newbigin, recovery of the gospel as public truth was critical for faithfulness and for the very survival of the western church. His methodology was based on several tasks. First, he sought to articulate the nature of the Christian tradition of rationality, so that reason and Christian tradition were not seen as mutually exclusive. Secondly, he called for the recovery of the gospel as 'metanarrative', and rejected the limited vision of the church as a place of private withdrawal from the world. Finally Newbigin called for Christian engagement in dialogue with pluralist society, including adherents of other faiths.

Newbigin's ideas were innovative, challenging many widely accepted paradigms. For example, he identified flaws in the traditional exclusivist–inclusivist–pluralist paradigm *vis-à-vis* other faiths:

> The position which I have outlined is exclusivist in the sense that it affirms the
> unique truth of the revelation in Jesus Christ, but it is not exclusivist in the
> sense of denying the possibility of the salvation of the non-Christian. It is
> inclusivist in the sense that it refuses to limit the saving grace of God to the
> members of the Christian Church, but it rejects the inclusivism which regards
> the non-Christian religions as vehicles of salvation. It is pluralist in the sense
> of acknowledging the gracious work of God in the lives of all human beings,
> but it rejects the pluralism which denies the uniqueness and decisiveness of
> what God has done in Jesus Christ.[45]

In *Faith and Power*, Newbigin addresses 'the secular myth'. He asserts that in earlier periods the British had a clear sense of identity, but that this is no longer the case. Multiculturalism, while offering certain advantages, poses a number of problems that British society has not yet resolved. Newbigin argues that the relativist thinking associated with the postmodern West tends to conceal the existence of absolutes. He associates these absolutes with the

Ten Commandments, and believes that they should not become a matter of individual choice.

Newbigin considers the vital link between the rise and decline of secular society, which provides a catalyst for the view that religion is anachronistic. The progressive discarding of the religious underpinning of western society, accompanied by progressive decay, has led to great pessimism in the United Kingdom, and to specific problems for which secular society has no answer. For Newbigin, the response to this loss of direction in the West has come in the form of a re-emergence of religion, particularly in the shape of religious fundamentalism, of which Muslim fundamentalism is the most prominent and most vocal form.

Newbigin discusses the possibility of re-establishing a Christian society. He calls for Christians to get involved in wide-ranging social issues rather than quarantining their Christian values within the realm of Sunday worship. He provides a set of useful recommendations to the church on how it can re-engage with the world. He draws a distinction between Christian and Muslim approaches to achieving a more religious society: 'Christians agree with Muslims that God's will is to be done in the public no less than the private sphere. The question is: what kind of obedience does God desire?'[46] Newbigin answers by stating that God desires obedience freely given as an expression of love, not given out of fear of divine punishment. He identifies the former with Christianity and the latter with Islam.

Thus, in concert with the general movement in Anglican evangelicalism in the second half of the twentieth century, Newbigin voices a strong call for Christian involvement in society, rather than withdrawal and separatism. He demonstrates an openness to engaging with other faiths in this endeavour, but at the same time articulates a message that reinforces the theme of the uniqueness of Christ, so central to evangelical writing.

Colin Chapman. Another Anglican evangelical who has written extensively on Christian–Muslim relations is Colin Chapman. In his 1998 work *Islam and the West*, Chapman expresses a set of views that similarly reflect changing times in traditional Anglican views of other faiths.[47]

Chapman is concerned that Christians should be able to hear Muslim views in order to reach balanced opinions: 'It is particularly important that people in the West should be able to listen with greater sympathy to Muslim interpretations of history.'[48] One way in which Christians can do this is by listening to Muslim perspectives on the Crusades and joining other Christians in issuing apologies for the injustices perpetrated by the Crusaders.[49]

In his work Chapman presents Muslim voices on key themes for Christian consideration. He largely focuses on Muslim modernizer authors who have chosen to settle in the West, such as Seyyed Hossein Nasr and Akbar Ahmed. There is little recourse in his work to radical Islamist authors, such as Ahmad Deedat, Abu'l A'la Mawdudi or Sayyid Qutb, whose anti-western, anti-Christian polemics are a beacon to large numbers of radical Islamists throughout the world.

On the theme of conversion, a key theme for evangelicals, Chapman presents factors that identify the appeal of Islam to non-Muslims and encourage them to convert to Islam. He thus provides a perspective from the viewpoint of Islam, rather than focusing on Muslims who convert to Christianity, an approach that has attracted much greater Christian attention in the past. Chapman does not shy away from the thorny issue of 'forced conversion' to Islam (widely denied by Muslims), concluding that there were definite cases of the practice, though stating that it was more the exception than the rule. He quotes Nehemia Levtzion: 'Forced conversions . . . seem to have weighed less than is implied in non-Muslim sources and more than is admitted by Muslims.'[50]

In aiming for a sense of balance, Chapman states: 'There are two particular dangers to be avoided. The first is that since some Muslims want to "convert the West", all Muslims must want the same thing. The opposite danger is for people in the West to listen only to the more liberal voices in the Muslim community, and to discount completely the missionary intentions of a proportion of the Muslim community all over the world.'[51]

On the issue of Islam and human rights, Chapman notes that some Muslims are concerned with violations of human rights in Muslim countries. He summarizes the content of the 'Universal Islamic Declaration of Human Rights' (1981)[52] and the 'Declaration on Human Rights in Islam' (1990),[53] commenting that 'in both these documents there are often significant differences between the official text, which is in Arabic, and the English translation'.[54] The implication here is that the different texts were moulded to fit the expectations of the different audiences.

On the question of methodology, Chapman is strongly opposed to polemics, favouring dialogue and apologetics as appropriate tools for interfaith contact. He poses a rhetorical question: 'Is it too much to hope, for example, that polemics can be ruled out on both sides?' Elsewhere, Chapman questions whether there is also too great a weighting placed on apologetics in Christian–Muslim relations, and too little on hearing Muslim voices through dialogue.[55] Chapman concludes his study with a strong call to the West to recognize the diversity of views among Muslims worldwide.[56]

We have thus again encountered evidence of winds of change in the Anglican Church. A greater measure of openness towards Islam has been in evidence than was historically the case with Anglicanism. At the same time, the evangelical tendency to include searching questions and robust scrutiny of certain features of Islamic practice sets such scholarship apart from the more pluralistic approach of writers such as Clinton Bennett.

Other significant Anglican writers and thinkers. This discussion of Anglican thinkers and writers on Islam is not intended to be exhaustive. Many other leading Anglican theologians and writers have made significant contributions to the discussion. J. N. D. (later Sir Norman) Anderson (1908–94), mentioned earlier, left in his many writings a valuable legacy to subsequent generations of Christian students of Islam. Mention should also be made of Bishop Michael Nazir-Ali, another prolific writer who has exerted an important influence on the Anglican Church's understanding of and approach to Islam.[57] Also significant is Bill Musk, who has made a crucial contribution to the study of the phenomenon of folk Islam.[58] Another influential Anglican writer is Vivienne Stacey, who has written extensively on mission history and methodology, with particular reference to Pakistan.[59]

Canon Patrick Sookhdeo has devoted his energies to advocating the cause of Christian minorities in Muslim-majority countries, and in the process has been an important influence in drawing attention to cases where Christians suffer discrimination and persecution at the hands of certain Muslim regimes.[60] Also engaged in important advocacy work is Baroness Caroline Cox, whose human-rights campaigning on behalf of Christians suffering in locations such as the Sudan and Nigeria has given much-needed public exposure to issues that would not otherwise have reached the headlines.[61]

Mission, freedom of religion and the World Evangelical Alliance

We have seen that the WCC, and denominations belonging to it, have moved away from an exclusivist approach to other faiths. Some voices have adopted an ostensibly pluralist position, while more have adopted inclusivist paradigms that nevertheless affirm the uniqueness of Christ's message for the whole world. Under the WCC, dialogue has come to be regarded as the normative instrument for Christian–Muslim contacts.

Nevertheless, there are many Christian Protestant groups that have not joined the WCC. These groups are chiefly evangelical, and they have come together to form the World Evangelical Alliance (WEA),[62] which functions as an umbrella body like the WCC, but bears a number of features that set it apart from the WCC.

The WEA traces its origins to 1846, when 800 Christian representatives from ten countries met in London to form 'a definite organization for the expression of unity amongst Christian individuals belonging to different churches'. This gathering resulted in the foundation of the Evangelical

Alliance of the UK. Just over a century later, a worldwide evangelical grouping was formed when, in 1951, representatives from twenty-one countries met to form the WEA. It functions as a global network of 114 national and regional evangelical church alliances, supplemented by ninety-two associate member organizations, together representing a constituency of approximately 150 million Christians in 110 nations.[63]

The WEA international office is located in Singapore, and the International Executive Council membership draws heavily on Third World representatives. The WEA General Assembly meets every four years. The WEA is structured according to various departments – the Church and Society Department, the Leadership Development Department, and the Publications Department – as well as various commissions: the Commission for Women's Concerns, the Theological Commission, the Youth Commission, the Missions Commission, and the Religious Liberty Commission.

Like the WCC, the WEA organizes conferences and consultations, such as the Cyprus Consultation held in late February 2000, which discussed challenges and opportunities facing the church in the twenty-first century and included a session discussing Islam and relevant Christian approaches.

The Missions Commission

The Missions Commission of the WEA fulfils an important function in that it offers an approach to Christian–Muslim relations, considered a priority by large segments of the Protestant churches but somewhat demoted as a priority by the WCC with its preference for dialogue. Thus the commission adds an important piece to the contemporary mosaic of Protestantism.

The commission defines its general goals as being to help to initiate regional and national evangelical alliances where they do not exist, and to strengthen existing ones 'in their role of assisting local churches to disciple the nations'.[64] It identifies three specific objectives:

1. To promote dynamic co-operation among existing and emerging national and regional missions associations
2. To strengthen and aid in the development of sending churches, training programmes and support/shepherding structures
3. To address critical concerns of international evangelical missions structures and their national and regional associations

The commission aims to achieve these objectives through a range of activities, including networking, establishing national missions commissions, forging strategic alliances and partnerships, facilitating the use of experienced consultant resources, publishing, training key Third World missions leaders, convening strategic international conferences and consultations, addressing critical needs within global missions, and administering projects and programmes.

The Religious Liberty Commission

The other WEA commission that bears directly on Christian–Muslim relations is the Religious Liberty Commission. The stated purpose of this body is crucial for understanding evangelical approaches to relationships with other faiths:

> The purpose of the World Evangelical Alliance Religious Liberty Commission (RLC) is to promote freedom of religion for all faiths worldwide as defined by Article 18 of the United Nations Declaration on Human Rights, and in accordance with Scripture. Our aim is to help all people, but especially Protestant Christians, to exercise their faith without oppression or discrimination.[65]

The phrase 'in accordance with Scripture' points to a characteristic feature of evangelicalism, namely the degree to which policy represents an outworking of the Bible. This is further emphasized by commission documentation, which identifies specific biblical references, interpreted as giving support to the approach and work of the RLC.[66]

The emphasis on Protestant Christians demonstrates the WEA's position of overtly identifying itself as a special-interest body. This contrasts with the approach of the WCC, for which a broad-based, ever-expanding ecumenism is the stated goal. Nevertheless, in the statement just quoted the RLC indicates that, beyond its primary focus on the Christian constituency, it also concerns itself with religious liberty for all, and this is emphasized in other documents:

> The World Evangelical [Alliance] . . . believes that its communities must not only seek to protect their own constituents, but should also assist others who suffer for their beliefs. It recognizes that the first act of violence recorded in the Christian Scriptures, the killing by Cain of his brother Abel, was the ill fruit of religious intolerance. Cain refused to accept Abel's mode of worship and therefore chose to kill him. WEA believes that in the religious freedom arena we are indeed 'our brother's keeper' and should proactively speak on behalf of others who suffer persecution.[67]

The primary focus on advocacy on behalf of the Christian constituency is justified on two counts. First: 'At the beginning of the 21st Century the largest faith group being persecuted is the Christian faith. It has been estimated that over 200 million Christians in at least 60 countries are denied fundamental human rights solely because of their faith.'[68] The second is based on an argument that advocacy for Christians will have positive spin-offs for other faiths: 'Persecution of Christians often serves as an indicator of the status of religious freedom for other minorities since where Christians are persecuted other religions tend also to suffer. Discrimination and persecution have been found to follow a distinct pattern regardless of who is being persecuted.'[69]

The RLC specifically targets freedom in a number of areas: religious education, public and private worship, sharing of one's faith, and the freedom to change one's faith. The RLC monitors infringements of religious liberty and reports on it on a regular basis via press releases and email notices. Furthermore, the RLC holds an 'International Day of Prayer for the Persecuted Church' each year in November.

The nature of the work of the RLC means that Muslim locations and authorities, especially where Islamists are in power, regularly appear in RLC reports. In *The Geneva Report 2001*, for example, twelve countries were highlighted as practising discrimination or persecution against Christians, and eight of these were Muslim-majority states. Other reports have focused on topics such as harrassment of Christians in Turkey, Christian victims of the push to implement Islamic law in parts of northern Nigeria, and Pakistan, with a special report entitled 'Pakistan: Forgotten on Death Row'. The common prohibition in Muslim-majority countries of non-Muslims' sharing their faith with Muslims, and the widely reported discrimination and persecution against Muslim converts to Christianity, mean that RLC comment on practice in Islamic countries is quite robust.

The work of the WEA, through both the Missions Commission and the RLC, supplements the differently orientated work of the WCC in Christian–Muslim relations. Though WCC consultations do address subjects such as religious liberty and freedom of religion, the dialogical focus and the mixed-faith presence at WCC interfaith meetings mean that some of the more challenging questions and statistics regarding persecution of religious minorities are not articulated in WCC contexts as they are in WEA contexts.

The Lausanne Committee for World Evangelization
The Lausanne Committee for World Evangelization, more commonly known as the Lausanne movement, is not a formal part of the WEA. Members of the Lausanne movement also tend to be members of the WEA, however, and both share an evangelical orientation.

The Lausanne movement originated in a congress called by a committee headed by Billy Graham, which took place in 1974 in Lausanne, Switzerland. Christian leaders from 150 countries and many denominations attended this gathering. The meeting produced a 'Covenant' that challenged churches and Christian organizations to engage in world evangelization for the remainder of the twentieth century and beyond.

The work of the Lausanne movement is carried out by a network of some twenty-five committees in different countries and regions of the world. In fulfilment of its objectives, the movement organizes small international consultations (of which more than thirty were held between 1974 and 2000), regional, national and international consultations and conferences (of which more than fifty were organized in the same period), and world congresses, held in 1974 and 1989, that bring together current and emerging leaders to consider world evangelization.

The Lausanne movement produces various publications. The Lausanne Newsletter appears quarterly, and carries news and analyses of current issues. Occasional papers and books are also published on subjects important for world evangelization, and together these publications provide an important forum for articulating Lausanne-movement perspectives on key events and for reporting on the movement's activities.[70]

Statements from the 1974 and 1989 Lausanne International Congresses on World Evangelization point to a certain evolution in evangelical policy towards other faiths. Article 3 of the 1974 Lausanne Covenant includes the following statement:

> We affirm that there is only one Saviour and only one gospel, although there is a wide diversity of evangelistic approaches. We recognise that all men have some knowledge of God through his general revelation in nature. But we deny that this can save, for men suppress the truth by their unrighteousness. We also reject as derogatory to Christ and the gospel every kind of syncretism and dialogue which implies that Christ speaks equally through all religions and ideologies. Jesus Christ, being himself the God-man, who gave himself as the ransom for sinners, is the only mediator between God and man. There is no other name by which we must be saved. All men are perishing because of sin, but God loves all men, not wishing that any should perish but that all should repent.

The 1989 second Lausanne Congress, held in Manila, issued what has become known as the Manila Manifesto. Clause 3 of this manifesto reflects a somewhat different approach:

> Because men and women are made in God's image and see in the creation traces of its Creator, the religions which have arisen do sometimes contain elements of truth and beauty. They are not, however, alternative gospels. Because human beings are sinful, and because 'the whole world is under the control of the evil one' (1 John 5:19), even religious people are in need of Christ's redemption. We therefore have no warrant for saying that salvation can be found outside Christ or apart from an explicit acceptance of his work through faith.

The inclusion of a scriptural reference in the above statement demonstrates the ongoing evangelical commitment to grounding policy statements and formulations in biblical teaching. The 1989 manifesto proceeded with a statement of repentance:

> In the past we have sometimes been guilty of adopting towards adherents of other faiths attitudes of ignorance, arrogance, disrespect and even hostility. We repent of this. We nevertheless are determined to bear a positive and uncompromising witness to the uniqueness of our Lord, in his life, death and resurrection, in all aspects of our evangelistic work including inter-faith dialogue.[71]

The 1989 manifesto reflected a wider movement of the 1980s towards a more inclusivist paradigm, with regard to perspectives on other faiths. The Manila declaration acknowledged that other faiths may 'contain elements of truth and beauty', and furthermore the note of repentance for past sins and excesses towards other faiths is much more explicit. Such inclusivist statements, however, are balanced by robust statements affirming the uniqueness of Christ's teachings, and the need for all to hear these teachings.

The Catholic Church and other faiths

Having taken a traditionally exclusivist attitude to other faiths, and indeed, other Christian denominations during most of its long history, the Catholic Church underwent a revolution at the Second Vatican Council. The sessions of this council ran from 1962 to 1965. It was after a rather stormy first session, characterized by tension between traditionalists and reformists, that Pope Paul VI was elected to the papacy on 21 June 1963. He guided the remaining three sessions of the council, which concluded on 8 December 1965. The decisions of the council were marked by revolutionary changes in wide-ranging areas, not least of which was the attitude of the Catholic Church towards other faiths.[72]

Vatican II
In *Ecclesiam suam* (6 August 1964), his first encyclical after ascending to the papacy, Pope Paul VI gave voice to the mood for change by calling for an extensive dialogue between the Catholic Church and the great religions of the world. The Pope pictured all humanity in a series of concentric circles, with Christ as the centre. The outer circle embraced all members of the human race. The second-to-outer circle included all those members of humanity who worshipped the one supreme God: the Jews, the Muslims, and the adherents of the 'great Afro-Asiatic religions'. Circles further inside referred to the

various Christian churches, with Christ as the centre. Pope Paul described the circle that referred to the non-Christian religions as follows:

> Then we see another circle around us. This too is vast in extent, yet not so far away from us. It comprises first of all those men who worship the one supreme God, whom we also worship. We would mention first the Jewish people, who still retain the religion of the Old Testament, and who are indeed worthy of our respect and love.
>
> Then we have those worshipers who adhere to other monotheistic systems of religion, especially the Moslem religion. We do well to admire these people for all that is good and true in their worship of God.
>
> And finally we have the followers of the great Afro-Asiatic religions.[73]

This statement represented a significant departure from the traditional approach of the Catholic Church to non-Christian religions. The Pope's words indicate that the church conceived of a hierarchy of religious truth, as it were, whereby the non-Christian religions contained elements that were true in themselves, though, in order to be fulfilled, these religions needed to accept Christ as their ultimate path. This latter caveat is encapsulated in the following paragraph of the encyclical:

> Honesty compels us to declare openly our conviction that the Christian religion is the one and only true religion, and it is our hope that it will be acknowledged as such by all who look for God and worship Him.
>
> But we do not wish to turn a blind eye to the spiritual and moral values of the various non-Christian religions, for we desire to join with them in promoting and defending common ideals in the spheres of religious liberty, human brotherhood, education, culture, social welfare, and civic order.

The Second Vatican Council was organized around four central poles: revelation, liturgy, the church, and the church in the modern world.[74] The declarations emanating from discussions relating to the fourth pole confirmed the approach contained in Pope Paul's first encyclical. Vatican II acknowledged that all the religious faiths represented humanity's search for God.

The Vatican II 'Declaration on the Relationship of the Church to Non-Christian Religions' (*Nostra aetate*) included sections specific to Islam, and presented what it described as five 'authentic elements of Muslim spirituality':

> The Church also looks upon the Muslims with respect. They worship the one God living and subsistent, merciful and almighty, creator of heaven and earth, who has spoken to humanity and to whose decrees, even the hidden ones, they seek to submit themselves wholeheartedly, just as Abraham, to whom the

Islamic faith readily relates itself, submitted to God. They venerate Jesus as a prophet, even though they do not acknowledge him as God, and they honour his virgin mother Mary and even sometimes devoutly call on her. Furthermore they await the day of judgment when God will reward all people brought back to life. Hence, they have regard for the moral life and worship God especially in prayer, almsgiving, and fasting.[75]

This statement is significant. Though 'Islam is not considered by the Church to be a revealed religion',[76] the *Nostra aetate* declaration did specify key areas of Muslim belief that the earlier papal encyclical *Ecclesiam suam* had referred to as 'all that is good and true':

1. Muslims adore the one, true, living and sustaining God, creator of heaven and earth.
2. Their spiritual attitude before God is to be completely submissive to his supreme will, as was Abraham, to whom they look.
3. They revere Jesus as a prophet.
4. Muslims honour Mary.
5. Muslims believe in the future life and the last judgment.
6. Muslims are bound by a moral law and worship God through prayer, almsgiving and fasting.

At the same time as it exhibited a greater degree of openness towards other faiths, the Catholic Church called on other faiths to reciprocate. A declaration on religious freedom was issued, which stated:

> The human person has a right to religious freedom . . . to deny man the free exercise of religion in society, when the just requirements of public order are observed, is to do an injustice to the human person and to the very order established by God for men . . . Religious communities have the further right not to be prevented from publicly teaching and bearing witness to their beliefs by the spoken or written word.[77]

Competing voices since Vatican II

For the decade following the Second Vatican Council and more, the study of mission within the Catholic Church was eclipsed while theologians reassessed traditional Catholic approaches. A number of Catholic theologians and writers were especially prominent in formulating post-Vatican II thinking. The legacy of Louis Massignon (1883–1962) was crucial. His thinking was built upon by writers such as Jacques Jomier,[78] Robert Caspar[79] and Henri Sanson.[80]

The Catholic Church moved quickly to allocate significant resources to building bridges of dialogue with the Muslim world after Vatican II. A book on guidelines for dialogue between Christians and Muslims was published in 1969 and revised in 1981.[81] Various research centres were established, one of the most active and notable being the Pontifical Institute for the Study of Arabic and Islam (PISAI) in Rome. The PISAI is active in organizing interfaith events and in publishing the journals *Islamochristiana* and *Encounters* as well as a prolific output of books.

Catholic theology in this period continued to move along the path initiated by Vatican II, focusing on the elements of truth in other religions; indeed, a strong movement developed within the relevant sections of the Catholic Church that regarded individual adherents of other religions as bearers of 'salvific values', though this movement did not go so far as to acknowledge that other religious traditions themselves offered alternative ways to salvation.

Regular conferences were held on the question of interfaith dialogue. One such, the Assisi Conference of 27 October 1986, was a key step in carrying forward the pronouncements of Vatican II. At the same time it affirmed the uniqueness of Christ, considered so essential to mainstream Christian doctrine.[82]

Pope John Paul II's encyclicals in the early 1990s contributed to a redefinition of substance of the traditional Catholic view of evangelism. Henceforth, this was to focus on three macro streams: inter-religious dialogue, inculturation/contextualization, and liberation theology.[83] The church had by now acknowledged that persons outside it could be saved by grace,[84] though not by other faith traditions themselves.

The spirit of Vatican II lives on in the Catholic Church. In February 2000, an international symposium was convened in Rome to continue a review of the Second Vatican Council. This review had been initiated by a synod of bishops in 1985. Symposium reports included one on discussion of the church in the modern world, particularly addressing 'dialogue and discernment in witnessing to the truth'.[85] The issue of dialogue has remained a central priority to church considerations.

Pope John Paul II

It would be inaccurate, however, to suggest that all Catholic voices have been singing from the same score since Vatican II. Indeed, papal statements have at times served to add a critical cutting edge to discussions, ensuring that a lively debate continues within the church about approaches to other faiths.

Thirty years after Vatican II, Pope John Paul II commented in 1994:

'The religiosity of Muslims deserves respect. It is impossible not to admire, for example, their fidelity to prayer.

Some of the most beautiful names in the human language are given to God in the Koran, but He is ultimately a God outside of the world, a God who is only Majesty, never Emmanuel, God-with-us . . . There is no room for the Cross and the Resurrection. Jesus is mentioned, but only as a prophet . . . not only the theology but also the anthropology of Islam is very distant from Christianity.'[86]

It is interesting to observe subtle differences between the various statements. Referring to the Muslim view of Jesus, the Vatican II declaration *Nostra aetate* had stressed a positive view: 'They venerate Jesus as a prophet, even though they do not acknowledge him as God.' By adding the word 'only', Pope John Paul II's statement created a more negative impression: 'Jesus is mentioned, *but only* as a prophet.'

Elsewhere John Paul II stressed the importance of proclamation of the Word as a partner with dialogue: 'Just as interreligious dialogue is one element in the mission of the Church, the proclamation of God's saving work in Our Lord Jesus Christ is another . . . There can be no question of choosing one and ignoring the other. Both are legitimate and necessary.'[87] He was thereby giving further weight to a statement on dialogue and proclamation issued in 1991 by the Pontifical Council for Interreligious Dialogue and Congregation for the Evangelization of Peoples, which had stated:

Interreligious dialogue and proclamation . . . are intimately related, but not interchangeable: true interreligious dialogue on the part of the Christian supposes the desire to make Jesus Christ better known, recognised and loved; proclaiming Jesus Christ is to be carried out in the gospel spirit of dialogue. The two activities remain distinct but, as experience shows, one and the same local Church, one and the same person can be diversely engaged in both.[88]

John Paul II's various statements and activities have reflected the diversity within the church on the issue of approaches to other faiths. In March 1995, John Paul II met with the Iranian President Muhammad Khatami, who had himself called for closer dialogue and contact between Islam and Christianity. This meeting has led to an annual series of Catholic–Iranian dialogues.

Further reflecting the church's commitment to openness, but echoing the invitation to reciprocate originally expressed at Vatican II, John Paul II issued a forthright call in 1995 for Muslim-majority countries to extend the same respect for religious minority rights as Muslim minorities enjoyed in predominantly Christian countries. This statement was issued to coincide with the opening of a large mosque in Rome.

Furthering the effort of the Catholic Church to open a new chapter in its relations with other faiths, the Vatican declared 12 March 2000 as a 'Day of

Forgiveness'. John Paul II addressed an audience at St Peter's Basilica and issued a public apology for the past sins of the church.[89] He identified seven categories of sins for which forgiveness was sought: general sins; sins in the service of truth; sins against Christian unity; sins against the Jews; sins against respect for love, peace and cultures; sins against the dignity of women and minorities; and sins against human rights.

Specific groups or historical events were not named in the Pope's address, but prayers during the mass were linked with the address and precise groups and issues were named, including sins against Israel and against gypsies, abortion, and persecution of Christian minorities. An interpretive key to the liturgy was released ahead of the mass, identifying specific wrongs for which the pontiff was seeking forgiveness.

In order to avoid any impression that the Catholic Church saw past wrongs as being one-sided, the Pope also mentioned that the church was willing to forgive others guilty of abuse of Christians over the centuries. Many observers interpreted this as referring in large part to Muslim history, though it was not specifically mentioned. The address by the Pope attracted criticism from various quarters, especially from those who saw it as not going far enough.[90] Nevertheless, the speech reflects the continuing process within the Catholic Church to build new bridges to former adversaries.

Variations on a theme

The push within the Catholic hierarchy for dialogue with Muslims has been tempered with forthright statements from various sources, supplementing a number of statements by the Pope, referred to above.

Cardinal Arinze, the Nigerian past President of the Pontifical Council for Inter-religious Dialogue, has invariably spoken with clarity of commitment. He launched a conference at Cumberland Lodge, Windsor Great Park, in March 2002, with the words: 'The religion which Jesus Christ founded was meant by him for every people, time, place, and culture.'[91] Furthermore, Cardinal Arinze has been outspoken in calling for religious freedom for all people, a freedom of which he conceives as including 'not only freedom of conscience, but also freedom to live, profess, and spread one's religion, alone or with others'.[92] He stresses that this freedom should not be restricted to the personal domain:

> Since the human person is social by nature, inner acts of religion require external expression . . . freedom should be exercised in common worship, with the possibility of forming religious associations and of allowing his religious convictions to shape his life in society. Religion is not just a private affair. Therefore religious freedom cannot be restricted to the purely personal domain.[93]

Cardinal Arinze articulated such a message of critical openness to Islam during a 1997 address at the influential Centre for Christian–Muslim Understanding at Georgetown, USA: 'A religion should not ask for [full acceptance] in a country where it is a minority and deny it to others when it is the majority.'[94] He proceeded to refer to Muslim-majority countries where there were reports that Christian minorities were suffering discrimination, such as Egypt and Pakistan. Discussing religious freedom, Cardinal Arinze stressed in his address that it included 'both the right to practice a religion and the right to share that religion with others'.[95] In this context, he was critical of certain Muslim countries that legislated against Christian evangelism, such as Malaysia, Pakistan, Kuwait and Saudi Arabia. These critical comments were counterbalanced with optimistic statements about the potential for Christian–Muslim co-operation in areas of shared theology and social concern, pointing to past mutual support in international forums discussing pro-family, anti-abortion issues.

Concern about the flourishing of Catholic–Muslim relations has been expressed by some elements in the church since Vatican II. For example, at the October 1999 synod of European bishops, Giuseppe Bernardini, archbishop of Izmir, Turkey, called on the Pope to convoke a special Vatican meeting to address what he called 'the problem of Muslims in Christian countries'. He accused Muslim countries of 'using petro-dollars not to create jobs in the poor countries of North Africa and the Middle East but to build mosques and cultural centres in Christian countries where Muslims have migrated, including Rome, the centre of Christianity'. Rome's first mosque was built in 1995 at a cost of US $50 million, of which $35 million was provided by Saudi Arabia and the remainder by twenty-two other Muslim countries.[96]

Archbishop Bernardini's comments drew criticism from some segments of the Catholic Church. With a veiled challenge, Sydney's Columban Centre for Christian–Muslim Relations wrote: 'Archbishop Bernardini of Izmir, Turkey, has accused Muslims of plotting to dominate Europe and de-Christianize the continent. His words clashed with the Pope's policy of promoting good relations between Christians and Muslims, one of the aims of his papacy.'[97] The archbishop's concerns found echoes, however, in statements by other leading Catholics, such as Jesuit Father Samir Khalil, a research specialist on the Islamic and Arab world, who commented in interview:

Many Spanish Muslims have the idea of re-conquering Europe . . . [reaffirmed] months ago by the Imam of Granada, at the laying of the first stone ceremony at the city's new mosque before the King of Spain! . . . there are hundreds [of churches converted to mosques] . . . Just think of Santa Sophia in Istanbul, the Ummayade mosque in Damascus and the Ibn Tulum mosque in Cairo built with remains of destroyed churches . . . the famous mosque of Cordoba – originally a church before it became a mosque – is still almost entirely intact, thanks to the Christians who took care to preserve it. In other cases, the buildings immediately underwent so much violence that the church's original structure is now almost unrecognizable.[98]

Theocentric inclinations

Like some Protestant theologians, a few Catholic theologians lean towards a pluralist perspective on Christian–Muslim relations. Such a voice can be heard clearly in *Muslim–Christian Relations: Past, Present, Future*, by Father Ovey Mohammed. This work was published by the Catholic publishing house Orbis Books in their 'Faith Meets Faith' series on inter-religious dialogue, and should be seen as providing a window into minority thinking among Catholic theologians on the challenging issue of Christian relations with, and attitudes towards, other faiths.

Father Mohammed, a Jesuit priest, devotes the first chapter to a thumbnail sketch of Islamic history, scripture and belief. He takes an approach that accords with orthodox Muslim dogma, accepting the traditional Muslim accounts of Muhammad's life and the compilation of the Qur'an, and describing sectarian differences.

Chapter 2 summarizes the historical background to modern-day Christian–Muslim relations, firmly linking European colonial expansion with Christian mission in a fairly uncritical manner.

The third chapter includes reference to past studies by Christians of Islam, as well as Muslim approaches to inter-religious relations. In this, Father Mohammed summarizes the approaches of both polemical and irenic Christian voices. However, he tendentiously chooses to discuss only moderate Muslim writers. In the latter part of this chapter, Father Mohammed flies a clearly pluralist flag, declaring acceptance of the prophetic claims of Muhammad and accepting the Qur'an as a word of God. This conflicts with the very spirit of Vatican II and the statements of Pope John Paul II.

Thus there are a few theologians within the Catholic fold who incline themselves less towards the orthodox Christocentric view and more towards a theocentric view, whereby the great religions of the world are considered as alternative responses to the unique divine reality. Adherents of this particular view have predictably encountered significant opposition from mainstream Catholicism.

Conclusions

We have seen in this chapter that Protestant churches by and large have moved from a position of exclusivism to inclusivism since the Second World

War. In spite of the push by certain groups within the mainstream churches to adopt a more pluralist position, this is still a minority viewpoint. Moreover, those Protestant churches that are experiencing greatest growth, namely evangelical churches, appear to have planted their flag firmly at the point where they acknowledge elements of truth in other faiths and seek to build bridges of understanding with other faiths, but draw the line at compromising the essential uniqueness of Christ as the ultimate and universal path to God.

In the last part of this chapter we have considered evolving Catholic attitudes to other faiths in the second half of the twentieth century. The church has more clearly articulated a view that acknowledges elements of truth within other faiths, as well as 'salvific values' borne by individual adherents of other faiths. A small minority within the Catholic Church has gone further, adopting a clearly pluralist line and acknowledging Muhammad as Prophet and the Qur'an as a word of God.

Nevertheless, these changes are driven more by pastoral than by theological concerns. At its core, Catholic theology holds fast to a belief in Christianity as the greatest bearer of godly truth, and to the unique role of Christ in leading people to salvation. On the question of religious freedom, the highest levels of the church frequently make forthright statements critical of certain Muslim authorities for the treatment of Christian minorities in Muslim locations.

Catholicism embraces divergent voices, which it holds in tension with one another. This contrasts with the Protestant churches, where one major grouping, the WCC, flies the dialogue approach at full mast, and the other major grouping, the WEA, stands apart and undertakes approaches based on traditional mission and pursuit of religious liberty. The Catholic Church can thus be seen as integrating more diverse voices, whereas Protestants tend to fragment according to their divergent viewpoints.

5. METHODS OF INTERFAITH ENGAGEMENT

The previous chapter focused upon evolving attitudes within the churches towards other religions, especially Islam. Our attention will now move from ideological paradigms to actual practice. In this chapter, our interest will fall upon practical ways in which the churches are engaging with other faiths, especially Islam, in order to realize their particular ideological paradigms.

A summary of the approaches of the churches

A distillation of the various ideological approaches at this point would be useful to see how far the 'inclusivist train' has travelled. Certain core elements have emerged from the policy statements made by the churches over the past forty years. We can summarize the six key positional statements as follows:

1. Other faiths may contain elements of truth and beauty.
2. Christians may learn something from people of other faiths.
3. Christians should allow themselves to be challenged by other faiths.
4. Other faiths are worthy of Christian affection, respect, and even admiration in certain ways.
5. Other faiths do not represent alternative gospels.
6. The biblical witness to God and Christ is complete in itself.

The six key positional statements apply particularly to those church groups that embrace an inclusivist position. They do not reflect the position of those who articulate pluralist perspectives, who would challenge points 5 and 6.

How do Christian groups turn these statements into actual practice in interfaith contacts?

A starting point that is agreed among the main church groups – the WCC, the WEA and the Catholic Church – is that 'proselytism', where it 'involves cajolery, bribery, undue pressure, or intimidation (even if in subtle ways) in order to bring about a seeming conversion', is 'a corruption of Christian witness'.[1] If such practice is considered unacceptable, what practices are considered desirable and worthy of promotion by the churches?

World Council of Churches dialogue meetings

The WCC focus on dialogue produced a substantial number of major dialogue meetings between Christians and Muslims during the last four decades of the twentieth century and into the twenty-first, whether under the direction of the Dialogue Unit or under that of the OIRRD.[2] Table 3 is not exhaustive, but it provides a representative selection of such meetings, demonstrating the kinds of topics considered worthy of promotion by the WCC.

Table 3 A selection of WCC dialogue meetings, 1970–2002

Date	Topic	Place
March 1970	'Dialogue between Men of Living Faiths'	Ajaltoun, Lebanon
July 1972	'The Quest for Human Understanding and Cooperation – Christian and Muslim Contributions'	Broumana, Lebanon
July 1974	'The Unity of God and the Community of Humankind'	Legon, Ghana
January 1975	'Muslims and Christians in Society: Towards Goodwill, Consultation and Working Together in South East Asia'	Hong Kong
June 1976	'Christian Mission and Islamic Da'wah'	Chambésy, Switzerland
November 1977	'Faith, Science and Technology and the Future of Humanity'	Beirut, Lebanon
December 1979	'Christian Presence and Witness in Relation to Muslim Neighbours'	Mombasa, Kenya
June 1985	'Implications of Inter-faith Dialogue for Theological Education Today'	Kuala Lumpur, Malaysia
June 1989	'Religion and Life'	Usa River, Tanzania
March 1993	'Peace for Humanity'	Vienna, Austria

Date	Topic	Place
November 1993	'Religion, Law and Society'	Nyon, Switzerland
November 1994	'Religion and Human Rights'	Berlin, Germany
September 1995	'Towards a Christian–Muslim Statement of Principles on Human Rights'	Malta
November 1996	'Religion in the Contemporary World'	Teheran, Iran
May 1997	'One World for All'	Vienna, Austria[3]
September 1997	'Interreligious Prayer'	Community of Bose, near Magnano, Italy
October 1997	'Religion and Co-Citizenship'	Cairo, Egypt
July 1998	'Religious Freedom'	Beirut, Lebanon
October 2000	'Multi-faith Consultation on Religious Education'	Bangkok, Thailand
November 2000	'Christian–Muslim Meeting'	Amersfoort, The Netherlands
November 2000	'Christian–Muslim Conference on Communal Tensions'	Limassol, Cyprus
October 2002	'Christians and Muslims in Dialogue and Beyond'	Geneva, Switzerland

Out of this set of dialogue meetings, several trends emerge. First, the WCC bodies responsible for organizing dialogue activities sought to move meetings around a wide range of locations. Secondly, activities were held regularly, with a major meeting occurring almost every year. Thirdly, the topics chosen were current and also touched upon certain controversial features, such as inter-religious prayer, religious freedom, and religion and human rights, the growing interest in the last two in the late 1990s reflecting the increasing prominence given to these issues at that time.

In addition to direct Christian–Muslim meetings, the WCC dialogue team has arranged a number of tripartite gatherings since the early 1990s. In May 1993 a Jewish–Christian–Muslim colloquium on Jerusalem was jointly sponsored by the WCC, the Pontifical Council for Interreligious Dialogue and the Lutheran World Federation in Glion, Switzerland. A similar event was sponsored in August 1996 in Thessaloniki, Greece.

The WCC also seeks ways to move beyond dialogue meetings into areas where ground-level activities will be sustainable in various ways. In August 1997 a meeting at the University of Balamand, Lebanon, on 'Mutual Views and Changing Relations between Christians and Muslims', led to plans for co-operation in Christian–Muslim studies. Tarek Mitri, head of the OIRRD, assessed the broad sweep of topics covered during this meeting:

> The papers presented by a large number of participants highlighted the changes in Christian–Muslim relations during the last thirty years. Some assessed the significance of dialogue and scholarship and its impact on those relations, privileging a thematic focus or a regional perspective. Others chose to concentrate on recent Christian and Muslim writings, dialogical and polemical, or on the intellectual and practical experience of their own institutions.[4]

A series of follow-up meetings dealing with human-rights issues led to a broad-based gathering in October 1999, when Muslims and Christians from fifteen countries met in Hartford, Connecticut, to discuss religious freedom, community rights and individual rights. This meeting gave birth to the idea of establishing a permanent Christian–Muslim forum on human rights, religious freedom and problems arising out of mission/*da'wa*.[5]

Contacts between the WCC and the Iranian government, initiated in the mid-1990s, have also been fruitful. In December 1999, a Christian–Muslim colloquium was held in Geneva on 'The Future of Religion', co-organized with the Islamic Organization for Culture and Communication in Iran. This meeting also addressed questions raised by the relationship between Iranian Muslims and Christians, at both the international and the national levels.

Although dialogue is the preferred format for Christian–Muslim contact by the WCC, this does not prevent joint meetings from engaging in discussion on sensitive issues such as human rights and religious freedom. Nevertheless, the mixed-faith nature of any such gathering, though providing distinct advantages in terms of a guaranteed audience, raises questions about the degree to which searching questions on the most sensitive issues can be discussed.

The practice of dialogue at the grass roots: the CCBI model

In addition to discussions held at the level of church leadership under WCC auspices, it is important to see how emerging WCC policies have been translated to action at the grass-roots level. Responsibility for policy implementation has been devolved by the WCC to local levels, with WCC publications, such as *My Neighbour's Faith – and Mine* and *Encounters in the Spirit* being designed to provide guidelines for interfaith practice.

The Council of Churches of Britain and Ireland (CCBI) has enhanced the outline of the Four Principles of dialogue (see above, p. 111) with a series of practical suggestions for ways in which Christians could form partnerships with adherents of other faiths. Areas of co-operation identified were: in community meetings, clergy action, social action and advocacy, education, and worship (see Table 4).

In the United Kingdom, the recommendations outlined in the table have been used in certain locations for increasing numbers of interfaith dialogue activities, particularly among the more liberal wings of the various Protestant churches.

Table 4 CCBI suggestions for partnership between Christians and adherents of other faiths

Areas of co-operation	Recommended action for Christians
Community meeting	Make an effort to meet adherents of other faiths: neighbours, work colleagues, parents of children's school friends.
	Contact a local interfaith group.
Clergy action	Christian clergy should provide counselling support to adherents of other faiths in times of crisis.
	Clergy should get to know religious leaders of other faith communities personally and involve these leaders in matters pertaining to the whole community.
Social action and advocacy	Co-operate in matters of common cause: racial harassment, drug abuse, inadequate housing.
	Provide assistance to other faith communities to procure worship facilities, and freedom to observe dress codes, dietary restrictions, etc.
	Address the issue of access to public broadcasting by other faith communities.
	Beware of linking Christianity with underlying racist attitudes. Religious argument can be used as a cover for racial prejudice.
Education	Rethink attitudes concerning religious education in schools.
	Revise Sunday school materials to eliminate attitudes seemingly critical of other faiths.
	Promote studies of world faiths and interfaith relations at tertiary levels.
Worship	Pray for people of other faiths.
	Pray with people of other faiths.

Activities of the Lausanne movement

Evangelical groups translated their focus on mission and religious liberty to a range of activities on the ground. The Lausanne movement sponsored several conferences relating specifically to mission among Muslims. October 1978 saw the North American Conference on Muslim Evangelization, with proceedings published in a substantial volume.[6] A summary entitled 'The Glen Eyrie Report: Muslim Evangelization', is available on the internet.[7]

In June 1980 the Lausanne movement sponsored the 'Mini-Consultation on Reaching Muslims' in Pattaya, Thailand. The report of this gathering is also available on the internet.[8] Its principal recommendations included calls for respect for other cultures, training in churches, sensitive proclamation, dialogue, and to work for justice issues. Thus these recommendations affirmed the evangelical call for mission and religious liberty, but fore-grounded a methodology based on respect, sensitivity and dialogue.

This report portrays the sharing of the gospel as an integral part of dialogue, finding scriptural support for this view in the New Testament, where 'the word "dialogue" often means a conversation conducted to convince another party of the truth (e.g., Acts 17:2; 18:4)'. The report refers to this as *discursive dialogue*, and adds that there are other forms of dialogue in use today:

> . . . *dialogue on religious experience*, in which members of different faiths seek to share their particular religious experiences with one another. There is also the so-called *secular dialogue*, in which representatives of different faiths discuss ways in which greater communal understanding can be developed, how common action can be taken to correct various social evils, and how followers of different faiths can co-operate in the task of community development and national reconstruction.[9]

The report affirms dialogue as 'a valid and even necessary activity for Christians'. It argues that through dialogue people learn how others appreciate the significance of life; they can gain an insight into the nature of other people's religious experience; and avenues can be explored for pursuing joint action on social issues. Emphasizing this spirit of openness, the report adds that 'it may be that the Christian can learn much from the life-style, devotion, or learning of the other'.

This 1980 report clearly enunciates the other voice of Christianity, however, affirming key beliefs as non-negotiable: 'We believe that Christians are called to witness at all times, and in all situations, to the new life which they have received through Jesus Christ by the operation of the Holy Spirit . . . People must be allowed to accept or to reject the claims of Jesus Christ in an atmosphere of freedom.' Issue is taken with a certain approach to dialogue, in which other religious systems 'complement' the Christian gospel – i.e., they have insights about the nature of God or the plan of salvation which the gospel lacks. To achieve a 'rounded' knowledge of God and his will, it is asserted, we must listen to the witness of other religions. Such a concept of 'mutual witness' we cannot accept, although personal appreciation of the nature of the gospel may become clearer through dialogue. The gospel itself is the full and complete revelation of God and his plan of salvation . . . dialogue is and should be an integral part of Christian mission . . . The aim of dialogue must most surely be to learn and to appreciate, but it must chiefly be to teach and to tell men and women about Jesus Christ, the Way, the Truth, and the Life.[10]

This statement is consistent with the essence of the Lausanne movement World Congress statements of 1974 and 1989. Thus, for the Lausanne movement, and for evangelicalism in general, dialogue has its place as part of the broad objective of transmitting the message of the gospel to all people. Freedom of religious choice is a key condition for this to happen, hence the emphasis of evangelicalism upon religious freedom and choice. Dialogue is seen as a means to an end, rather than an end in itself.

Case studies: Muslim–Christian dialogue in practice

Dialogue among religious leaders
Dialogue is being pursued at the highest levels of the Christian and Muslim communities. There have been ongoing contacts between Sunni Muslim and Anglican leaders, one of the leading participants being Dr Muhammad Sayyid Tantawi, Shaykh of Al-Azhar University and former Grand Mufti of Egypt. Shaykh Tantawi met with the former Archbishop of Canterbury, Dr George Carey, on several occasions, both in Britain and in Egypt. In these meetings Dr Carey emphasized that Christian–Muslim relations should take precedence over dialogues with other faiths, given the tenuous nature of the relationship in the past.[11] These contacts between the respective leaders of their religious communities have encouraged local contacts between Islamic leaders and Anglicans in Egypt. In October 1997 Shaykh Tantawi joined mourners at the head of the funeral procession for the late Bishop Samuel Habib, head of the Egyptian Anglican Church.[12]

Similarly, contacts between Sunni and Catholic leaders have been developed. Shaykh Tantawi has met Pope John Paul II for dialogue discussions. Furthermore, Shaykh Tantawi was instrumental in the establishment of a Sunni inter-religious dialogue committee for reinforcing dialogue contacts with the Vatican.[13] In October 1999, Shaykh Tantawi joined the Egyptian Coptic Pope Shenuda III in attending a dialogue conference at the Vatican.

Jewish religious leaders also attended. The conference included discussion groups 'aimed at reconciling the religions and confronting ethnic and factional fanaticism'.[14]

Such dialogue gatherings have not been without their controversies, however. The third meeting of the Anglican Communion/Al Azhar Joint Dialogue Commission was scheduled to be held in New York on 10–11 September 2003, the second anniversary of the 9/11 attacks. The dialogue was being administered by the Anglican Communion's Network for Inter Faith Concerns (NIFCON), the Episcopal Diocese of New York hosting the event. Just before the dialogue was to take place, it was postponed, Muslim representatives citing unease in Egypt about the election of Canon Gene Robinson as bishop of New Hampshire.[15] Robinson's election just weeks before had caused worldwide debate in the Anglican Communion because of his open admission of a homosexual past.

Controversy has also occurred where meetings between Muslim and Jewish religious leaders have taken place. When Shaykh Tantawi met with the visiting Chief Rabbi of Israel at Al-Azhar Mosque in Egypt in December 1997, this meeting received statements of support from bodies such as the Islamic research academy of Al-Azhar,[16] but also attracted much criticism from student groups. Moreover, a private lawsuit was filed against Shaykh Tantawi, claiming that he sanctioned an illegitimate meeting within 'one of the holy homes of God'.[17]

Such dialogue activities among religious leaders have become increasingly prevalent within Britain, and have carried official sanction. For example, on 3 January 2000, the government's Department for Culture, Media and Sport, in conjunction with the Inter Faith Network for the UK, hosted a shared faith communities' event in London as part of the millennium festivities.[18] The event, broadcast nationally by the BBC, was held in the Royal Gallery in the Houses of Parliament. It was attended by representatives of Britain's nine major faith communities, and included presentations by faith leaders and young people from the communities, with readings from sacred scriptures and appropriate musical contributions. Its content was developed by the faith communities, through the Inter Faith Network for the UK. The event culminated in the signing of 'A Shared Act of Reflection and Commitment by the Faith Communities of the United Kingdom'.[19]

Dialogue among scholars

Christian–Muslim dialogue activities among scholars have become increasingly common as well. An example occurred in May 2000, when a dialogue meeting of around eighty Christian and Muslim scholars was held at Cumberland Lodge in the Great Park, Windsor. The theme was 'Christians and Muslims in the Commonwealth'. It was jointly sponsored by the King

George VI and Queen Elizabeth Foundation of St Catherine's and the Altajir World of Islam Trust. Notable features included small-group discussion of themes raised in plenary sessions.

Separate worship activities were held, but several Muslim participants also attended worship in the Queen's Chapel, which was very close to Cumberland Lodge. Participants met and chatted with the Queen on an impromptu basis after one such worship service.

A volume of papers delivered at the conference was subsequently published.[20] In addition, a number of the presentations were summarized and published in the Muslim periodical *Discourse*.[21]

Dialogue on religious experience

It is important to consider the nature and effectiveness of dialogue gatherings at the grass roots. One such grass-roots dialogue activity relates to a group engaging in dialogue on religious experience in Birmingham, UK. Outcomes have been published by the WCC.

Andrew Wingate, an Anglican minister and former missionary in India, initiated a series of dialogue encounters between his parishioners and Muslims in Birmingham. Wingate writes: 'My time in India convinced me that we come to understand other faiths not from books and texts, but from meeting people . . . we meet with people who follow Hinduism or Islam, not with Hinduism and Islam.'[22] This statement is consistent with the first principle of dialogue as drawn up by the WCC and enunciated by the CCBI, which states: 'Dialogue begins when people meet each other.' Furthermore, Wingate discusses the exclusivist–inclusivist–pluralist paradigm,[23] and concludes that he is an inclusivist. Again, this is broadly consistent with the principal documentation produced during the last decades of the twentieth century by the WCC.

In order to initiate meetings, Wingate first approached the local Islamic Centre in his area of Birmingham. After he received a positive response, the first meeting was convened between about fifteen Christians and Muslims, and the agreed topic of discussion was 'prayer'. The second dialogue meeting was held at a local mosque. For this meeting, the Christian women and the Muslim women sat apart from the men, in accordance with standard mosque practice.

During subsequent years, many meetings were held in private homes of members of the dialogue group. The third meeting was held at the home of one of the Muslims. The focus for this session was on readings from the Bible and the Qur'an, but discussion covered a wide range of topics. At Christmas time the Christian participants paid a visit to the homes of Muslim contacts and shared a meal. A further meeting was held in one of the Christian homes. On this occasion, the family dog was kept away from the group out of respect for Islamic scriptural portrayals of dogs as unclean animals.[24]

One meeting was held in Wingate's house. The Muslim participants were all men, whereas the Christian group included women. This meeting centred around the place of Jesus in personal Christian faith. The meeting included personal testimonies by many of the Christians present, though a measure of Christian diversity was recorded on this point, some Christians being less inclined to speak of a personal relationship with Jesus.[25]

As relationships developed, there were increasing opportunities for expression of heartfelt views. For example, on one occasion one of the Christian women described Islamic worship as sombre and Islam as a sad religion on the basis of what she had observed. This led to considerable discussion. Moreover, as the dialogue meetings continued, Wingate records that the meetings between women tended to be on a one-to-one basis, in accordance with Muslim wishes.

It is interesting to read Wingate's conclusion. He pondered key questions that regularly arise from such interfaith gatherings: 'I am faced with the question whether they are worshipping the same God as me. Intellectually, I know they must be, as there is only one God, and that is a basic tenet of both our faiths. But deep in my heart, can I feel that they are doing so, even though they do not see God in his complete fullness (if I felt they did, then I would be a Muslim)?'[26]

This local activity successfully brought together Christians and Muslims to engage in dialogue discussions on respective religious experiences. Meetings were carried out with due regard to issues of sensitivity and mutual respect, but nevertheless discussion on controversial topics arose. The overall tone seems to have been inclusivist rather than pluralist, with an emphasis on seeking to identify truths and shared beliefs without necessarily calling on either faith community to compromise on certain central tenets.

Dialogue for conflict resolution

A dialogue of a different form was the WCC Encounter Youth Exchange Project. This represented an interfaith initiative of the Anglican Diocese of Chelmsford, England, with the Maronite Diocese of Haifa and the Holy Land.

The aim of the project was stated as seeking 'to promote a better understanding of, and to work towards, reconciliation between, Christians, Jews and Muslims by offering young people an opportunity for encounter by way of educational exchange visits between the Holy Land and England'.[27] Thus the purpose was not so much a deep exchange of respective theological perspectives as conflict resolution achieved by showing the human face of communities in adversarial situations, in the hope that cycles of negative stereotyping would be broken. In the words of project co-ordinator Anne

Davison: 'We're using them as role models – an awareness-raising thing. It will be a chance for our kids to see something positive.'[28]

The project's first encounter occurred in September 1998 in the form of an interfaith meeting in East London, attended by students and staff from King Solomon High School (Jewish), the Ursuline School and Canon Palmer School (Roman Catholic) and Muslim students from Newham College of Further Education, all based in Britain.

In August 1999, twelve young British people between the ages of sixteen and eighteen (four Christians, four Jews and four Muslims), with an equal balance between boys and girls, travelled to Israel to meet a similarly constituted group for a ten-day encounter. They participated in workshops at Neve Shalom (Wahat as-Salam in Arabic), a unique village[29] where Jews and Arabs live side by side, committed to working through their differences.[30]

Prior to the encounters, the respective groups participated in a preparation programme involving both cognitive and experiential activities. Both the preparation programme and the encounters included activities focusing on basic principles of dialogue and conflict-management techniques. The encounters also allowed time for visits to places of worship and historical interest and for fun.

This programme was funded by sponsorship and participant resources, and carried the stamp of the WCC as its promotional body. This shows another dimension to WCC interfaith activities, moving beyond the dialogue on religious experience to engaging with some of the most intractable inter-community conflicts.

Dialogue on social concerns
Dialogue initiatives have not been restricted to WCC-inclined church groups. Indeed, evangelical Christian contact with Muslim communities has witnessed an increasing variety of approaches, including dialogue. One of the most significant initiatives in this regard has been the Faith and Society dialogue group in Britain.

The Faith and Society group derived from an increasing perception among evangelical groups that there were many areas of shared social concern among Muslims and Christians, and that the potential for partnership on these issues was not being addressed through existing methods of Christian–Muslim interaction. Accordingly, a pilot conference was held at the London Institute for Contemporary Christianity in November 1997, called 'Faith and Power'. The stated aim of the conference was 'to reflect on areas of public life in which Christians and Muslims seek to work out the social and political implications of their faith in an increasingly secular society in Britain today'. This conference included plenary presentations on issues of social concern by Christian and Muslim speakers, followed by meetings of focus groups addressing specific themes. The ratio of Christians to Muslims at this initial conference was 90:10. Organizers deemed the conference a success, but it was felt that effort should be devoted to achieving a greater sense of numerical balance between the faiths in future gatherings.

A second conference for what was now called the Faith and Society group was held in October 1998 at the Islamic Foundation in Leicestershire. The theme was 'People of Faith in Britain Today and Tomorrow'. It was attended by 110 people, the Christian-to-Muslim ratio being approximately 60:40.[31] Of this number, around thirty-five expressed interest in participating in regular meetings of focus groups.[32] As a result, focus groups on family, sexuality and gender, education, and religion and public life were convened in February and March 1999 to discuss these issues of concern common to Christians and Muslims.[33]

In October 1999 the Faith and Society group held its third annual meeting in Birmingham, and attracted around 100 Christians and Muslims, of whom around 80% were Christian.[34] The theme was 'Seeking the Common Good'. The Right Reverend John Austin, bishop of Aston, Birmingham, delivered a plenary presentation on behalf of Christian participants. He called on the audience to learn to tell their respective stories in 'an inclusive way'. He further lamented the state of economic imbalance in the world and called on people of faith to overcome jointly 'the idolatry of economic concerns' in the modern world. Imam Abduljalil Sajid, a leading figure in the Muslim Council of Britain, set his plenary presentation firmly within an Islamic theological framework. Imam Abduljalil argued that the notion of the 'common good' was heavily embedded within the vocabulary of the Qur'an, and the five pillars of Islamic duty were an effective device for encouraging Muslims to build concern for others into their daily lives. He called on people of faith to work together to increase the public role of religion.

Both keynote speakers agreed that dialogue did not demand complete compromise, and that different faiths involved in interfaith co-operation should take care to preserve their distinctive features and beliefs. There was also agreement on the need to tackle the worldwide imbalance in the distribution of resources and wealth.

During the afternoon, participants broke into five focus groups, addressing a range of social issues: the media; family, sexuality and gender; religion and public life; education; and law. The media group based its discussion around the question 'How to get God into the headlines'. Members agreed to seek to identify people of faith in the media who could help to increase the public profile of religion. Members also agreed to lodge complaints when material offensive to religious concerns appeared in the media.

The group discussing family, sexuality and gender considered a practical case study of family breakdown, and underlined the importance of support and education in the early stages of family formation. In a similar vein, the 'religion and public life' group considered several practical case studies, showing co-operation between Christians and Muslims in various British cities. The education group initiated plans for Christians and Muslims to visit each other's places of worship. The law group addressed the different philosophical bases to English and Islamic law, and considered the challenge ahead with the advent of European laws in Britain.

The annual day conference for the Faith and Society group for the following year was held on 28 October 2000 at the Carlisle Business Centre in Bradford. The theme was 'Faiths in Society: A Challenge to Policy Makers', and the particular focus fell on Bradford, which contains a significant Muslim population. The event attracted around ninety participants, of whom approximately one quarter were Muslim.

The day began with reflections on Christian and Muslim scriptures. This was followed by a Christian plenary session, given by Guy Wilkinson, Archdeacon of Bradford. He spoke of the church's perception of its own place and of that of the Muslim community, and then considered the public-policy perception of religions. He concluded by suggesting ways in which Christians and Muslims could together engage with public society, calling for joint action on social issues, co-operation to address negative media images of religious communities, and efforts to overcome territorial separation (stating that 'white flight' is the church's responsibility and that Muslims should not encourage territorial separation).

The Muslim plenary address was given by Mohammed Ajeeb, former Lord Mayor of Bradford. He called for frankness and honesty in dialogue, and cited instances of how Muslims had been victims of Islamophobia in Bradford and elsewhere in Britain. He stressed that Muslims perceived the church as influential in public society, and called on the church to assist the Muslim community in its situation of relative disempowerment.

In small-group discussion, responses were given to the plenary talks. Some participants commented that significant public resources were channelled into the Muslim community and other minority communities in Bradford. One Asian Christian present asked how Muslims in Bradford contributed to the common good, rather than merely focusing on Muslim rights. This led to considerable discussion between the Muslim and Christian speakers present. Focus groups met in the afternoon, assembled according to the topics of law; media; education; religion and public life; and family, sexuality and gender.

Faith and Society is an example of how evangelical Christian approaches to other faiths have diversified beyond traditional mission activities. In its first three years Faith and Society facilitated significant and ongoing contacts between evangelical Christians and Muslims in Britain. Though such dialogue activities fall broadly into the category termed 'secular dialogue' in the

Lausanne movement report (mentioned above), such a label is misleading. Faith and Society discussions have ostensibly addressed issues of social concern, but scriptural and theological references have been frequent, embedded within the topics discussed, and presented as the basis of specific views and recommendations.

Catholic–Muslim dialogue

Dialogue between Catholics and Muslims became increasingly frequent at the grass-roots level around the world during the last quarter of the twentieth century.

In Sydney, Australia, St Columban's Mission Society established the Columban Centre for Christian–Muslim Relations in Turramurra in the mid-1990s. Explaining the motivation for establishing the centre, staff write: 'The Columban Centre for Christian–Muslim Relations contributes to the ongoing work of building better relations between the two faith communities in Sydney and beyond . . . We know people have experienced God in so many ways and have experienced the spiritual dimension of the human within many different cultural and symbolic systems.'

Official endorsement of the work of the centre came in July 1997, when Cardinal Arinze, head of the Pontifical Council for Inter-religious Dialogue, visited the Columban Centre and addressed a group of 100 people who represented some fourteen different faiths and denominations. Emphasizing the centrality of dialogue to Catholic policy, and reminding readers of church authority, a statement on the cardinal's address by staff of the Columban Centre said: 'A clear message [of the address] is that anyone who is not in favour of inter-faith relations is singing outside the choir of the church.'[35]

The Columban Centre for Christian–Muslim Relations undertakes a range of activities. It organizes conferences and meetings between Christians and Muslims to discuss respective beliefs and practices. It maintains a library and resource centre on Islam and inter-religious dialogue. It arranges in-service sessions for teachers, seminars and workshops on Islam for Christians, visits to mosques, and other relevant activities. The centre co-ordinates a network of women who wish to develop stronger contacts with Muslim women. Finally, it publishes a newsletter, called *Bridges*, informing others of activities and advertising events.

The Columban Centre women's dialogue network was formed in 1997 by nuns who were working there full-time. Liaison with the Muslim community mainly takes place in the western suburbs of Sydney, around the large Muslim community in Auburn. Christian members of the women's dialogue network visit mosques, invite Muslim speakers to talk to their group, and undertake studies of Islam. The women's dialogue network has established links with the Muslim Women's National Network of Australia. Both groups attend each other's functions. In October 1998, five Catholic women from the Columban Centre's women's dialogue network attended the Annual National Seminar of the Muslim Women's National Network of Australia. The topic of the seminar was 'Issues of Concern to Muslim Women'. Writing on the experience, Sr Pauline Rae, head of the Columban Centre, says, 'We are women of faith, worshipping the One God and acknowledging the essential element of prayer in our lives.'

The Catholic–Muslim women's partnership has also increasingly involved Sydney Anglican women in interfaith women's dialogues. A dialogue session in early 2000 at St James's Church, King Street, centred upon a panel of speakers drawn from the Catholic, Anglican and Islamic communities. Sr Pauline Rae wrote of the event in inclusivist terms, saying, 'If two of the world's great faith traditions, Islam and Christianity, comprising more than 50% of the world's population, can meet each other in friendship and respect here, what great things can Allah/God do through us?'

In Ghana, a very different setting records a similar sense of partnership and openness between Catholics and Muslims, fulfilling official policy of the Catholic Church. Father Aloysius Nuolabong promotes Christian–Muslim dialogue in the diocese of Wa, Ghana.[36] He first seeks to gain Muslim confidence by setting aside funds to provide medical and educational support for the Muslim poor. He then visits Muslim villages and holds meetings with imams and their Muslim constituencies. Father Nuolabong speaks about the need for dialogue between Muslims and Christians.

In one village, the imam's son spoke in response and 'urged both Christians and Muslims to embrace the idea of dialogue. He further called on his fellow Muslims to take note of the difference between Christianity and Western civilisation.'[37]

Thus Catholic clergy and parishioners in diverse parts of the world have been working to implement Vatican policy regarding attitudes to other faiths in recent decades. The dialogue approach is integrated, including both dialogue on religious experience and dialogue on social concerns.

Christian–Muslim debate

The preceding discussion has focused upon a range of dialogue activities, undertaken by a wide number of Christian groups. It is noticeable that such dialogue activities produce positive Muslim interest and engagement from two of the three Muslim categories described at the outset of this present study: namely traditionalist and modernizing Muslims. In terms of our examination of British Muslim responses to British society, it is noticeable that interest in Christian–Muslim dialogue comes from those of a participatory mindset. On the Christian side, interest in dialogue has been seen to come from liberal, traditionalist and evangelical wings of the churches.

There is one Muslim voice that has not yet been heard; namely, that of those Muslims of a separatist mindset, including radical Islamists. Where do they fit into Christian–Muslim relations? Do they have a part to play in increasing Christian–Muslim dialogue activities?

Muslim radicals pose a particular set of challenges to the Christian faith. Many Islamic student groups on university campuses in western universities were engaging in increasing levels of anti-Christian polemic in the 1990s and into the twenty-first century, as part of their mission (*da'wa*) activities. In their effort to pose searching challenges about the reliability of the biblical materials they distribute material written by such famous Muslim polemicists as Ahmed Deedat. An example of anti-Christian polemical writing drawn from materials prepared by the University of Sheffield Islamic Circle runs: 'To propagate the Gospel, it is its present form [*sic*] is as dangerous and irresponsible as handing out any harmful, addictive substance, for error delights its followers and the consequences are eternal . . . From the foregoing, it is clear that the existing Bible, together with the beliefs and the practices of Christianity, are full of unauthorised innovation.'[38]

Besides producing their own polemical writing, such student groups distribute works produced by past generations of Muslim polemicists. One such, written in India in the nineteenth century and widely distributed among Muslim student groups on British university campuses, concludes:

> The gradual realisation of the distortions present in a number of their holy books is bound to lead the Christians, sooner or later, to admit to the truth of the fact that the greater part of the Judeo-Christian Scriptures have undergone great changes and distortions.
>
> We have shown that the Christians do not possess any authentic records or acceptable arguments for the authenticity of the books of either the Old Testament or the New Testament.[39]

Maurice Bucaille's *The Bible, The Qur'an and Science* is another favourite among Muslim polemicists. This excerpt provides a taste of its approach to the gospels: 'Matthew's phantasms, the flat contradictions between Gospels, the improbabilities, the incompatibilities with modern scientific data, the successive distortions of the text – all these things add up to the fact that the Gospels contain chapters and passages that are the sole produce of the human imagination.'[40]

While such Muslims are willing to ask searching questions of Christian sacred texts, they are not usually willing to ask such questions about the Islamic primary materials. This leaves the way open for others to do so. In the words of the Catholic scholar Anthony O'Mahony, 'Islam still needs to ask itself fundamental questions regarding its nature and origins, and not let these questions be asked only by people outside Islam.'[41]

Such challenges from Islamists have been ignored by most Christian groups engaged in multifaith contacts, whether liberal, traditionalist or evangelical. Some evangelical groups, however, have responded by accepting challenges to public debates, a practice used in earlier periods by Christian missionaries such as Carl Pfander, the great Christian missionary debater in India in the mid-nineteenth century.[42]

Such public debates are increasingly frequent on British university campuses. They are typically organized by student Islamic societies, and are designed around a strictly enforced structure. These debates attract large numbers. For example, a debate arranged by the Manchester University Islamic Society and the Christian Union on 19 April 1997 attracted 500 people, filling the hall to capacity and disappointing many would-be attenders who were not able to gain entry. The Christian speaker was Jay Smith, a prominent debater on Christian–Muslim topics in Britain and the USA. Muslim arguments were articulated by Shabir Ali, a leading debater from the Da'wah Centre, Canada. Three topics were discussed: 'Similarities and differences between Islam and Christianity'; 'The nature of sin'; 'What does Islam or Christianity have to offer the campus?'

Each speaker spoke without interruption for ten minutes, then each was given five minutes to respond to the other. Questions were then received from the floor, with the chairman enforcing strict rules of discussion and debate.

Since that event, Christian–Muslim debates have been taking place with increasing frequency in Britain and overseas. These have included debates between Jay Smith and Sheikh Omar Bakri Muhammad of Al-Muhajiroun in London in November 1999, a repeat encounter between Smith and Shabir Ali in Atlanta in October 2000,[43] and a debate between Smith and Azzam Tamimi of the London-based Institute of Islamic Political Thought at Cambridge University in January 2003. In addition to these widely publicized events, debates between other evangelical Christians and Muslim militant spokesmen have increased in number. Keith Small debated with Shabir Ali in Bradford in March 2000, and with another Muslim speaker at the University of Edinburgh in February 2004, on the topic 'Who was the real Jesus: that of the Bible or of the Qur'an?' Other such debates took place at the universities of Birmingham and Glasgow in 2000, and at Coventry University in 2001. A place of regular debating interaction between Christians and Muslims is Speakers Corner at Hyde Park, where militant Muslims had come to dominate the scene until challenged by the evangelical Hyde Park Christian Fellowship since the late 1990s.

This approach tends to be more apologetic and polemical than dialogical in methodology. Arguing for the importance of this approach, Smith
calls for a redefinition of 'dialogue' based on the biblical example of Paul's
methodology:

> Paul's premise for dialoguing was not simply to learn from others, and from
> there to compromise his beliefs in order to evolve another set of beliefs. He
> knew this would bring about syncretism . . . he sought to prove what he said
> (Acts 17:3). He marshaled arguments to support his case, provided evidence, and
> therefore engaged in argument . . . His job was to persuade [his hearers] of the
> truth of the gospel. What they did with that truth was then their own
> responsibility.[44]

Elsewhere Smith argues for this approach as being the most appropriate way
for Christians to respond to the phenomenon of radical Islamism:

> Today it is the radical Muslims who are attacking our Christian foundations
> more vociferously and more comprehensively than any other Muslim group.
> Their passion is amazing, even impressive, though misguided. It does no good
> to dismiss them as simply irrelevant extremists, representing a small minority of
> Muslims. The statistics . . . show that they are growing in numbers and ability,
> and prepared to die for what they believe, and take as many as possible with
> them . . . Christians cannot wish them away . . . Some of us will have to stand
> our ground and confront them, publicly, face-to-face, in debate if need be.[45]

In this methodology we encounter a measure of confidence in the message
of the Christian gospels as was manifested in the statement by William Carey
cited in chapter 1. This methodology is highly controversial, however, and is
attracting much opposition from within Christian circles, including evangelical opposition.[46] Yet it also attracts considerable support. It requires a large
dose of courage, both to face a particularly intimidating manifestation of
Islam as well as to deal with hostility from certain Christian individuals and
groups. At the time of writing, the debate methodology leads the way among
Christian approaches to Islam in specifically addressing anti-Christian
polemic from radical Islamist groups.

Activities following 11 September 2001

We have already noted that after the terrorist attacks of 11 September 2001,
the incumbent Archbishop of Canterbury, George Carey, devoted increased
attention to Christian–Muslim relations. In January 2002 he joined Jewish,
Muslim and other Christian leaders in signing a multifaith accord in Cairo,
condemning violence in the Middle East. This accord included the

statement that, 'according to our faith [and] traditions, killing innocents in the name of God is a desecration of His holy name, and defames religion in the world . . . we call upon all to oppose incitement, hatred and the misrepresentation of the other'. The different faiths were represented at the highest level, including, along with Archbishop Carey, Shaykh Muhammad Tantawi of Al-Azhar Islamic University in Cairo, and two leading rabbis from Israel. This meeting of faith leaders also received statements of strong support from political leaders in the Middle East region, including Prime Minister Ariel Sharon of Israel, Chairman Yasir Arafat of the Palestinian Authority, and President Husni Mubarak of Egypt.

Following the Cairo multifaith meeting, Shaykh Tantawi visited London, where a further bilateral dialogue agreement was signed in January 2002 between the Church of England and Al-Azhar.[47] This event accompanied the first of a series of dialogue meetings, which came to be referred to as the 'Building Bridges' seminars.

The 'Building Bridges' seminars

London, January 2002. A dialogue meeting of forty prominent Christians and Muslims was held in January 2002 at Lambeth Palace in London. The meeting was prompted by the shadows gathering over the Christian–Muslim relationship following the terrorist attacks of 11 September 2001. The volume received the sanction of the Archbishop of Canterbury, Dr George Carey, of Prince Hassan of Jordan, and of Prime Minister Tony Blair.

The conference was structured around specific themes. Each was addressed by a Christian and Muslim, with another Muslim and Christian responding respectively. In the published proceedings, Michael Ipgrave, advisor to the Church of England Archbishop's Council on Interfaith Relations, adds his comments throughout.

The initial theme, 'Christians and Muslims Face to Face', was addressed by Mustafa Ceric, Grand Mufti of Bosnia and Herzegovina, and the prolific writer and scholar Bishop Kenneth Cragg. Ceric drew on the Qur'an in stressing that 'we are to adopt an inclusive, not an exclusive approach, to the worlds of faith'.[48] Cragg, in his characteristically penetrating style, contrasted the confidence of Islam in the use of political power with Christian eschewing of a formal political role since the Enlightenment. He posed a rhetorical question about the Islamic approach: 'Does it not oversimplify the whole business of religion in the world and tangle religious integrity in these political auspices?'[49]

Conference participants also addressed the thorny issue of how to deal with past history. Michael Ipgrave saw a possibility of controlling the memory of the past by deliberately focusing on certain key episodes in order to shape the future. Professor David Kerr of Edinburgh University provided a Christian voice in addressing this theme, followed by Professor Tarif Khalidi of the University of Cambridge.

Justice Nasim Ahmad Shah of Pakistan and Professor Michael Banner of King's College, London, gave consideration to the respective approaches to religious minorities. Justice Shah acknowledged that 'Christians in practice face many difficulties in Pakistan',[50] frankly detailing some instances of discrimination. In response to this paper, Archbishop Henri Teissier asked whether the ambiguity of the teachings of the Qur'an regarding religious minorities fuelled abuse of minority rights in certain countries.

Discussions also addressed the theme of 'Faith and Change'. Cambridge professor David Ford proposed six items for a future agenda in the Christian–Muslim relationship. Seyed Amir Akrami of Iran presented an interesting threefold typology of Muslim responses to change:[51] (1) those who reject it or assume that traditional ways of dealing with change are sufficient; (2) those who embrace change and dispense with religious tradition and heritage; and (3) those who accept change and allow religious positions to move where appropriate.

Participants considered the best means of setting an agenda for the future. Dr Rabiatu Ammah of Ghana commented that 'one way Muslim communities can seriously curb fundamentalism and extremism is for the authorities to give them a voice and constantly to engage in dialogue with them on critical issues'.[52] Professor Tarek Mitri of the World Council of Churches stressed the importance of setting the agenda together. Bishop Michael Nazir-Ali pointed out that both faiths had well-developed mystical traditions attesting to 'the true worth of inwardness', and Brunel University professor Gillian Stamp gave voice to this mystical tradition in Islam by quoting from the great Persian Sufi Jalal al-Din Rumi.

Qatar, April 2003. A second 'Building Bridges' seminar was held on 7–9 April 2003 in Qatar.[53] Fifteen Christian scholars, led by Dr Rowan Williams (who succeeded Carey as Archbishop of Canterbury in 2003) joined with fifteen Muslim theologians to explore the use of scripture in the two faiths. This event coincided with the Iraq War.

After the seminar Dr Williams issued a statement that clearly expressed the degree of self-reflection prompted by the meeting:

> Our work here involved examining the use and understanding of scripture in Muslim and Christian thought. We were sent back to our own and to each others' sacred texts to deepen our understanding. Muslims confess their belief in the God who 'brings the living out of the dead and He brings the dead out of the living' (Qur'an, Sura 30 v 19–30). Christians strive to live 'in the presence of the God who gives life to the dead and calls into existence the things that do not exist' (Romans 4:17).

A common concern expressed by both Christians and Muslims about interfaith dialogue is a fear of compromising of central tenets of faith. Archbishop Williams' statement sought to address this concern: 'Without compromising our respective convictions, we found it possible to listen to how each tradition of faith understood this fundamental vision of the creator's presence and action.' The Archbishop also took the opportunity in his statement to explain how dialogue served a key role in building bridges in times of international tension and difficulty:

> The seminar is part of a continuing process of dialogue between Muslims and Christians. It is the very strong conviction of those involved in this dialogue at a time of international tension, when both faith communities are sometimes criticised and caricatured and when disagreements are presented in dramatic and exaggerated ways, [that] it is all the more important to give time and energy to sustained efforts towards better understanding of the spiritual and intellectual heart of each tradition.
>
> We hope that our work here will contribute to the drawing together of our traditions in a commitment to work together for a just and reconciled world.[54]

A further seminar took place from 29 March to 1 April 2004 at the Center for Christian–Muslim Understanding, Georgetown University, continuing the study of sacred texts from both faiths.

The Archbishop's Initiative in Christian–Muslim Relations

Another legacy of Archbishop Carey was the Archbishop's Initiative in Christian–Muslim Relations. This initiative traces its origins to a reception given by the Archbishop at the time of a visit to London by Shaykh Tantawi in 1997. At this reception the Archbishop spoke generally of the need for a structured dialogue between Christians and Muslims in Britain. This led to calls by British Muslim leaders for a national body where Muslims and Christians could meet to compare views and discuss issues of common concern. Such a body was seen as paralleling the Council of Christians and Jews, which had been set up in 1942 and provided an effective forum for Christian–Jewish co-operation.

A group of Christians from diverse denominations met at Lambeth in October 2000 to discuss ways of developing these ideas. A joint Christian–Muslim Planning Group was drawn together to carry forward the initiative, and a larger Reference Group of Christian and Muslim leaders was identified in 2001 to meet from time to time and provide advice to the Planning Group.

In 2002 and 2003 the Planning Group conducted a series of visits to key towns and cities in England: Blackburn, Bradford, Leicester, east London and northwest London. These visits took the form of 'listening exercises', involving over 500 people in around 100 separate meetings. They brought together Christians and Muslims from diverse backgrounds, other faith communities, local authorities, police, media and others with an interest in community relations. Two primary issues were addressed: first, 'What were considered to be the most important issues on which Muslims and Christians need to work together?' and second, 'What could a national forum do to help Muslims and Christians locally meet, talk and act together?'

The initiative was co-ordinated from Church House in London, the administrative headquarters of the Church of England. It was stressed from the outset by both Christian and Muslim representatives that any Christian–Muslim body emerging from this initiative should not replace local activities, but should rather work alongside existing Christian–Muslim and interfaith groups.

During this process, Archbishop Carey retired from his post and was replaced by Dr Rowan Williams, who expressed his support for this initiative from the start.

A final meeting of the Reference Group was held in January 2004, at which the Planning Group reported on the outcome of the listening exercises. The decision was taken to proceed with the development of a national Christian–Muslim Forum. This initiative is still in an advanced planning stage at the time of writing.

High-level Catholic responses in the wake of 9/11
Catholic authorities also moved quickly to try to address turmoil in the relationship between Islam and the West following the 9/11 attacks. In his message for the World Day for Peace in December 2001, Pope John Paul II declared: 'Jewish, Christian and Islamic religious leaders must now take the lead in publicly condemning terrorism and in denying terrorists any form of religious or moral legitimacy.'[55]

He invited religious leaders from diverse faiths to Assisi in January 2002 to renounce violence publicly and to commit themselves to peaceful co-existence. This 'pilgrimage for peace' on 23 January gathered together 200 world religious leaders from the Christian, Jewish, Muslim, Buddhist and Sikh faiths and from others. It undertook to oppose the use of violence in God's name.[56]

The Faith and Society conference, June 2003
The annual conference of the Faith and Society group planned for October 2001 was cancelled, given the uncertainties following the terrorist attacks of the previous month. The group remained in abeyance during 2002, but late that year a decision was taken to resurrect it. This decision was partly

connected with initiatives from the Archbishop of Canterbury; the Faith and Society chairmanship had resided in Church House since its establishment, so it was inevitable that it would be seen as germane to the broader Archbishop's Initiative. Furthermore, the perceived fragility of the relationship between Islam and Christianity in Britain at the time suggested that a revived Faith and Society could play a part in building bridges between Christians and Muslims.

As a result, the fifth annual day conference of the group was held on 26 June 2003. It addressed the theme 'Faith-full Citizens: Christians and Muslims in Britain'. The venue was the London Central Mosque and Islamic Cultural Centre, which was chosen in the specific hope of attracting a higher level of Muslim attendance than had been the case at previous conferences.

The format tried and tested at previous conferences was followed. The day began with two plenary presentations. Ahmed Thomson, a barrister and convert to Islam, provided the Muslim plenary presentation. He explained faith (*iman*) in terms of the core Islamic doctrines: oneness of God, angels, messengers, revealed scriptures, judgment and God's decrees. He then articulated a distinction between a believer (*mu'min*) and an unbeliever (*kafir*). He argued that *kafir* states do not survive, citing Pharaonic Egypt, the Incas and Stalinist Russia as examples. In contrast, he maintained, states ruled by believers have no difficulty ruling the masses as 'the believers control themselves from the inside'. He called for people of faith to unite, saying, 'If we people of *iman* make a stand when people of ignorance control society, we can transform society.'

Dr Derek Tidball, Principal of London Bible College (now the London School of Theology), presented the Christian plenary. He stressed that it is not possible to read straight off the page from the Bible to the modern world, since a process of interpretation is necessary. He drew on four 'moments in scripture': Israel as a theocracy, the period of exile, the period of Jesus Christ, and the period of the apostles and mission. He then demonstrated how these biblical references can provide wisdom and insight in addressing issues and challenges in modern Britain, in terms of eschewing a division between sacred and secular, living as people of faith in an anti-faith society, challenging governing authorities at certain times, and subordinating human authority to the divine authority of Jesus Christ. He concluded by stating that 'we owe it to Britain to continue to speak on spiritual issues and values'.

After lunch participants broke into small groups, to address issues of citizenship as they relate to the media, education, local communities, and civic society.

Several features of the conference were noteworthy. First was the disappointing attendance. Only forty-seven people took part, of whom only seven were Muslim, five of these being presenters on the day. There was thus virtually no participation of the rank and file from the Muslim community. The reasons are unclear at the time of writing, though there seems to have been no attempt to promote the event in the British Muslim community.

Another feature of note was the willingness of both plenary speakers to ground their presentations clearly in their respective sacred writings and to articulate the central tenets of Muslim and Christian faith and belief. At previous conferences Muslim speakers had done this, but Christian speakers had given only passing attention to biblical content and reference.

Furthermore, the practical relevance of much of the discussion was evident, both in the plenary presentations and in other activities. For example, one presentation focused on a practical project of co-operation between Christian and Muslim youth in Birmingham, which has been running successfully for several years and could serve as a model for Christian–Muslim activity in other locations.

Catholic–Shi'a dialogue, York, July 2003

A Christian–Muslim engagement of a specific type is seen in the Catholic–Shi'a dialogue held in York in July 2003. This event was the outcome of a set of friendships established between Iranian students studying at British universities and monks of the Catholic abbey at Ampleforth, near York, in the late 1990s. A visit to the Iranian holy city of Qom by the abbott of Ampleforth and one of his staff ensued in April 2002. This visit generated reciprocal goodwill and an agreement jointly to plan and hold a Catholic–Shi'a dialogue conference the following year.

The conference was held at two venues: the Jesuit Heythrop College in London, and Ampleforth Abbey. The initial day at Heythrop attracted around ninety people, with a 60:40 ratio of Christians to Muslims. An invited group of thirty-five carried on the dialogue at Ampleforth, including seventeen Iranians, over four subsequent days.

A set of themes was addressed, with a Catholic and a Shi'a paper delivered in turn on each theme, followed by questions and discussion. Themes were the remembrance of God, the challenge of living a life of faith today; moral problems of life and death; the Word of God and the idea of sacrament; prayer and contemplation; the challenge from outside; Abraham as a man of faith; the family; and religion and education.[57] Besides gathering in plenary presentations, participants met in small groups to discuss issues arising from the papers.

A number of features of the conference were noteworthy. First, there was considerable frankness on the part of both Christian and Muslim speakers in the exchanges and presentations. Public prayers by adherents of both faiths were identifiably Christian and Muslim respectively, rather than being a neutral, multifaith kind of prayer. Catholic speakers were forthright in referring to Jesus as 'Son of God' and praying accordingly. In return, Muslim participants did not hesitate to ask challenging questions about the Trinity, prayer to Jesus, and other doctrines that were alien to Islam.

Furthermore, a forthright call for freedom of religion was made by the Revd Dr Justo Lacunza Balda, Director of the Pontifical Institute for the Study of Arabic and Islam. He stated that 'religious freedom must be discussed openly. It is the most essential question that Christians and Muslims must debate today . . . Religious freedom is a sacrosanct right of the individual, regardless of faith.' Though this issue was not addressed by Muslim speakers during plenary presentations, Ayatollah Araki from the Shi'ite delegation commented in small-group discussion that if a person has the truth and then rejects it – that is, he becomes an apostate – he would be punished in hell for ever.

A second feature of note was the friendly spirit in which these frank exchanges took place. At no time was friction evident or offence taken. It should be recorded at this point, however, that some key thorny issues were not addressed. There was no substantial discussion of the death and resurrection of Christ or of the authenticity or otherwise of the writings sacred to each faith. Key questions that are virtually taboo in Islam, such as those probing the character of Muhammad and his claim to prophecy, received no attention.

A third characteristic was the contrast between the frequent quoting from sacred scripture by Muslim speakers and the almost total absence of this by Catholic speakers. This led to frequent Muslim questions to Christian speakers regarding the need for standard criteria for theological doctrines, and questions seeking to identify standards on which Catholic speakers were drawing.

A fourth, very positive, feature of the conference was the willingness of Muslim participants to attend Catholic worship services in Ampleforth Abbey along with Catholic participants. The conference's location in a living, praying community, rather than in a secular conference centre, facilitated this.

The conference concluded with a statement of willingness by both sides to build on discussions in tangible ways, through follow-up meetings, joint publications and other possible avenues.

Multifaith dialogue in Watford, March 2003

Following the outbreak of the Iraq War in March 2003, the Watford Inter-Faith Association called for a multifaith meeting in the community to affirm co-operation at a time of international crisis. This meeting provides a good example of how dialogue at the local level can play a role in striving for peace and reconciliation.

The event was billed as seeking 'peace, harmony and co-operation in our community', and aimed 'to express our solidarity in response to the outbreak of hostilities in the Middle East, and to reaffirm our determination to continue to work together to strengthen interfaith and inter-community relations in our town'. The gathering attracted around fifty representatives from many faiths: Christians of various denominations, Muslims, Hindus, Buddhists, Jews, Bahais, Zoroastrians, and others. It was hosted by the Watford Council at the town hall.

The WIFA chairman, a Zoroastrian, laid the foundations for the gathering in his welcoming speech. He stressed that inter-religious co-operation was no longer 'a luxury or an option, but rather an absolute necessity'. He called for all the groups represented to be faithful to their own faith traditions while shunning the temptation to disparage the traditions of others. He also emphasized that the meeting should focus on Watford issues and not be deflected on to war talk.

Most of the speakers adhered to these guidelines. The mayor of Watford said that the key ingredients for community harmony were tolerance and love. She read from 1 Corinthians 13 to illustrate the kind of love needed to achieve such harmony. Speakers from different faith traditions similarly drew on passages from their own sacred scriptures to argue for shared values of neighbourliness, tolerance, and desire for peace.

Discussion inevitably touched upon the nexus between faith and the war. One Christian speaker stressed that the Iraq War was not a crusade, and that 'it was not being waged in the name of Jesus Christ, the Prince of Peace'. A Muslim speaker, in similar vein, pointed out that weapons of mass destruction were not sanctioned by Islamic belief.

Several speakers who drifted into discussing contentious matters, however, put the external façade of unity on such themes to the test. One Muslim representative questioned the motives of western leaders who had taken the US and Britain into war. Another argued passionately that the Israeli–Palestinian conflict was the root cause of the current conflict. These comments prompted the Watford civic mayor to ask what price should be paid for peace, and at what point the international community should act when faced by evil tyranny.

Although such opinions did risk politicizing what was intended as a non-political meeting, they did nevertheless remind the audience of real debates likely to take place in the broader community. To this extent, these speakers added a note of reality to the gathering.

The meeting concluded with the signing of a Statement of Commitment, drawn up by the Inter Faith Network of the UK. This was based on the 'Shared Act of Reflection and Commitment by the Faith Communities of the United Kingdom' developed at the shared faith communities event held in January 2000 as part of the millennium festivities.[58]

The meeting highlighted both the successes and challenges of interfaith dialogue. Much good came out of it. Name cards were exchanged and laughs were shared across faith lines. Each participant inevitably came away with an increased awareness of other faith perspectives, whether through hearing selections from various sacred texts or simply through being reminded of the human face of other faiths.

Tripartite dialogue in Australia, 2004

In Australia, a tripartite dialogue body grouping together Christians, Jews and Muslims, called the Jewish–Christian–Muslim Conference of Australia, was formed in 2003. Its first significant event was to be a residential conference, to include forty-five people drawn from the three faiths in equal numbers, with a wide range of interests; it was to be held in Brisbane on 23–26 August 2004. The event took as its model a series of interfaith conferences held in Europe annually since the initial gathering at Bendorf, Germany, in 1973.

Participants were drawn from the clergy, lay people active in congregational life, academics, welfare and community support professionals, and tertiary students. The programme included time to share personal experiences and approaches to worship, and to have group discussions on differing religious beliefs and community life under the guidance of fellow conference participants with experience in interfaith dialogue.

The aims of this conference were to 'encourage better understanding of each other's faiths through personal contact, extend contact between leaders of the Abrahamic religions, and encourage closer cooperation. An additional hope is to see the development of a growing pool of people who are committed and able to lead interfaith dialogue programmes and therefore help reduce tension and improve cohesion within the Australian community.'[59]

Conclusions

We have seen that interfaith dialogue represents the central plank for realizing in practical terms the increasingly inclusivist attitudes in the churches towards other faiths. This dialogue can take various forms. Dialogue on religious experience is attracting the participation of all streams of the church, but especially World Council of Churches and Catholic groups. Dialogue on social concerns is similarly attracting all streams of the broader church, and on this score the Faith and Society initiative in Britain represents an important evangelical activity that may serve as a forerunner of other such evangelical enterprises in the future.

Christian–Muslim debate has also appeared as one piece in the mosaic of Christian–Muslim interaction in recent years. This activity relates to a specific subset of the Muslim community, namely radical Islamists, for whom other dialogical approaches have not proved effective in building bridges between communities. Those who participate in debates from the Christian side argue for such interaction to be seen as part of dialogue, on the basis of the biblical record.

Christians who seek to engage with Muslims thus have many routes open to them. The path selected will depend both on the interests and gifts of the person concerned and on the identity of the Muslim partners in the interaction.

PART 3
ASKING QUESTIONS AND SEEKING ANSWERS

6. ISSUES IN CHRISTIAN–MUSLIM RELATIONS TODAY

We began our study by considering factors that facilitated a movement towards greater inclusivism in British attitudes to other faiths, especially Islam. We also considered how advances have been set back by a series of developments at the beginning of the twenty-first century.

We then looked more closely at Islam in Britain, engaging with its diversity, its internal debates, and its various responses to British society. This discussion was informed by a consideration of the issue of globalization, which looms large in Muslim consciousness in considering approaches to the non-Muslim West. We then proceeded to examine more closely the church in its diversity, both within Britain and beyond. We saw that a diverse church produces diverse methods of engagement with other faiths, although all major church blocs have moved towards more inclusivist attitudes to other faiths.

Discussion of these issues raises a host of questions that need to be addressed regarding the future relationship between Christianity and Islam in the twenty-first century. This final section will be devoted to a consideration of some of the most important questions that arise out both out of the preceding discussion and from my many encounters with Christian and Muslim groups in Britain and elsewhere.

Muslim plurality

Are there serious dialogues between radical Muslims and other Muslims?
In the wake of 9/11, a gathering of Muslim scholars in Europe meeting on 16 October 2001 denounced the al-Qa'ida network, saying: 'The so-called Qa'ida Organization . . . is not in any way an Islamic organization and its activities should not be linked to Muslims. The statements of the spokesmen of this organization are not in keeping with the teachings of Islam and have nothing to do with the Sunna. Not one of the leaders of this group enjoy [*sic*] the attributes that give him the right to issue fatwas.'[1]

Osama bin Laden responded to statements that rejected his Islamic credentials by issuing some rejections of his own:

> The fatwa of any official aalim (religious figure) has no value for me. History is
> full of such ulema (clerics) who justify Riba (interest [on loans]), who justify the
> occupation of Palestine by the Jews, who justify the presence of American
> troops around Harmain Sharifain (holy places in Saudi Arabia). These people
> support the infidels for their personal gain. The true ulema support the jihad
> against America.[2]

This exchange is a good example of the relationship between radical and
moderate voices within the Islamic community. They usually talk past each
other, with the result that meaningful dialogue between radicals and the more
moderate mainstream is rare. In such cases, when Muslim radicals and moderates dismiss each other's credentials as Muslims, a related question arises.

Should Christians decide who the real Muslims are?

Evangelicals, with their firm commitment to the Bible as the ultimate yardstick of theological orthodoxy, tend to apply the same criteria in evaluating
Muslims. Thus Muslim radicals are often seen by Christian evangelicals
(especially fundamentalists) as 'real Muslims' because of their scriptural-
literalist approach. This response, however, is really more of a window into
the mind of the Christians concerned than into that of the Muslims on whom
they claim to comment.

Christians should avoid passing judgment in such intra-Muslim debates.
It is up to Muslims to resolve their differences. While Christians may hope
that certain views will prevail in intra-Muslim arguments, it is not the
responsibility of Christians to adjudicate, declaring any particular group to
be the 'real Muslims'.

So what is Islam?

My view of Muslim identity is derived from my engagement with Muslims
in vastly different contexts around the world.

Islam is a Hui Chinese peasant popping occasionally into his mosque,
which resembles a pagoda and has the Islamic creed (*shahada*) on the wall in
Chinese, not Arabic. Islam is equally a Javanese peasant going straight from
Friday prayers to the rice fields, where he will leave an offering to the goddess
of the rice, Dewi Sri. Islam is also a Lombok folk Muslim who tells me that
Islam has only three pillars, not five. Islam is the Iranian gentleman I met one
evening in a street café by the Caspian Sea who was not in the least interested
in answering my questions about his faith, preferring to talk about the last
time Iran played Australia at football. Islam is the faith of modernizers such as

Anwar Ibrahim, Mohammad Arkoun, Mohammad Talbi, Nurcholish Madjid, Benazir Bhutto and others who are outspokenly critical of Islamist radicals, who argue for a separation between mosque and state, and who want to develop an updated Islamic hermeneutic.

Of course, Islamist radicals will point to the Islamic primary texts – indeed, will dwell on those texts – and say that such people are not true Muslims. But such a response itself represents only one face of the mosaic that is Islam.

Christian plurality

Is the creation of a truly multi-ethnic church in Britain the key to overcoming the guilt-for-colonialism phenomenon?

We saw in the first chapter that the guilt burden for Britain's colonial past has had a knock-on effect on attitudes within the British church, where mission has come to be seen in the minds of many as an arm of the discredited colonial policy of the past.

The solution to this may well lie in the co-operation of churches to achieve a truly multi-ethnic identity. If churches, especially in urban areas, were to work to include more Afro-Caribbean and Asian Christians, they might not feel so vulnerable to accusations of hypocrisy from non-Christians around them.

This is easier said than done, of course. In many instances churches assume a distinct ethnic identity, not so much because of a policy of exclusion of other ethnic groups, but rather because people of a particular group wish to congregate together.[3] Overcoming this tendency will mean paying close attention to policy at the level of church leadership, and allocating of resources to campaigns designed to educate the laity in the churches.

Do denominational divisions within the Christian body provide fuel for some Muslims who seek to discredit Christians and their faith?

There is a widespread perception among Muslims that Christians are hopelessly divided. This is reinforced by specific references within the Qur'an, such as Q98:4: 'Nor did the People of the Book make schisms, until after there came to them Clear Evidence.' In explaining this verse, the modern commentator Yusuf Ali suggests that the fragmentation among the People of the Book[4] is a direct result of their having rejected the message of Islam.[5] The great schism between Orthodoxy and Catholicism in the eleventh century, and the later Catholic–Protestant divisions, are considered to represent the fruit of Christians' having rejected Islam centuries before.

In this context, continuing public bickering along Christian denominational lines is seen by many Muslims as further evidence of modern

Christianity's lack of validity as a revealed faith. Thus Christians who cannot build bridges among themselves cannot hope to reach out successfully to Muslims *en masse*.

What is the general Christian perception of Islam and vice versa?

There is no such thing as a 'general perception'. Some Muslims view Christianity positively; others view it as debased and corrupt. A position commonly held by Muslims is that expressed by Shagufta Yaqub, editor of *Q-News*, who commented in interview: 'I see most Christians – or, at least, people who were born into a Christian family – as having come very far from their religious beliefs. When I think of the church, I think of it as such a loose thing now . . . Christianity has tried so hard to stay alive by changing with the times, it's lost a lot of its original message.'[6]

Some Christian pluralists are willing to argue for a measure of divine involvement in the Islamic prophet and in the texts associated with him. We have already quoted the words of Clinton Bennett, Anglican priest and scholar: 'I do not know *how* the Qur'an was communicated by God through Muhammad, but I can accept that it was.' He continues: 'As I view the incarnation as a mystery, so I view the *bookification* of the Qur'an.'[7] Most Christians, however, would not support such a statement, and would consider that any recognition of the Qur'an as divinely sourced and of Muhammad as a genuine prophet would be tantamount to accepting Islam's claim to be the final revelation.

Christian–Muslim relations in other contexts

What is the attitude of the Orthodox churches in relation to dialogue with Islam?

So far we have not focused specifically on the Orthodox churches, given their relatively minor presence in Britain.[8] It would be appropriate at this point, however, to make some comments regarding engagement between the Orthodox Christian churches and Islam, in order to provide a comparative perspective. We shall focus on the Russian and Greek churches, which represent the two poles of world Orthodoxy.

The Russian Orthodox Church has been experiencing a significant revival since the fall of communism. At the beginning of the twenty-first century the church included 128 active dioceses, compared with sixty-seven in 1989; there were 19,000 parishes, compared with 6,893 in 1988; and almost 480 monasteries, compared with eighteen in 1980. In the year 2000, pastoral activities for the Russian Orthodox Church were carried out by 150 bishops, 17,500 priests and 2,300 deacons.

The church was not only active in meeting internal Christian needs. External relations with other faiths, including Islam, were receiving increasing attention, though Russian Orthodox activities in this regard were directed to Muslim communities outside the country rather than to Russia's own fifteen-million Muslim minority, which did not seem to be of great interest to the church.[9] For example, the year 2000 witnessed the holding of the third colloquium of the Joint Russian–Iranian Commission on 'Islam–Orthodoxy' Dialogue. It took place in Tehran on 24–25 January 2000.[10] The delegation of the Russian Orthodox Church was headed by Bishop Alexander of Baku and the Caspian Region. The Iranian delegation was headed by Hojat ul-Islam Noumani.

The participants in the colloquium discussed the theme 'The Role of Inter-religious Dialogue in International Relations'. Papers by Orthodox and Muslim speakers addressed a range of topics: 'Conditions and Rules of Intellectual and Cultural Dialogue', 'Religion and Conflict: the Roots of the Problem and the Ways to Its Solution', 'The Orthodox View on Freedom', 'The Role of Inter-religious Dialogue in International Relations', 'The Situation with Inter-religious Dialogue in Russia at Present', and 'Inter-religious Dialogue in Iran: History and Some Thoughts on the Themes'.

In its structure and thematic focus, this Russian–Shi'a encounter resembles the dialogue interactions that are taking place between Anglican and Catholic churches and Muslim interlocutors, discussed earlier in this study.

The Greek Orthodox Church has interacted closely with the Islamic world for centuries, especially through the steadily shrinking Orthodox communities in Muslim-majority Middle Eastern countries. Anastasios Yannoulatos sees four phases in this engagement while Islam swept through the region. The first phase (eighth–ninth centuries) was characterized by Eastern Christians who were 'taunting and undervaluing Islam'. The second (ninth–fourteenth centuries) saw a flourishing of anti-Islamic polemical writings in the face of ongoing threats to Eastern Christendom. The third phase (fourteenth–fifteenth centuries) was marked by 'mild criticism and objective evaluation of Islam'. With the fall of Constantinople to the Turks in 1453, Orthodox Christianity entered a fourth phase (fifteenth–eighteenth centuries), one of 'silence and monologue'.[11]

More recently, Eastern Orthodoxy has been devoting its attention increasingly to a new phase of dialogue with Islam. This has coincided with changes in the Catholic Church since Vatican II (which Orthodoxy has observed) and developments within the World Council of Churches (in which Eastern Orthodoxy has participated).

The Greek Orthodox Patriarch Petros VII of Alexandria, in a 1998 speech, articulated his view of the origins and value of Orthodox–Muslim dialogue:

Dialogue between Christianity and Islam springs from the essence of Christianity, which is the foremost religion of dialogue . . . There are basic and essential differences between the religions of Christianity and Islam, which cannot be ignored . . . Subjects concerning man and the world, especially matters which deal with everyday problems, can lead in this dialogue . . . Communication and co-operation between religions make an essential contribution to the abolition of religious fanaticism, an intellectual sickness of the religious person . . . Productive dialogue can help realise heavenly peace on Earth, and protect the holiness of life and man's dignity . . . Dialogue which is based, not only on theological matters, but on worldly issues, can be both hopeful and fruitful.[12]

In the same speech, however, Petros VII reflected the historical concerns of Eastern Orthodox Christians in Arab lands in alluding to issues of religious freedom:

Orthodoxy coexists and seeks dialogue with Islam; dialogue which presupposes freedom of speech and equality between the two parties . . . In Eastern Christianity one sees respect towards the religious experience of others, forbearance and mutual understanding . . . For centuries, a large part of Orthodoxy lived in the Islamic world, although not always as an equal member of its society . . . dialogue is necessary, and indeed, is the only acceptable way to bring our two religions closer . . . Dialogue is necessary if we are to overcome the past and the present of alienation, confrontation, enmity and hatred.[13]

In certain circumstances the Orthodox Church interaction with Muslims has been coloured by factors falling outside areas of church authority. A case in point is found in Bulgaria, where the communist government forced the Turkish and other Muslim minority groups[14] to adopt non-Muslim names in 1985. This caused an outcry among Bulgarian Muslims at the time, but the Bulgarian Orthodox church authorities remained largely silent on the issue, in contrast with the active role the Bulgarian church had played in saving Bulgarian Jews from deportation to Nazi camps during the Second World War. This silence contributed to an atmosphere of mistrust and bitterness between Bulgarian Muslims and the Orthodox Church.

The engagement of the Orthodox churches with Islam is particularly interesting, given that their historical interaction is much closer than has been the case with western Christianity. Our primary focus on the British context, however, precludes our taking this discussion further in this study.

International crises

How central is the Israel issue to Christian–Muslim relations around the world?

Analysis of this much-discussed issue is driven in large part by different perspectives and angles on the Israeli–Palestinian conflict.

Muslims widely consider the establishment of the State of Israel in 1948 as an attempt to reassert European colonial control by means of a latter-day Crusader state. M. Shahid Alam expresses this in condemning suggestions that Pakistan might recognize Israel: 'If Zengi,[15] Nur al-Din, Salahuddin and the Egyptian Mamluks refused to recognize the Crusader states, can Muslims today be expected to choose differently?'[16] Many Muslims also see European and American economic and military links with Israel since its creation as evidence of the West's expansionist goals. The humiliating defeat of Arab armies by Israel in several wars since 1948 is thus considered to have been facilitated by the West.

Many non-Muslims challenge such views as oversimplifications of a very complex conflict. Many argue that the historical presence of a Jewish community in the Holy Land for thousands of years entitles the Jews to a state on part of the land, at least. It is further pointed out that western, and indeed, American support for Israel is not monolithic. Moreover, Muslim perspectives tend to ignore how Palestinian and other Arab actions and policies have contributed to the intractable nature of the conflict over the years. They also ignore the vigorous debate within Israeli society concerning policies towards its Arab neighbours.

Nevertheless, from a Muslim perspective, support for the Israeli–Palestinian peace process among Palestinians in the West Bank and Gaza plummeted during the first years of the twenty-first century. Support for rejectionist radical Islamist groups rose by 12% to 31% during 2001. In contrast, support for the mainstream Fatah organization, which had been guiding the Palestinian participation in peace discussions with Israel, fell from 33% to 20%.[17] This reflects a widespread feeling among Palestinians, shared by Muslim masses in other countries, that a two-state solution would be a sell-out of Palestinian rights. Their preference would be for Israel to disappear as a state, as they consider it to be an alien western implant in the Muslim heartlands.

Does this mean that the conflict surrounding the State of Israel is a root cause of Islamic radicalism? The response must be in the negative. While the conflict fuels the radical Islamist movement, it is not a root cause. If Israel ceased to exist tomorrow, Muslim radicals would find other arenas of conflict where military engagement was seen as appropriate: Chechnya, the Sudan, Kashmir, the southern Philippines, eastern Indonesia, to name a few. In the words of the radical group Al-Muhajiroun: 'Muslims will proclaim that the only solution to the atrocities being committed against them in Palestine, Kashmir, Chechnya or Afghanistan is Jihad; an obligation to engage in physically upon those nearest and an obligation upon the Muslims around the world to support verbally, financially and physically!'[18] In essence (and this is key), their literalist reading of Islamic scripture leads radicals to conclude that non-believers (that is, non-Muslims) are 'infidels' and should be fought. They draw their inspiration from Qur'anic verses such as Q9:5: 'Fight and slay the Pagans wherever ye find them, and seize them, beleaguer them, and lie in wait for them in every stratagem.' The issue of Israel is not so much a root cause of the radicals' conflict with the West as a manifestation of it.[19]

It should be noted, however, that many, perhaps most, Muslims would disagree with this assessment, opting to identify Israel as the root cause of diverse conflicts in the Middle East. Such a view of Israel is shared by many Europeans, according to an opinion poll of October 2003, conducted by the Eurobarometer organization, and based on interviews with 500 people in each of the (then) fifteen states of the European Union. It found that 59% of those surveyed considered Israel to be the greatest threat to world peace, followed closely by the United States and North Korea in joint second place.[20] It seems that Muslim views on this issue find considerable support among the masses of the European Union.

How should Christians respond to the international political crises of the early twenty-first century?

Christians should consider a number of factors in responding to current international political crises. At the outset it is important to sift critically through a mass of issues, distinguishing the primary from the secondary.

Matters such as the diversity of Muslim opinion and the need to condemn anti-Muslim public reaction are important and require a response. In a key sense, however, they are peripheral to the central issue, from which our attention must not be deflected. The fact is that there is an international network of radical Muslims, committed to terrorism, that must be stopped. This network, built loosely around the al-Qa'ida group led by Osama bin Laden, has come into public view since 9/11, but it was far from dormant prior to that date.

Christians should acknowledge from the outset that Islamic radicalism does pose a threat that cannot and must not be ignored. It must be confronted, and immediately. As part of this action, Christian leaders should recognize that, if the Muslim majority is brought within the circle of friendship, the Muslim radicals will be cut off from the base of support they desire.

First, then, churches should be encouraged to develop their contacts with modernizing Muslims at times of crisis. This can be done through engaging in dialogue at community level, forming individual friendships, co-operating on social issues, and offering hospitality to Muslim neighbours or colleagues.

Secondly, Christian leaders should continue to urge their governments to distinguish publicly between different kinds of Muslims. They should stress that most Muslims do not bear responsibility for the terrorist attacks of 9/11. In this way, governments may create a climate that is less conducive to racist attacks against innocent members of Muslim communities in different countries.

Thirdly, and in recognition of the fact that western governments and allied states need to take appropriate action against the radical Islamic groups, Christian leaders should support government moves to strengthen anti-terrorist legislation, arrest and detention, and limited military action. Such measures received the sanction of the United Nations Security Council on 28 September 2001, when it adopted a wide-ranging, comprehensive resolution with steps and strategies to combat international terrorism.[21] Nevertheless, such statements of support should be tempered by asking searching questions of governments, to ensure that the action taken is proportionate and effective.

Fourthly, Christian leaders should encourage their governments to seek partnerships with moderate Muslim governments in the ongoing response to the radicals. Furthermore, US efforts to draw together and maintain a broad coalition, including Muslim nations, provide hope for a resolution to the present world crisis. This crisis should not be allowed to become a general conflict between the West and Islam.

Fifthly, Christian leaders should counsel caution in response to calls to negotiate with radical jihadi Islamists. Such a well-intentioned but naïve call was made in April 2004 by former Northern Ireland Secretary Mo Mowlam, who urged the British and American governments to open talks with Osama bin Laden and al-Qa'ida around a negotiating table.[22] The fact is that Muslim radicals are driven by a literalist reading of Islamic scripture that leads them to conclude that non-Muslims are 'infidels' and should be fought; such groups would see negotiations merely as a stratagem towards their ultimate goals.

A sixth and essential step in identifying right responses to the current world crisis involves turning to the pages of the Bible for wisdom and guidance. The responses outlined above are eclectic, combining irenic approaches with measured support for the use of force. This conforms to biblical standards. In Matthew's Gospel, Jesus told his disciples to turn the other cheek when struck,[23] but later in the same book he also overturned forcefully the tables of the money-changers in the temple.[24] We therefore need to select our response wisely, according to the circumstances: sometimes dialogue and humility will be the best course, but on other occasions (when the former does not bring about a godly environment) a more forceful response will be required.

Is Christianity more supportive of globalism, industrialization and capitalism than Islam is?

Christianity is not inherently more supportive of globalism than Islam. As we saw in an earlier chapter, many Muslim writers condemn globalization, but a close reading of their writings shows that they are not opposed to globalism *per se*, arguing rather for localism or regionalism. Indeed, these writers are typically driven by a desire for *Islamic* globalism: they promote Islamic banks around the world, seek to empower the Organization of Islamic Conference (which includes over fifty Muslim nations in a kind of mini-United Nations), and urge Islamic women around the world to stop wearing jeans and to don the headcover. That is globalism under a different guise.

The same is true of industrialization. Muslims of most varieties favour economic progress, for which a prerequisite is industrialization. The concern of many is not with industrialization *per se*, but rather that it should seek to advance the Islamisation of society. Malaysia is a classic case in point. It made massive strides in industrialization during the last quarter of the twentieth century, exactly when Islamization was being promoted both from above (by the governments) and at the grass-roots level.

As for capitalism, there certainly are aspects of it that go against the grain of Islamic economic theory. The obvious one is the dependence upon interest on loans for financing further economic activity. (Muslims are forbidden to charge or pay interest on loans.) But, such details aside, there are many Muslim-majority countries around the world that seek Islamization within a largely capitalist framework. Malaysia is again a good example.

Is a clash between the West and Islam inevitable?

There is certainly great potential for ongoing rivalry between Islam and the West. Islam is a total package for life, covering the religious, political, social and economic domains, whereas the West vigorously enforces a separation between sacred and secular. It is difficult to reconcile the two worldviews. Moreover, Islamic doctrine is most comfortable when it is the majority, and Islamic law assumes that situation. Muslim minorities in western countries have proved to be among the most awkward. They often argue that conflict with the non-Muslim majority is due to exclusion and alienation. While this is true in part, there are deeper issues, deriving from inbuilt rivalry and competition between western and Islamic ideologies. But rivalry need not turn to conflict if carefully handled, with goodwill on both sides. Rivalry can be good; conflict is rarely good.

Are all Muslims united in opposing the War on Terror?[25]

On a trip to Washington DC in July 2002, I met Shaykh Muhammad Hisham Kabbani. We were both speaking at a public symposium, held at the Center for Religious Freedom, that focused on the spread of radical Islamism in different parts of the Muslim world.

I was particularly struck by Shaykh Kabbani's outspoken critique of radical Islamism. He showed a degree of candidness that is uncommon among moderate Muslims in condemning the ideology of *jihad*-driven Islamists. Absent was the implicit justification one hears so often, which sees Islamist radicalism merely as a product of failed western foreign policy. This was a hard-hitting internal critique by one of the Islamic world's most courageous figures.

Shaykh Kabbani is head of the Islamic Supreme Council of America (ISCA). He also enjoys a senior position in the worldwide Naqshbandi-Haqqani Sufi mystical order, and is a favourite to become head of this group in the future.

An article by a prominent ISCA representative in the *National Review Online* in 2002[26] shows just how fractured is the Muslim community both in the West and elsewhere. Dr Hedieh Mirahmadi, an aide to Shaykh Kabbani, wrote with concern about the activities of radical Muslims, whom she terms 'jihadis', who set up a mini-Islamic state in the mountains on the Iraq–Iran border around a dozen Kurdish villages. They received funding and weaponry from bin Laden's al-Qa'ida, as well as increased fighting strength as they were joined by jihadi warriors who fled Afghanistan on the fall of the Taliban.

These jihadis desecrated ancient Sufi tombs that had served as sites of local pilgrimage for the inhabitants of the region for centuries. In a particularly gruesome development, the radicals stole corpses of revered saints from these tombs, beheading them in the streets as a mark of defiance of local custom. Furthermore (based on the Qur'an's prohibition of the creation of images, lest they be worshipped), a blanket ban was placed on any public or private display of photos of deceased relatives and living friends and families. A set of edicts placed restrictions on the public movement of women.

Such radical activity adheres to a well-established pattern. Mirahmadi points to the depth of its roots in saying that 'these extremists follow a 200-year-old radical doctrine that has brought only injustice, oppression, and violence to those brought under its sway'.

The ISCA, representing as it does one prominent Muslim group with a considerable international Muslim support base, debunks the myth of Muslim solidarity in opposition to America and the West. This particular Muslim group calls on the West to act in confronting the Muslim radical networks. Mirahmadi warns that 'if the West remains silent while these militants conquer centuries-old communities of devout yet moderate Muslims, then they will continue to spread'. She is clearly at odds with both Muslim and western commentators who see American foreign policy as the ultimate source of international tensions.[27] She insists that 'the greatest danger to the freedoms of Muslims everywhere in the world, including the U.S., is not the war on terror, but the oppression and intolerance of radicals who continue to commit atrocities in the name of religion'.

As the fierce debate among western commentators continues over the best method to respond to the challenge of radical Islam, we should be mindful that similar debates are taking place among Muslims themselves. In this context, bridge-building with such moderate Muslim groups is a necessity.

Psalm 33:16 ('No king is saved by the size of his army; no warrior escapes by his great strength') reminds us that military solutions are not a quick fix. Armed campaigns are no doubt necessary, in certain circumstances, to evict oppressive forces from power. Clear cases in point are the war against Nazi Germany, and the more recent campaign in Afghanistan. But such military activities do not produce solutions in themselves. They only bring about a change in circumstances that can facilitate the identification of solutions.

The War on Terror is not just about military pursuit. In the long run it is more about providing ongoing support to communities that have suffered from long-term oppression, such as the people of Afghanistan. Such support should empower those who are dedicated to improving the lot of the masses, not to oppressing them.

Human rights under Islam[28]

The issue of the treatment of Christian minority communities in Muslim-majority locations receives regular attention from Christian churches and other bodies advocating religious liberty,[29] and leads to questions such as the following, posed at the 2003 London Lectures: 'One is free to become a Muslim, but not free to leave Islam. How is it possible to have a two-way dialogue with a partner who is not willing to reconsider his own point of view; that is, when freedom is available to only one of the dialogue partners?'

There are significant differences between Islam and Christianity regarding conversion away from one's original faith. If a Christian renounces Christianity and becomes a Muslim, his or her family and community would probably be disappointed. Some negative comments may be made, or, in the most extreme cases, the convert may be disowned by his or her family. There is, however, no enforceable religious prohibition on conversion away from Christianity. In contrast, Islamic law does not allow Muslims to renounce their faith. The punishment for apostasy according to Islamic law is severe. While 'some modernists have argued against the traditional death penalty for apostasy on the grounds that the Qur'an only specifies other-worldly punishment',[30] in more conservative or remote Islamic locations capital punishment is still often implemented, both by officialdom and by radical Islamists.

Article 18 of the Universal Declaration of Human Rights states: 'Everyone has the right to freedom of thought, conscience and religion; this right includes freedom to change his religion or belief.'[31] Human-rights agencies and certain national governments have lobbied hard for widespread implementation of this provision in recent decades. These efforts have led to an increasing openness in traditionally Christian countries in the West to expanded worship and missionary activities by non-Christian faiths. Muslim majority countries, however, even those that are signatories to the Universal Declaration of Human Rights, have resisted full implementation of this provision. Their opposition is based on a range of factors: guidelines relating to apostasy in Islamic scripture and legal texts; recent legislation drawn up by governments in some Muslim countries; and unwillingness by Muslim populations to countenance the spread of non-Muslim faiths in Muslim lands.

Teachings in Islamic scripture

The Qur'an, the ultimate scriptural authority of Islam, believed by Muslims to be the Word of God, says of those who abandon Islam for another faith: 'Those who turn back as apostates after Guidance was clearly shown to them – the Evil One has instigated them and buoyed them up with false hopes' (Q47:25). The second most authoritative scriptural source within Islam, the prophetic Traditions or Hadith, says: 'Narrated Abdullah: Allah's Apostle said, "The blood of a Muslim who confesses that none has the right to be worshipped but Allah and that I am His Apostle, cannot be shed except in three cases: In Qisas [retaliation] for murder, a married person who commits illegal sexual intercourse and the one who reverts from Islam (apostate) and leaves the Muslims." '[32]

Islamic law schools drew on such statements in the Qur'an and Hadith to formulate precise guidelines for punishing those guilty of apostasy. The Hadith stipulation just quoted is incorporated into the legal text *al-Risala* of the Malikite school in the words: 'An apostate is . . . killed unless he repents. He is allowed three days' grace; if he fails to utilise the chance to repent, the execution takes place. This same also applies to women apostates.'[33] The legal texts prescribed that apostates were to undergo other punishments before suffering the death sentence. This is again specified in *al-Risala*: 'If either of a couple apostatises, the marriage shall be judicially dissolved by a divorce. But according to the view of other jurists, such a marriage is to be dissolved without a divorce.'[34]

Application in the modern world

Many countries with majority Muslim populations have implemented Islamic law, or s*hari'a*, to varying degrees in the modern world. Some countries have proclaimed the s*hari'a* as the overriding basis of their legal systems.

Other countries have made Islam the official religion, but implementation of the *shari'a* has been restricted to specific areas.

Those countries which have been most forthright in basing their legal codes on Islamic law, and therefore in taking action against apostasy, include Pakistan, Saudi Arabia, Mauritania, the Sudan and Iran. The latter, though Shi'ite and therefore drawing on different Hadith collections and legal codes, nevertheless takes a view on apostasy from Islam similar to that discussed above. Other countries that draw on *shari'a* to a lesser degree include Malaysia, which nevertheless has passed legislation forbidding non-Muslims to attempt to convert Muslims (though allowing and, indeed, giving official sanction to conversion in the other direction).

In the context of *shari'a* prohibitions against apostasy, those Muslims who have renounced their faith in countries that follow Islamic law have often undergone great suffering, discrimination and persecution.

In Pakistan, human-rights agencies have documented many cases where converts away from Islam have been targeted by local Islamic and civil authorities. The case of Tahir Iqbal serves as an example. After converting from Islam to Christianity in 1988, Iqbal was accused by local Islamic leaders of defiling a copy of the Qur'an. He was arrested, and imprisoned for over eighteen months. Repeated requests for bail by his counsel were refused, and he was found dead in his cell in suspicious circumstances in July 1992.[35]

Cases of harassment, discrimination or persecution of converts have also been documented by human-rights or church groups in Egypt, Morocco, Somalia, Sudan, Saudi Arabia and Iran. In the last of these, several pastors who were actively involved in evangelizing Muslims were murdered during the 1990s, with church groups strongly suspecting the complicity of local government and Islamic authorities.

Muslims living in the West, too, can experience difficulties if they choose to convert to Christianity. Though the threat of death is less prevalent than in Muslim societies, converts in western countries often face rejection by their families and communities, disinheritance, and possible divorce if their marital partner remains a Muslim.

Conversion represents one of the greatest obstacles in Christian–Muslim interaction in the modern world. This should not, however, be swept under the carpet, as it were. Indeed, it cries out for sensitive discussion. Western societies are increasingly playing host to Muslim immigrant communities, and Muslim mission activity in the West is becoming more widespread and sophisticated, and is benefiting from freedom of speech and multicultural policies in western countries. At the same time, Muslim-majority countries typically impose stringent restrictions on mission activity to Muslims by non-Muslim faith adherents. Thus Muslim-majority communities are denied the free access to a range of faiths that is enjoyed by non-Muslim majorities in western countries.

Dissenting Muslims voices

As signalled above, a few prominent Muslims do not adhere to the standard line that prescribes death for apostates. For example, the former leader of the Sudan, Dr Hasan al-Turabi, argued that the scriptural prohibition against apostasy was time-bound:

> The Prophet, peace be upon him, explained that one who abandons his religion and deserts his fellows should be killed. Regrettably, people of subsequent generations have taken the Prophet's saying out of its historical context and generalised it. In so doing they deny one of the basic truths of Islam: the freedom of faith. How can it be imagined by a rational person that Allah, Who had compelled none to believe, allows us the right to compel others and force them to believe? The Qur'anic verses that prohibit compulsion and coercion are numerous and so are the sayings and practices of the Prophet, peace be upon him. That is why I do not hold the common view on the question of apostasy.[36]

Such views are encouraging, but in the early twenty-first century they are held by a tiny minority of Muslims. Moreover, they have attracted severe condemnation from many Muslim scholars who take a more traditional Islamic view on the question.

How should Christians respond?

Christians both outside and within the Muslim world can respond to this situation in various ways:

- by supporting human-rights groups engaged in advocacy on behalf of Christian minorities experiencing discrimination
- by expressing support through letters to newspapers, politicians, and so on, for the full implementation in Muslim countries of the Universal Declaration of Human Rights provision relating to religious freedom
- by bringing these issues to the attention of their local churches for action through prayer, support for missions outreach, and similar means
- by sensitively discussing these issues with individual Muslim friends, neighbours and work colleagues, urging them to take up such matters with Muslim representative bodies
- by encouraging their churches to engage in dialogue on these issues with local mosques and Islamic centres

What about the anti-reciprocity argument?

The report quoted below raises the much-discussed issue of reciprocity. It is drawn from *Asia Times Online*, and refers to an interview with Abdul Hadi Awang, former Chief Minister of the Malaysian State of Terengganu and

President of the conservative Islamic political party, PAS, which governed in
Terengganu from 1999 to 2004:

> Hadi was asked if it was true that an application to build a new Catholic church
> in Kuala Terengganu had not yet received a favorable reply. Hadi said the state
> had studied the matter and found out that the place currently being used was
> adequate for the church's requirements (Catholics there have been using a
> chapel belonging to a local convent). 'To build a new church, with a tall steeple
> and *lambang* [symbol or cross], in a public place would be a sensitive issue,' he
> said. 'They [the church] have to consider the sensitivities of the community
> around them. They have a place of worship now; we think it is adequate. We
> would allow them to build a *dewan* [hall], but not a prominent steeple. It's for
> their own safety.' When asked why this issue should be 'sensitive', Hadi said
> there were certain quarters, a small minority, in society who were *jahil*
> (ignorant) and that they could create problems. He also said the state
> government could not guarantee security against such problems as it does not
> control the security forces, which come under federal jurisdiction.[37]

Those readers familiar with London might find themselves comparing this
proposed church building with the imposing East London Mosque, which
broadcasts the Islamic call to prayer throughout that part of one of the great
capitals of the Christian world. It would seem that majority Christian
London is far more open to overt expressions of alternative faith adherence
than were the Muslim PAS authorities in the Malaysian state of Terengganu.

Does this case raise issues of reciprocity that call for Christian attention
and discussion? It would appear so. Christians involved in dialogue with
Muslims need to speak not only for the masses they represent directly in their
own countries, but also for the faceless minorities from their own faith tradition who live in lands where the Muslim dialogue partner is in the majority, such as in Malaysia. It seems only fair that the efforts extended by western
countries, home to nominally Christian majorities, to provide equal opportunity to Muslim minorities should be reciprocated by Muslim-majority
countries in relation to their Christian minorities.

Not all Christians agree with this. In February 1997 the Islam in Europe
Committee of the European churches produced a document that rejected
the use of the term 'reciprocity', arguing that 'reconciliation' was a more
desirable goal of Muslim–Christian bridge-building.[38] At the same time, in
a letter to Dr Ataullah Siddiqui of the Islamic Foundation in Leicester,
Dr Christopher Lamb, former Secretary of the Council of Churches of
Britain and Ireland, wrote: 'We have . . . decided to reject the whole concept
of reciprocity as a basis for Christian/Muslim relationships.'[39] Tarek Mitri
of the World Council of Churches asserts in a similar vein that 'the call for

"reciprocity" in the treatment of minorities is problematic'.[40]

Affirming the line taken in the European churches' document, Muslim authors at the Islamic Foundation in Leicester lamented that 'so often European Christians contrast the allegedly good treatment of Muslims in European countries (apart from Bosnia) with the allegedly bad treatment of Christians in Muslim countries. The way the comparison is made usually suggests that since Muslims treat Christians badly (it is said), then there is no reason for Christians to treat Muslims well or even justly.'[41]

In fact, however, this statement does not accurately articulate the argument for reciprocity. Reciprocity does indeed call for advocacy on behalf of Christian minorities in Muslim-majority lands, but certainly does not urge discrimination against Muslim minorities in Christian-majority lands. Nevertheless, such Muslim statements and the views of the anti-reciprocity exponents in the churches seem to indicate a meeting of minds on this point.

While the eloquent arguments of those Christians who reject the notion of reciprocity may persuade certain Christian scholars and please some Muslim interlocutors, it is hard to ignore a sense of disloyalty and abandonment when western Christian leaders refuse to speak out forcefully on behalf of any Christian minority in a Muslim-majority location that is experiencing discrimination. In this context, the views of Cardinal Arinze of the Catholic Church should be strongly affirmed:

> The right to religious freedom . . . applies wherever there is a human being. People of the majority religion in a country should not therefore deny to religious minorities in that country the very freedom of religion that they claim for their coreligionists in another country where they are in the minority. This is what reciprocity is all about. In order to build for peace, we need the acceptance and practice of reciprocity.[42]

Similarly, the forthright statement of the former Archbishop of Canterbury, George Carey, deserves support: 'During my time as archbishop, this was my constant refrain – that the welcome we have given to Muslims in the West, with the accompanying freedom to worship freely and build their mosques, should be reciprocated in Muslim lands.'[43]

An Eastern Orthodox voice would be appropriate at this point, given the daily experience of much of Eastern Orthodoxy under Islamic rule:

> Greater care should be taken in the future to avoid a new mistake: that in the name of cultivating a good climate for the Muslim–Christian dialogue, the poor and miserable Orthodox minorities who live in Muslim majorities are forgotten or even sacrificed. Parallel to the polite stance and respect for the Muslims who live in the West, similar support is needed for Christians who are oppressed in intolerant

Islamic environments in Africa and Asia. The contemporary Muslim–Christian dialogue should take into consideration these international situations that require coexistence and mutual dependence.[44]

Religion, society and the public discourse

Is religion now back on the public agenda in the West?

In 1993 Harvard professor Samuel Huntington wrote an article, and later a book,[45] in which he foresaw a coming clash of civilizations. A centrepiece of Huntington's vision was based on conflict between the western and Islamic worlds. This argument may well have gathered cobwebs along with count-less other scholarly theories if it had not been for 9/11. That event gave the Huntington theory a new lease of life, and represented the watershed moment in the revival of interest in and discussion about religion in the west.

The tragedy of 9/11, plus the ensuing War on Terror, has given new impetus to flagging efforts to bridge Christian–Muslim divides. There has been a surge in Christian–Muslim dialogue activities at all levels: at that of political leadership and religious leadership as well as at grass-roots level among Christians and Muslims. In that respect, 9/11 has had a positive effect, though this is offset by the fact that the tension between the West and Islam is worse than it has been for perhaps a hundred years.

In sum, religion is now a hot topic, especially where the Christian–Muslim interface is concerned. Those who work as Christian specialists in the study of Islam now find that describing their work is no longer a conversation-stopper in social gatherings; quite the reverse.

Nevertheless, in the current climate officialdom sees some faces of Christianity as more respectable than others. The movement towards greater Christian–Muslim bridge-building means that the favour of government officialdom falls on those sections of Christianity that are inclined to the dialogue paradigm rather than to traditional mission or more robust methods of exchange. In other words, Christianity is now more firmly on the public agenda in the West, but it is a particular face of Christianity that has bene-fited in the current climate. Evangelicalism has not been the beneficiary, according to Giles Fraser, Vicar of Putney and lecturer in philosophy at Wadham College, Oxford, who asserts that 'the word evangelical is now firmly linked in the public imagination with intolerance and bigotry'.[46]

How should Christians respond when a mosque is to be built in their neighbourhood?

The construction of mosques has been a source of considerable debate throughout Britain for many decades, with the increased presence of non-Christian faiths in the country. Numbers of mosques have increased from eighteen in 1966 to over 1,000 at the turn of the twenty-first century. The concern felt by many people is reflected in a question submitted for discussion at a public lecture in 2002: 'How do we stop small Islamic towns spreading in our own country? Certain areas have Islamic councils, schools, Muslim enclaves, etc. Shouldn't we be just as concerned about the situation in our own backyard as we are in international events?'

This raises challenging questions, because it has to do with the identity of the neighbourhoods concerned. Whether the issue is the construction of a mosque, or of a house of worship of a faith other than our own, or indeed of some landmark which is going to alter the existing identity of the community in some way, it is a fact that people feel threatened. The British are no different from other societies in wishing to preserve intact what they perceive to be a long-held identity. It is natural for Christians to feel uncomfortable when mosques are created in the midst of communities unused to them.

But, at the same that time, societies evolve. Neighbourhoods change in their make-up in a host of ways, and no community can be frozen in time and form. We cannot accept the establishment of a system that says that one type of British citizen will live in a particular neighbourhood and a different type of British citizen will not. This would be tantamount to apartheid. There is always going to be movement of populations, and all people want to bring the symbols of their faith with them. So, if Muslims move in growing numbers to a particular neighbourhood, they will want to establish a mosque. It is understandable that Christians feel threatened in such circumstances, but the fact is that they need to adjust to the reality of a new situation. In a free society, adherents of different faiths should have the right to set up their own places of worship.

At the same time, it is important that immigrant communities show sensitivity in the way they establish the symbols of their faith within a community for the first time. For example, it would not be tactful for the first mosque erected in a town to dominate the skyline. Local councils should design new planning guidelines or implement existing ones[47] to ensure that houses of worship of a faith previously not represented in a town or neighbourhood are constructed in such a way as to blend in with, rather than dominate, an existing community.

An example of the way insensitive actions by minority groups can arouse hostility from a majority community that feels that its identity is being threatened took place in the central Italian town of L'Aquila in October 2003. A Muslim-rights advocate launched a court case in which he called for the removal of crucifixes from the state primary school his children attended. The judge, ruling in favour of the Muslim complainant, stated that 'the presence of the symbol of the cross shows the will of the state to put Catholicism at the centre of the universe as the absolute truth'.[48] The ruling drew critical responses from some Catholic Church figures, with Cardinal Ersilio Tonini saying, 'You cannot remove a symbol of the religious and cultural values of a people just because it can offend someone.'[49]

Furthermore, immigrant communities should not themselves practise a kind of apartheid. Towns should not become largely Muslim towns. Interaction is important; faith communities should mix together in order to build an atmosphere of understanding and tolerance, reflecting the fact that Britain is a multi-religious community. Governing authorities must ensure that a system of apartheid does not develop. In order for this to happen, both national and local governing authorities should consider appropriate means of intervention.

Is the term 'multifaith' appropriate for Britain?

One question I was asked at a public lecture was: 'Bearing in mind the fact that in Britain the ratio of Christians to adherents of other faiths is 71% to 6%, is not the use of the word "multifaith" – implying an equal spread – unfortunate, leading to a case of the tail wagging the dog in the formulation of national policies?'

If the term 'multifaith' is used descriptively to reflect the fact that multiple faiths are represented in Britain in the early twenty-first century, its use is entirely appropriate. Indeed, this would be the case for virtually any period of past British history, since at no time has only one religious faith been represented among Britain's citizens.

The question I was asked, however, implies another dimension; namely, that faiths representing a relatively small minority of Britain's population have come to exercise a disproportionate amount of influence in the formulation of government policy regarding faith matters. There is a widespread perception in the Christian community of Britain that this is the case. A perusal of the BBC Religion and Ethics website[50] quickly creates the impression that different faiths are given equal space, without any suggestion of proportional differences among the population at large. This leads me to comment further on the 'people of faith' notion.

Should Christians embrace the 'people of faith' notion?

In the first chapter we encountered a phenomenon that is gaining widespread currency in interfaith circles. People who hold this view, which we have termed the 'people of faith' notion, argue that there should be a substantial measure of common identification between people of different faiths who actively practise their faith, as opposed to the broad masses of the British community, who either declared themselves to have no faith in the 2001 population census or were nominal adherents of a faith (mostly Christianity) but did not practise it on a regular basis.

Christians should give careful thought to the ramifications of this 'people of faith' notion, which is based on the implicit argument that the 9% of the population who practise Christianity should identify themselves first and foremost, not with the 62% of the population who also express some allegiance to Christianity, but rather with observant Muslims, Hindus, Buddhists, Sikhs, Jews and so forth.

This has considerable significance for the access to the corridors of power currently enjoyed by Christians, especially by the Church of England. The head of state in Britain, the Queen, is also the head of the (Anglican) Church of England and of the (Presbyterian) Church of Scotland. Twenty-six Anglican bishops sit in the House of Lords. State funding is available to vast numbers of Christian schools (and in lesser measure to Jewish and Muslim schools). There are many other ways in which Christianity has a privileged position among the faiths in Britain.

Arguments in favour of the *status quo* can be articulated (though not without challenge) if Christianity is seen as the faith of the majority. If, however, practising Christians present their faith as representing a small minority of the British population, reflecting the situation of other faiths in Britain, then the current privileged position enjoyed by Christianity will be unsustainable in the short to medium term. The outcome is likely to be either disestablishment of the Church of England or an adjustment of the *status quo* so that the instruments of power and influence currently wielded by Christians, especially by the Church of England, are shared with other faiths present in Britain. This latter scenario has been advocated by some representatives of other faiths.

A sub-category of the 'people of faith' notion has made an appearance on the multifaith stage; namely, the 'Abrahamic faiths' category. There is an increasing tendency to lump together Jews, Christians and Muslims, drawing attention to their common link with Abraham and, in the case of Christians and Muslims, common figures such as Jesus. Toby Howarth engages with this view:

> Some Christians warmly embrace this idea of kinship between the three religions, taking it as the starting-point of their relationship, while others reject out of hand the idea that Muslims might be their religious 'cousins'. But whatever their feelings, Christians need to take seriously the Muslim *claim* to Abrahamic religious descent. They also need to acknowledge the clear kinship of *religious ideas* that binds Christianity with Islam and Judaism, and distinguishes these three from other great world religions such as Buddhism and Hinduism.[51]

This approach, however, potentially lends support to a view of Muslim supercessionism, the Islamic doctrine of People of the Book allowing Muslims to say, 'Yes, of course we accept you Jews and Christians . . . But Muhammad was the seal of the prophets.' Here is another reason why the 'people of faith' notion must be closely scrutinized by Christians and not swallowed wholesale.

In summary, if Christians do not want to be in the position of realizing after the event that decisions have been taken for them, they need to think through these issues carefully, so that future scenarios will reflect the understanding and will of the church.

What is the future of multifaith Britain?

In a recent volume, the Revd David Pawson prophesied that Britain would be an Islamic society by the middle of the twenty-first century.[52] Discussion of such a scenario in various organs of the print and electronic media has become increasingly prominent. In one particularly well-argued piece, Peter Hitchens reports on the case of a white British non-Muslim family who live in a predominantly Muslim neighbourhood in a British city. The two daughters of the family, aged twelve and nine, elected to wear Muslim headcovering and to attend mosque worship and Qur'anic instruction, reflecting the practice among their local peer group. Hitchens suggests that this case may well be a window into the future of Britain, where social and moral decay make a religious revival ultimately inevitable, but where Christianity is no longer the leading candidate to lead such a revival.[53]

Some see such views as driven by a sense of alarmism, as well as by a failure to see Muslims in their diversity. Nevertheless, there clearly is a debate to be had on this topic, and it should be aired freely, rather than being muzzled when those articulating views such as Hitchens' are shamed into silence. Discussing the future of multifaith Britain is a legitimate and necessary exercise. Moreover, it is appropriate to comment on this debate at this point in the present study.

As for the short-term future, it is likely that multifaith Britain will see a number of changes of a relatively minor nature, but the macro picture will probably not alter substantially. In the middle of the twenty-first century, Britain will still be a majority Christian country, given a very broad definition of 'Christian'. The minority faith communities will grow somewhat, including the Islamic community, but Islam will not become a majority faith within Britain.

Reports of British conversions to Islam tend to capture media interest. Dani Garavelli wrote in 2002: 'About 20,000 British people have converted during the last decade. At Edinburgh's central mosque, there have been

80 'reverts' – Muslims believe that everyone is born into Islam — over the last four years.'[54]

The British Muslim writer Yahya Birt[55] disputes the figure of 20,000, based on his analysis of conversions to Islam taking place in Scotland, and on the 2001 British census results. He writes: 'The Scottish example . . . provides us a substantial base upon which to speculate about the total number of converts [to Islam] in the UK. If we take the percentage of Scots converts against the total population, we get a figure of 14,200 converts, which sounds about right.'[56] Birt breaks down the figure of 14,200 as in Table 5, suggesting that fewer than 9,000 white British have converted, less than half the commonly quoted estimate of 20,000. His analysis leads him to another conclusion which is of direct relevance to our study:

> The first myth to be exploded was the claim that Islam is Britain's second largest (and it is asserted fastest-growing) religion. But this growth has everything to do with immigration and birth rates rather than conversion. In percentage terms, the Scottish figures show us that out of all the minority religions and the main Christian denominations, Islam is the religion people are least likely to leave or convert to . . . In other words, it is the least attractive to others and yet paradoxically the most resilient . . . In the marketplace of faiths, Islam would not appear to be offering an attractive prospect.[57]

Table 5 Estimated numbers of Muslim converts in the UK, 2001 (Birt)

Religious/racial origin	Numbers	Percentage
White/Other	8,700	61
Originally Hindu	700	5
Originally Sikh	400	3
Black Caribbean	4,400	31
TOTALS	14,200	100

There are in fact many more conversions to Buddhism in Britain than to Islam. Of the total number of Buddhists in Britain, 50% are converts.[58] Buddhism carries a New Age appeal in a pluralistic culture. It is likely that Buddhism will rise significantly in its proportion of faith adherence in this country. But, overall, Britain will remain unchanged for the forseeable future as a country where the majority profess Christianity.

The longer-term future is more difficult to predict, given the range of factors and variables involved. But key requisites if Britain is to shore up its

Judeo-Christian heritage for the long term and disprove the scenario advanced by David Pawson and Peter Hitchens will be

- the churches' ability to strike a balance between loyalty to revealed truth and relevance to its social context
- the churches' commitment to reaching out to vast numbers of nominal Christians in the British population
- the churches' ability to minimize intra-Christian rivalries and disputes
- Christians' involvement in the public arena through political activity, participation in the media, and social advocacy
- a national rediscovery of confidence in its past
- controlling social, ethnic and religious change that results from immigration, so that the majority community feels that its overall identity is not under threat[59]

Approaches to dialogue

Because of the replacement theology that Islam in general holds with regard to Christianity, it will often (although not always) be Christians who initiate the dialogue.[60]

What are the objectives of interfaith dialogue?

Many Christians and Muslims are seeking opportunities for dialogue, especially in western countries where Muslim minorities have settled in increasing numbers since the Second World War. Why bother? This is a question many people from both religious communities ask. If dialogue participants are not convinced of the value of dialogue, they will be ineffective dialogue partners.

Four principal objectives of dialogue between Christians and Muslims can be identified. The order of priority will differ according to the requirements and perspectives of the participants concerned.

1. *Mutual understanding.* Dialogue about faith and cultural differences facilitates mutual understanding. Human history has witnessed many conflicts which have resulted from ignorance between communities. Many might have been avoided if there had been a greater degree of mutual knowledge and understanding.
2. *Understanding God.* Dialogue should provide an opportunity for participants to advance in their knowledge of God and of his plan of salvation for all humanity. In this context, dialogue on religious experience has a particular part to play.

3. *Witnessing.* Interfaith dialogue should give the participants a forum in which to express their faith. Both Christianity and Islam consider speaking about one's beliefs and passing on these beliefs to others, or 'witnessing', to be a significant and integral part of faith. As Cardinal Francis Arinze comments, 'For the Christian it is not only a right but a duty to share the faith.'[61] Dialogue should take this fact into account and provide a forum for such witnessing to occur. Open and frank sharing of religious experience is important.

4. *Co-operation in relevant areas.* Dialogue should also result in some benefit to all parties involved. A fruitful dialogue between Christians and Muslims will form the basis for joint activities for the advantage of all concerned. A particular case concerns humanitarian relief and development. Like Christianity, Islam teaches the importance of helping the poor and underprivileged, the orphaned and other disadvantaged groups. This shared concern should be explored to determine possible areas for co-operation.

Muslims and Christians might enter a dialogue with different objectives. Ataullah Siddiqui expresses Muslim motives in engaging in dialogue: 'Muslims have seen dialogue, in some respects, as a plea to explain their faith, but more than that they have viewed dialogue as an opportunity to face the growing challenge presented by atheism and materialism. Therefore, the theological dialogue for Muslims has received little attention.'[62]

None of these objectives needs entail compromising the central tenets of one's faith. This is a position on which Christians and Muslims can and do agree. As Douglas Pratt has perceptively observed, 'the first and primary goal of dialogue is understanding, not agreement'.[63] Mohamed Talbi, a prominent Muslim modernizing thinker of the late twentieth century, concurs with this view: 'Never conceive of [dialogue] in terms of negotiation, in terms of concession, in terms of persuading the other. We only may conceive of it as a species of state of mind of somebody who tries to understand.'[64]

In this context, two questions posed during the 2003 London Lectures are relevant: 'Do you agree with the Kandy statement that "the result of dialogue is the work of the [Holy] Spirit?"', and 'How can Christians approach Christian–Muslim dialogue genuinely or sincerely when the ultimate hope is for Muslims to be won over to our side?'

On the first, it should be noted that the results of dialogue events are many and varied. A perusal of the many Christian–Muslim dialogue events organized by the World Council of Churches since 1970 suggests that varying degrees of co-operation, or lack of it, flow out of the activities. The involvement of the Holy Spirit in such a process is very difficult to measure. What can be measured is the level of human effort expended in dialogue, both during and after specific events. While the Holy Spirit may be involved in such events, it is going too far to suggest that the Holy Spirit is necessarily involved in the outcomes of every Christian–Muslim dialogue event that is organized.

On the second question, the dialogue objectives listed above provide for a central role for witnessing to one's faith, be it Christianity or Islam. Witnessing implies an eagerness on the part of Christians or Muslims to share their faith in such a way that the other may choose to change faiths. This is perfectly legitimate, as long as it is done on a level playing field. According to the WCC Guidelines on Dialogue discussed earlier, 'Dialogue assumes the freedom of a person of any faith . . . to be convinced by the faith of another.' The unresolved issue here, of course, is the lack of freedom for Muslims to change their faith, as we have seen.

Are there any prerequisites for interfaith dialogue?

In order to achieve the objectives listed above, thought must be given to defining the rules of engagement. This issue has arisen regularly in Christian–Muslim interactions organized by the church bodies. The value of agreed formats applies equally to dialogues on religious experience or social concerns as to discursive dialogue or Christian–Muslim debate.

Claude Geffré argues for two essential conditions if genuine dialogue is to take place.[65] First, in entering a dialogue, the otherness of the dialogue partner within the partner's cultural and religious identity should be respected. Both parties must leave ingrained prejudices behind. Secondly, each party must respect its own faith by speaking honestly and candidly about their own faith perspective. As Michael Barnes observes, this loyalty to one's own faith position 'is much more likely to get well-motivated liberal hackles rising'.[66] Nevertheless, it is important not to enter a dialogue wearing a figurative mask, leaving behind essential elements of one's faith and taking into the dialogue only what one thinks will be palatable to the dialogue partner. It is only if faces are unmasked that parties can serve as effective partners in the dialogue. In this context, Christians must ensure that any sense of guilt for colonialism that they might feel does not translate into coyness or diffidence as they present the Christian message in dialogue situations.

Leonard Swidler develops this further by presenting the ground rules to be followed by participants in dialogue.[67] The ideas of both Geffré and Swidler are consistent with the WCC's Four Principles of dialogue discussed in previous chapters.

With whom should Christians engage in dialogue?

The headlong rush to promote Christian–Muslim dialogue and contact in western countries since 9/11 has been of benefit to both Christians and

Muslims in many ways. This process is, however, having one particularly negative spin-off. Other religious minorities are feeling sidelined in the process. Hindus, Buddhists, Sikhs and even Jews are asking why Muslim minorities are receiving so much attention, and why so much emphasis is now placed on improved Christian–Muslim relations rather than on multifaith harmony. Some are suspecting that the previous pattern of exclusion has merely been adjusted to accommodate Muslims in the inner circle, while others remain outside. Some even suggest that this is ironic, claiming that other minorities are more likely to work with the western majority in a way that builds social cohesion, rather than seek to separate from it.

The point is illustrated by a conversation I had with a Hindu woman who is involved in Hindu theological education and training with the youth of her community.[68] She explained that the young people she works with often express a sense of extreme frustration at what they observe to be preference in dialogue given to Muslims by church leaders at the expense of other faiths. On one occasion, a group of Hindu youths she was speaking with asked: 'What do we have to do to attract the same attention as Muslims? Do we have to hijack airliners and fly them into tall buildings to get noticed?' The woman stressed that the question was in no way meant as an expression of intent; rather, it reflected the increasing sense of exclusion felt by Hindus in Britain at what they consider to be favouritism accorded to Muslims in dialogue situations with Christians.

Nevertheless, leaders of the churches often argue that the fragility of relations between Christians, Jews and especially Muslims means that they should be the primary partners in dialogue in the post-9/11 environment. This was the position taken by the former Archbishop of Canterbury, George Carey. He launched the Archbishop's Initiative in Christian–Muslim Relations, which took precedence over a similar initiative towards Hindus, Buddhists and others. Likewise, Catholic statements have been offered along similar lines: 'The event of the year 2000 will provide a great opportunity . . . for interreligious dialogue . . . In this dialogue the Jews and the Muslims ought to have a pre-eminent place.'[69]

At the first 'Building Bridges' seminar, held in January 2002 (see above, pp. 153–154), Bishop Kenneth Cragg pointed out that 'there is much that is elitist about dialogue, and remote from the passions in the street'.[70] Here he has put his finger on one of the big challenges of dialogue activities, especially those undertaken by erudite scholars and prominent public figures. This problem can be compounded when certain groups are excluded from the dialogue. In the volume that emerged from the same seminar, Michael Ipgrave aptly states: 'People and communities of other faiths hold many of the same concerns and values [as Christians and Muslims]; there is much scope for fruitful interaction on a wider inter faith basis.'[71]

It is a weakness of many dialogue activities that the massive surge in attention to Christian–Muslim dialogue is somehow pushing the Hindus, Buddhists, Jews, Sikhs and others to the margins of British religious discourse. In expanding the boundaries of the inner circle to accommodate Muslims, there is a risk that other faiths may feel shunned and relegated.

To which Muslims should Christians be talking?

Both Islam and Christianity are vast mosaics, made up of diverse elements of many shades and colours. Some Muslims and some Christians are getting on better than ever, and work closely together to build bridges between the two communities. There are also some Muslims and some Christians who figuratively draw down the shutters on each other and are very suspicious of interfaith activity, seeing it as a sellout of their faith.

In many ways, the important aim of interfaith relations is not so much to focus on those who are already willing to cross lines, but rather to find ways of involving those Muslims and Christians who refuse to do so. The situation will not be much helped if three groups emerge: one of Christians who refuse to work with Muslims, one of Muslims who refuse to work with Christians, and a third group of 'professional dialoguers'. Our discussion in the previous chapter therefore focused on methods of engagement between Christians of different ideologies and inclinations and Muslims of various types. There should be engagement between *all* Christians and *all* Muslims, the type of engagement being determined by the nature of the groups involved in each case.

How can Christians best deal with their own lack of confidence?

In order to build confidence, Christians should become more aware; they should study the other faiths, learn more about their own faith so that they feel confident in their knowledge of Christianity, and use their gifts appropriately to do what God has gifted them to do.

One reason for lack of confidence among Christians is a lack of knowledge about their own faith. Just as Christians should learn about other faiths, so they should learn more about their own faith, through distance learning programmes if full-time study at theological college is not possible, or through courses in churches, such as the Alpha course. Before Christians take part in dialogue they must be educated. They need to learn about the faith of those with whom they are engaging in dialogue, but they must also be very clear in their own minds why they are doing so.

Should Christians pray with people from other faiths?

Prayer with adherents of other faiths should be recommended, on condition that it is honest prayer. Christians should pray as they would normally pray, allowing the others to pray as they would normally pray. Christians should not pray in a way they think might please the other. If they normally pray through Christ to God, then that is what they should do when praying in front of Muslims; they should not pray differently because Muslims are present.

Should Christians watch their language?
Choice of language can produce a negative reaction in certain circumstances. Consider the following report from a Christian periodical:

> Leading Muslim organizations say it's time for Americans to stop using the phrase 'Judeo-Christian' when describing the values and character that define the United States. Better choices, they say, are 'Judeo-Christian-Islamic' or 'Abrahamic', referring to Abraham, the patriarch held in common by the monotheistic big three religions. The new language should be used 'in all venues where we normally talk about Judeo-Christian values, starting with the media, academia, statements by politicians and comments made in churches, synagogues and other places,' said Agha Saeed, founder and chairman of the American Muslim Alliance, a political group headquartered in Fremont, Calif. . . . Others take offense, arguing that to alter the phrase 'Judeo-Christian' is political correctness and revisionist history at its worst.[72]

Interestingly, there has been some non-Muslim support for the suggestion:

> The movement to drop or change the phrase has some non-Muslim support, including the head of the National Council of Churches. The Rev. Bob Edgar, general secretary of the council, which represents 36 Christian denominations, said he prefers 'Abrahamic' to 'Judeo-Christian-Islamic' because it 'rolls off the tongue a little easier . . . The more inclusive we can be, the more committed we are to the founding fathers and mothers who struggled with the issue of respect for each other's religious faiths,' Edgar said.[73]

Such a suggestion is potentially highly emotive, as it can be considered to be challenging the very foundations of the identity of western societies. Objections can be expressed in various ways. The proposal could be taken to mean that Christians should watch their language in order not to offend Muslims by using phrases such as 'Judeo-Christian', but that it is acceptable to offend some Christians and/or westerners by using terms such as 'Judeo-Christian-Islamic' or 'Abrahamic'. Furthermore, some Christians point out that in citizenship education for newly arriving immigrants, imparting a sense of Britishness involves identifying the values underpinning the society adopted by the new arrivals, and this necessarily includes a recognition of the Judeo-Christian heritage of Britain.

It is hard to escape the impression that this discussion finds its context in a loss of confidence in much of the West regarding its history, and a willingness to reinterpret that history in order to embrace minority viewpoints.

Nevertheless, there is clearly a need to watch one's language in certain interfaith contexts. This particularly applies when referring to individual adherents of other faiths. Anti-vilification legislation is designed to protect people more than books, just as are laws relating to libel and slander. While it is legitimate to ask challenging questions of texts considered sacred by particular faiths, and even of the doctrines arising from those texts, great care must be exercised in publicly criticizing an individual or a group of adherents of a particular faith.

A case that illustrates this point is a review on the Friends of Al-Aqsa website[74] of a book written by Baroness Caroline Cox and Dr John Marks.[75] The first part of the review focused on the book itself, challenging its interpretation of events in a range of ways. This is perfectly valid literary criticism. The second part of the review, however, launched into a cutting critique of Baroness Cox's mindset and advocacy activities, an issue quite separate from the book in focus. At this point the review itself lost much of its impact, and the reviewer would have been well advised to have watched his or her language in this regard.

Do Christians have the right to ask critical questions about core Islamic beliefs?

This question serves as an umbrella for numerous specific questions regularly asked in non-Muslim discussion about Islam, such as two posed at the 2003 London Lectures: 'In dialogue, what is an appropriate measure of challenging core aspects of Islam, such as (a) certain aspects of Muhammad's lifestyle (looting, numbers of wives, inconsistency, etc.) and (b) the Qur'an, its inconsistencies and doctrines, all of which are ignored by many Muslims?', and 'Is there a place for polemics in Christian–Muslim dialogue?' These questions hover on the boundaries of insensitivity in terms of Christian– Muslim relations. If posed in a clumsy fashion to Muslims, they could cause great offence and ill will. At the same time, the issue of sensitivity should surely not be the only factor involved in determining the dynamics of Christian–Muslim engagement. Freedom of speech, especially in a western social context, should also be taken into account.

A particular case which led to legal action in Australia is relevant here. A Christian Pakistani migrant to Australia, Daniel Scot,[76] delivered a seminar on 9 March 2002 to an audience of between 250 and 300 in a church in Melbourne. The event was arranged by an organization called Catch the Fire

Ministry. In his address Scot discussed a range of topics: salvation in Islam; *jihad* in all its forms, especially holy war; deception in the Qur'an and Hadith; roles assigned to non-Muslims in the Qur'an and Hadith; women in Islam; and how to share the gospel with Muslims and answer their questions about Christianity.

The audience at the seminar included three white Australian converts to Islam, who were encouraged to attend the seminar by contacts within the Islamic Council of Victoria.[77] They lodged a complaint to the Victorian Equal Opportunity Commission, in the context of the Victorian Racial and Religious Tolerance Act of January 2002. The commission then organized a conciliation meeting. The terms of conciliation were that Scott should apologize for what he had said and promise not to teach these subjects again in any form, oral or written. An extensive list was given of statements for which he should apologize.[78]

The conciliation meeting was unsuccessful, so the matter was then sent to mediation as the next stage before the Victorian Civil and Administrative Tribunal. In the mediation stage, the Islamic Council of Victoria described Scot's teaching as inflammatory, and called for an apology and an undertaking not to teach again in like manner. This mediation stage was also unsuccessful. The case then went to a formal court hearing in October 2003, and is ongoing at the time of writing. During the court hearing, Scot showed an encyclopaedic knowledge of the Islamic sacred texts, far more than the three complainants.[79]

The comments by Scot that triggered the formal complaint included, first, challenging questions about the Islamic sacred texts, and secondly, challenging questions about interpretation of the sacred texts by Muslim people. The case prompted a spate of articles in the Australian press, with writers arguing the case from various angles.

In a contribution to the debate, one Australian Muslim writer, Amir Butler, questioned the wisdom of the complainants in bringing the matters to public attention through formal legal proceedings against Scot. He argued that the decision to appeal to anti-vilification legislation was the wrong reaction:

the only way to fight offensive ideas is to confront them intellectually. Legislation, punishments and smear campaigns cannot make bad ideas disappear. Instead, everyone must be allowed to express their views freely – good ideas will drive out bad. Political correctness has encouraged minorities to play the victim card, to vie for political influence by overstating and exaggerating being a victim. It's undignified, ineffective, and only serves to build resentment among the broader community that will quickly tire of being lectured as to how terribly racist it is – especially when that's untrue.[80]

Butler's identifying of political correctness as an instrument in causing interfaith friction resonates with our discussion in chapter 1. He concluded his article with a forthright call for honest dialogue:

> One can justifiably doubt a religion that can only exist within a fortress of anti-vilification laws and political correctness, a religion that cannot stand up to public scrutiny or criticism. A society based on this notion of political correctness is a society based on a foundation of lies – that all cultures, races, creeds and genders are the same and equal and that the state can, through legislation and ham-fisted social engineering, create cohesion among vastly different groups. The real key to social cohesion is honest dialogue. A dialogue, unfettered by political correctness, that is based on recognition that we have different ideas.[81]

The Scot case provides a good basis for answering questions about how forthright Christians should be in challenging core Islamic beliefs. Butler's comments also provide a very reasonable set of guidelines.

This case raises important issues relating to freedom of speech. In a society that values freedom of speech, there must be room to ask hard questions of sacred texts, be they Christian, Jewish, Islamic, Hindu or other. Indeed, such questioning is surely necessary in order to ensure that interpretation of those texts keeps pace with modern life, and is not frozen in time in a fundamentalist manner. At the same time, these questions should be posed in such a way, and at such time, that reasoned discussion rather than offence is more likely to result. In other words, the issue is not so much which questions are asked, but rather *how* they are asked.

How should Christians and Muslims report history?

In the volume arising from the first 'Building Bridges' seminar, Michael Ipgrave writes: 'While the past cannot be altered, the way in which it is remembered is not beyond our control. By their choice of key episodes on which to focus, and by their interpretations of those episodes, historians can significantly influence perceptions and attitudes in the present, and so help to shape the future.'[82] Ipgrave's approach seems to be embraced in David Kerr's thumbnail sketch of past Christian–Muslim history in the same volume.[83] He mentions what he sees as the two eras of European imperialism: the Crusades and the imperial expansion of the sixteenth to nineteenth centuries. No mention is made of the Ottoman conquest of Constantinople, Turkish imperial expansion into the Balkans and central European states, or the massacres of the Armenians.

Questions should be asked about this approach to history-writing. The task of the historian is essentially to report and interpret past events,[84] not deliberately to report some of them in more detail in order to facilitate present-day ideological whims and preferences. If the latter becomes the case, subsequent generations are likely to conclude that history gave way to propaganda and indoctrination in the name of better interfaith relations.

It is true that no school or university course in history can cover all areas of the field, and a large measure of selection is required. The decision then should become how this selection can be carried out in a way that does not merely feed one particular ideological approach, but rather reflects a suitable diversity of viewpoints.

Where does spiritual warfare come into Christian–Muslim relations?

> For our struggle is not against flesh and blood, but against the rulers, against the authorities, against the powers of this dark world. (Ephesians 6:12)

How are Christians to interpret this verse in regard to their attitudes to other faiths, especially in the context of the current War on Terror? Two responses present themselves. The first is simply to ignore such passages as irrelevant. The second, in contrast, is to apply them too readily to the world around us. Neither of these approaches is satisfactory.

The too-liberal approach

The first response typically derives from an uncritical acceptance of other faiths as equally valid variations on a divine theme. This is a product of our postmodern context, where subtle but powerful pressures are continually put on populations in western countries to accept all forms of diversity without question. Thus approaches that are most acceptable to current received wisdom are those that are multifaith, multi-ethnic, multi-cultural, multi-sexual and so forth.

Furthermore, this response is a cop-out. It ignores certain phenomena found in other faiths that, instincts suggest, may derive from forces for evil. A clear example is the al-Qa'ida phenomenon within Islam, which plans and rejoices at atrocities such as those carried out in New York and Washington on 11 September 2001. There is something very dark about this excerpt from a recorded conversation between Osama bin Laden and two of his colleagues:

> *bin Laden*: After a little while, they announced that another plane had hit the World Trade Center. The brothers who heard the news were overjoyed by it.
> *Shaykh*: . . . We stayed until four o'clock, listening to the news every time a little bit different, everyone was very joyous and saying 'Allah is great,' 'Allah is great,' 'We are thankful to Allah,' 'Praise Allah.' And I was happy for the happiness of

my brothers. That day the congratulations were coming on the phone non-stop. The mother was receiving phone calls continuously.

Shaykh: Fight them, Allah will torture them, with your hands, he will torture them. He will deceive them and he will give you victory. Allah will forgive the believers, he is knowledgeable about everything.[85]

The too-literal approach

The second response is equally unsatisfactory, but for different reasons. It leads to a knee-jerk dismissal of other faiths as lost in every way, often extending to a view of other faiths as instruments of Satan *per se*.[86] This attitude ignores the fact that adherents of other faiths are driven by a sincere desire to seek, know and please God. Christians might disagree with them about the extent to which Christians and Muslims respectively find God. To dismiss them automatically as being on the path of 'the powers of this dark world', however, seems to be taking issues of disagreement too far.

This attitude too is a cop-out. It avoids our responsibility to think about the degree to which godly truth may be found in other faiths. To think along such lines might make us feel vulnerable. Christians should, however, have sufficient confidence in their own faith to be prepared to be a little vulnerable in the challenges they tackle.

Reflections

Let me ground my comments in a live case study. It concerns my Indonesian friend Zayn ud-Din. He was brought up as a Muslim and was imbued with the values of his faith by devout parents. He was the eldest of nine children in a poor Javanese family. At twenty-one he set out for Australia in search of work to assist with the support of his family. We met as he began his journey.

Over a period of thirty years Zayn ud-Din became perhaps the most faithful friend I have ever had. He was devoted to my parents, who helped him when he was struggling on his arrival in Australia. He is a dedicated son, brother, husband and father to his own family.

Zayn ud-Din's name means 'the beauty of the faith'. He has always exhibited a quiet faith. He prays at home. He attends mosque on significant occasions. He never attempts to proselytize. He finds great sustenance in his faith in times of trouble and sorrow.

Zayn ud-Din is not is under the control of 'rulers and authorities'. Like many other ordinary Muslims, he manifests most, perhaps all, of the qualities called for by the apostle Peter: goodness, knowledge, self-control, perseverance, godliness, brotherly kindness, love.[87]

Christians should recognize that adherents of other faiths are also in quest of God.[88] At the same time, we should be prepared to ask hard questions of other faiths, and to have hard questions asked of Christianity in return. In short, Christians should be willing to live with difference. This is far better than either seeking a trite compromise formula based on the lowest common denominator of all faiths, or automatically dismissing adherents of other faiths as controlled by 'the powers of this dark world'.

Evaluating Islam

Preceding discussion has addressed some of the most thorny issues in Christian–Muslim relations. Sensitive areas have been touched upon, and explorations of both Christian and Muslim communities have revealed both positive and negative features. This inevitably leads to questions such as the following, which I was asked at a public lecture: 'How can we evaluate Islam, Muhammad and the Qur'an?' I shall answer it by addressing several related and frequently asked questions.

Is Islam a religion of peace?

A question posed during one of my public lectures in late 2002 has often been repeated in other such events: 'Can you comment on statements made by politicians and the media that Islam is a religion of peace? What in the Qur'an or *shari'a* law condones or allows the behaviour of radical Islam?' A variation on this question was posed at the same event: 'In the Qur'an, does Allah call for war? If so, under what circumstances?'

It is true that, since 9/11, Muslim moderates and many non-Muslim political spokespeople have repeated on numerous occasions that Islam is a religion of peace. For example, British Foreign Office minister Mike O'Brien expressed the official view of the British government in November 2002: 'Islam is a religion of peace. The vast majority of Muslims deplore violence and terrorism and condemned the events of 11 September . . . I intend to talk about that minority on the fringes who adopt a distorted view of Islam. A minority that is violent and is a threat to Islam and to the rest of the world.'[89] At the same time, radical Islamists have issued statements calling for violence and *jihad* in certain contexts, usually quoting Islamic scriptural reference in support of their calls. This can be confusing for non-Muslim observers, who hear two opposing viewpoints expressed by Muslims who draw on the same scriptures in support of their positions.

In fact, the answer lies not in an 'either . . . or' response, but rather in a 'both . . . and' one. The Islamic sacred texts offer the potential to be interpreted in both a peaceful and a militaristic way. It depends on how individual Muslims wish to read them.

On the BBC radio programme 'Thought for the Day' on 13 September 2001, Dr Zaki Badawi rejected the actions of the 9/11 terrorists by citing

Qur'an 5:32: 'We ordained that if anyone killed a person . . . not in retali-
ation of murder or in punishment . . . it would be as if he killed all Mankind.
And if anyone saved a life it would be as if he saved the life of all Mankind.'
Muslim moderates would wish to affirm Dr Badawi's use of this verse to
condemn violence and killing. It seems unambiguous. But if one continues
to the verse immediately following, the message is significantly different.
Qur'an 5:33 states: 'The punishment of those who wage war against Allah and
His Messenger, and strive with might and main for mischief through the land
is: execution, or crucifixion, or the cutting off of hands and feet from opposite sides, or exile from the land: that is their disgrace in this world, and a
heavy punishment is theirs in the Hereafter.' Thus, while Dr Badawi has
chosen to emphasize a more compassionate interpretation of these verses,
someone inclined to a more literalist reading of the Islamic scriptures could
easily emphasize verse 33, which talks of execution, crucifixion and the cutting
off of hands and feet.

On the one hand, one mindset, that of the Muslim moderates, takes a
subtle and reason-based approach to the Islamic sacred texts, reading them in
the light of the modern world and adapting them accordingly. Radicals, on
the other hand, read the texts in a literalist way, focusing on the surface
meaning. For them, the specific struggles such as are taking place in Palestine,
Iraq and Chechnya are not the main issue; rather, they read their Islamic texts
as calling for non-Muslim infidels to be fought, regardless of the cause. In
effect, a titanic struggle is taking place between moderates and radicals for the
hearts and minds of the Muslim masses in the middle.

Is terrorism more likely to flow out of Islam than out of Christianity?

Terrorism is more likely to flow out of Islam than out of Christianity, for the
simple reason that the Islamic sacred texts lend themselves more easily to justifying violence if they are read in a certain way.

While there is no shortage of passages referring to violence and war in the
Old Testament, the direction of progressive revelation in the Christian scriptural canon is clear. It is next to impossible to find scriptural justification from
Jesus' statements in the New Testament for hijacking airliners and flying them
into crowded buildings. By contrast, both the 9/11 hijackers and the radical
Islamist groups around the world who praised them grounded their statements in abundant references to the Qur'an and Hadith, where there is no
similarly clear progression from a message encompassing war to one encompassing peace.[90]

Of course, more moderate Muslim voices reject these radical readings of the
verses concerned, as seen above. They reinterpret them in their assertions that
Islam is a religion of peace. That is helpful, but needs to be taken further – for
moderate reinterpretations will not stop radicals reading the same verses to

justify violence. Muslim moderates need rather to tackle the verses used by radicals to justify violence – especially where the Hadith collections are concerned – and to recognize that it is time for some of the Hadith materials to be downgraded in importance. Some moderate Muslims have made this suggestion, but it has not yet been met by much positive response. It has to be Muslims who do this. Non-Muslims cannot do it for them.[91]

How should we study Islam?

Adherents of all faiths should have the option of studying other faiths. Moreover, the study should be carried out in a spirit of openness and honest critique where necessary.

There should be no whitewashing, such as is identified in the report 'Islam and the Textbooks', published by the American Textbook Council. This report evaluated the coverage of Islam and the Middle East in widely adopted history textbooks in American schools. It found that 'on controversial subjects, world history textbooks make an effort to circumvent unsavoury facts that might cast Islam past or present in anything but a positive light. Islamic achievements are reported with robust enthusiasm. When any dark side surfaces, textbooks run and hide.'[92]

This is political correctness at its very worst. The report further found that, unlike the treatment of Islamic and other non-western history, western history was subjected to the harshest scrutiny and critique. Paradoxically, this is a mirror image of the treatment of western, Christian and Jewish themes in Saudi Arabian school textbooks, where these themes are often expressed in vitriolic and hateful terms, according to another study.[93]

Truth and Christian–Muslim relations

'Since the Qur'an declares that "Jesus did not die, it was only made to appear so!", and Muslims are required to declare this and not to discuss it, in what way can there be any hope for reconciliation between the two faiths?'

The essence of this question, posed at the 2003 London Lectures, relates to conflicting truth claims between Christianity and Islam. One of the characteristic features of postmodernism has been a pervasive sense of coyness in using terms that suggest a value judgment. Modern scholarship has tended to blur the lines, especially in the context of postmodernist thinking, which sees virtually any doctrine as valid within its own context, and which retreats from assigning labels such as right, wrong, good, bad, mainstream or fringe.

A substantial body of terminology expressing opposites has been increasingly ruled 'out of court'. Western society seems to have advanced in its perception of the complexity of the world, but has also developed a growing reluctance to evaluate that complexity. It is increasingly unacceptable in postmodern times to state a position or to declare an opinion if it is at variance with contemporary received wisdom, which declares that all things are equal and that positions, attitudes, ideologies and faiths must not be dismissed as wrong or false – rather, they should all be seen as equally valid variations on an ideological or godly theme. This situation derives from the postmodernist approach to truth.[94] Truth has come to be seen as subjective, changing, and relative.

A paradox arises from the fact that this contemporary received wisdom on the meaning of truth has assumed a tyranny of its own. It became the dominant ideology in the late twentieth century, smothering alternative perspectives like a blanket. Those who do not swim with the current tide risk being dismissed as fossils, beyond redemption, rather than being seen as proponents of an equally valid ideology – which is what one could reasonably expect in terms of postmodernist ideology. Bruce Kaye writes that 'the great danger in postmodernism is that sovereignty will be reconstructed in terms of its caricature tyranny, while on the other hand in the secular mind difference will be so construed that religion has no place at all'.[95]

Thus the important boundary-markers that help us negotiate our way through a complex world have been increasingly denied to us. A resulting sense of disorientation is captured neatly by J. R. Middleton and B. J. Walsh, who paint a portrait of the 'crisis of our times': 'It is the kind of chill you feel on the top floor of the tower of modern civilisation . . . it is a floor with shattered walls, broken windows and the roof torn off by the postmodern winds of these icy heights . . . it feels as if our whole culture has the willies.'[96]

How is this relevant to Christian–Muslim relations? Muslims are experiencing similar kinds of stresses and irritations with what seems to them to be postmodernist anarchy. Seyyed Hossein Nasr writes of

> the reassertion at this late hour of human history of tradition which itself is both of a primordial character and possesses continuity over the ages, made possible once again by access to that Truth by which human beings have lived during most – or rather nearly all – of their terrestrial history. This Truth had to be stated anew and reformulated in the name of tradition precisely because of the nearly total eclipse and loss of that reality which has constituted the matrix of life of normal humanity over the ages.[97]

In approaching another great faith – Islam – which has certain exclusivist claims like Christianity and which is experiencing similar stresses in these postmodernist times, the challenge for Christians is to find a way to harness this commonality without being forced into adopting the extreme relativist view championed by postmodernism.

Muslims are no less concerned with seeking truth than are Christians. One of the ninety-nine names of Allah in Islam is *al-Haqq* (the Truth), and this underpins much Muslim writing that expresses exclusivist claims about truth as understood by Islam. Many Muslims feel a sense of great pain at the degree to which their faith is being eroded by postmodernist values in the West.

Christian writers articulate similar concerns. For example, Michael Green, in *The Truth of God Incarnate*, decries what he sees as the progressive dismemberment of the truth of the Christian faith: 'How much can you remove from a car, and still possess what is properly called a car? Lights may be a luxury; you can do without bodywork in warm weather; brakes may be dispensed with, at all events on the level; but if you remove the engine or the chassis it is questionable whether we are still talking about a car at all.'[98] In other words, Green feels that the very essence of Christianity has been discarded by many in the church in order to 'move with the postmodernist times', as it were. He is responding to views such as those expressed at a gathering of over seventy Anglican clergy of the Sea of Faith group, who do not 'believe in the authenticity of the Christmas story, as related in the New Testament, or the resurrection. Instead, [the group] believes that God is a mystical and personal experience which has no physical incarnation.'[99]

Green's views of truth is at one with traditional views of truth, which formed the basis of modern scientific thinking and are summarized by Peter Hicks:[100]

- truth is outside of us; it does not depend on us
- truth is discoverable; we can ask questions, investigate, form theories, etc.
- truth is authoritative; we do not control truth
- truth can be communicated; we can learn truth from one another
- truth is universal; the same the world over
- truth is eternal

We shall thus proceed with our dialogue on the basis of this understanding of truth, whereby certain non-negotiable truth kernels are taken as existing. Our task is to identify such kernels and relate them to the discussions between Islam and Christianity.

How do we deal with conflicting truth claims?

Nevertheless, we need to recognize from the outset that truth claims can be relativized to some degree, depending on the subject.

On the subject of *prayer*, there is a common claim among Christians that Islam is legalistic and rule-bound, as evidenced by the five daily Islamic prayers containing virtually identical content. It is difficult to accept this as a statement of absolute truth. Some Muslim groups, such as Sufis, have developed devotional formats that seek communion with Allah, based on unstructured prayers. Similarly, some Christian groups prefer heavily liturgical worship; their prayers are no less structured than those of the standard Muslim prayer. The *creation story* is similar in both the Bible and Islamic scripture. There are minor points of difference, but they relate to peripheral matters and should not deflect us from a primary focus on the overall similarity of the two accounts. Moreover, in certain of the *prophetic accounts*, such as the story of Joseph, the narrative detail is largely the same in both the Bible and Islamic scripture. The differences in detail that do occur seem to be minor in relation to the overall structure, didactic function and narrative thrust of the two accounts. Thus the topics of prayer, the creation story and some prophetic accounts demonstrate that wide-ranging subjects may allow for a degree of relativism in approach. We might even go so far as to say that there are various orthodoxies, and various truths on these topics.

But beyond areas such as these, there must be what Seyyed Hossein Nasr calls 'perennial truths'. For him these are found in tradition, which relates to the realm of the absolute:

> Tradition implies truths of a supraindividual character rooted in the nature of reality . . . Tradition, like religion, is at once truth and presence . . . It comes from the Source from which everything originates and to which everything returns . . . Tradition is inextricably related to revelation and religion, to the sacred, to the notion of orthodoxy, to authority, to the continuity and regularity of transmission of the truth . . . the meaning of tradition has become related more than anything else to that perennial wisdom which lies at the heart of every religion.[101]

How are we to identify these 'perennial truths'? It could be argued that this is the realm where we must vigorously oppose compromise or dilution. It is perhaps easier to identify such perennial truths in a secular context: for example, the truth that murder for personal financial gain is always wrong. But when it comes to perennial truths in the sphere of religious belief, post-modernist society has made religious people much more cautious.

Peter Cotterell[102] suggests that truth claims should be divided into two categories: those that are verifiable as fact, and those that are verifiable only notionally. He gives the example of the statement 'Christ died for our sins' (1 Corinthians 15:3). The first part, 'Christ died', is in principle verifiable as fact. The second part is verifiable only notionally.

Cotterell's concept of 'verifiable as fact' truth claims is readily reconciled with Nasr's notion of perennial truths. But there are some fundamental tensions between Christianity and Islam in this area. To take Cotterell's example, there is a basic opposition between (on the one hand) Christianity's account of Jesus' death on the cross and his resurrection, and (on the other) Islam's rejection of the crucifixion, death and resurrection of Jesus at Q4:157–159.[103] As Harold Netland points out, 'While it is logically possible for both [Christians and Muslims] to be wrong about the identity of Jesus . . . both cannot be correct. At least one view of Jesus must be false.'[104]

If all world religions depended on claims that were verifiable notionally, then a relativist approach would be much more appealing. But where claims verifiable as fact conflict between the religions, a special challenge lies in trying to reach the truth.

With regard to the second proposition in 1 Corinthians 15:3 – that Christ died *for our sins* – again, this is at variance with Islamic dogma, which holds that Jesus, like other prophets, was sent to show his community the truth through transmitting God's word, and to inform his community of the reward awaiting the righteous and the punishment awaiting the ungodly. By contrast with the historicity of Christ's death, on this part of the statement, however, we cannot assemble empirical evidence in support of either the Christian view or the Muslim view. Here it becomes rather an *experiential* matter (through the working of the Holy Spirit) or a matter of *faith* (declaring one's position without being able to assemble scientific evidence).

The quest for perennial truths, or those truths verifiable as fact, is important. Where the religions disagree on these perennial truths, however, a special challenge is posed, which should not be ignored. As Cotterell comments: 'It does no credit to scholarship to do other than admit to the fundamental and irreducible contradictions that exist among the myriad propositions of the world's religions.'[105] Nasr would seem to agree:

> Islam does not accept the idea of incarnation or filial relationship. In its perspective Jesus . . . was a major prophet and spiritual pole of the whole Abrahamic tradition, but not a God-man or the son of God . . . The Qur'an . . . does not accept that he was crucified, but states that he was taken directly to heaven. This is the one irreducible 'fact' separating Christianity and Islam, a fact which is in reality placed there providentially to prevent a mingling of the two religions.[106]

Similarly, Mohamed Talbi, a prominent Muslim modernizer of our era, writes:

> In a dialogue, we need to give attention to making evident our differences for the purpose of being able to avoid illusions. To avoid the illusion that already tomorrow we will be able to move towards a more and more integrated unity. We practise different religious which, even though they converge on the upper level, are very different in the manner of choosing the paths towards it.[107]

CONCLUSION

We began our study by referring to an 'inclusivist train' that has been influential in changing Christian attitudes towards other faiths over the last fifty years and more. We considered contextual factors that have played a role in these attitudinal changes, including social and political factors. In referring to other faiths, our primary focus throughout the study has fallen upon Islam.

We then looked at Muslim responses to the West, both in terms of British society and more generally in terms of a perceived western-driven globalization. These responses were seen to be varied, from a willingness to participate in various ways to a more separatist response that included a determination to develop an alternative, Islamic, model of globalism.

This was followed by a closer examination of various church umbrella groups: the World Council of Churches, the World Evangelical Alliance and the Catholic Church. Changing attitudes towards other faiths were considered in greater detail, as were practical activities recommended and pursued by the various churches.

Such a study triggers a multitude of questions and issues, and in the previous chapter we addressed some of the most common questions posed by audiences at public lectures during the period 2001–2003.

Revisiting exclusivism, inclusivism and pluralism

As we conclude our study, it would be appropriate to comment further on the relative merits of the exclusivist, inclusivist and pluralist approaches to other faiths, discussed at the outset.

In our engagement with biblical references in the Introduction, we identified four key themes that offer guidance to Christians as they formulate their views of other faiths:

1. God's universal blessing was bestowed originally on all of the human race, regardless of creed, ethnicity, geography and other factors.

2. Some people turned away from God, and developed aberrant religious beliefs and practices.
3. God seeks to re-establish the original relationship with all of humankind. The key to this is the kind of faith preached by Jesus Christ and found both among those who profess to be his followers and among some who come from outside this group.
4. It is incumbent upon Christians to take this message out to all people, in fulfilment of the Great Commission in the Gospel of Matthew.

It would also be helpful at this juncture to reconsider the six-point summary of the principal ideas arising from the policy statements of the various churches, which we looked at earlier (see above, p. 135):

1. Other faiths may contain elements of truth and beauty.
2. Christians may learn something from people of other faiths.
3. Christians should allow themselves to be challenged by other faiths.
4. Other faiths are worthy of Christian affection, respect, and even admiration in certain ways.
5. Other faiths do not represent alternative gospels.
6. The biblical witness to God and Christ is complete in itself.

Christians need have no problem with the four biblical themes or the six-point perspective on Christian relations with other faiths. They provide a sense of orientation on the issue, and both lists cohere. Any acceptance by Christians of these two lists as a basis for interaction with other faiths, principally Islam, however, will be conditional upon seeing these lists as a total package.

In other words, to take the four biblical themes, the concept of a universal blessing is inextricably linked with the other three themes. As for the six points, it is appropriate for Christians to seek to identify elements of truth and beauty in other faiths, to learn from other faiths, to allow themselves to be challenged, and to respect other faiths, providing that there is no compromise on points 5 and 6, namely the uniqueness of the Christian message and the completeness of the biblical witness to God and Christ.

Such a holistic approach is fully consistent with the position taken by many Christian groups. The statements presented previously by the Lausanne Congress of 1989 and the Anglican Evangelical Assembly of 1992 were unambiguous in calling for this holistic approach, which involves respecting other faiths while underlining the uniqueness of the Christian message. Key statements by Catholic authorities affirm this position as well.

How should we view religious pluralist approaches?

Religious pluralists, by contrast, typically use these themes and concepts in a selective fashion. For example, pluralists will stress the 'universal blessing' element of the biblical themes, but tend to downplay the other three elements. At the same time, they are likely to concentrate on the first four points of the second list and to ignore or retreat from points 5 and 6.

In this context, it should be noted that the 'universal blessing' theme in the Bible, as well as points 1–4 of the six points based on church statements, are very much in harmony with the predominant ideology in the West. In contrast, the other three biblical themes, plus points 5 and 6, represent more of a challenge to western pluralist norms.

In contemporary postmodern western society, it is far easier to adopt a form of uncritical universalism than to resolutely state that Christianity does have a unique message to proclaim and that Christians will not be deterred from proclaiming this message. But this difficulty in the context of surrounding social norms should not dissuade Christians from taking up this challenge.

This study rejects a pluralist approach based on a belief that all faiths are merely equally valid variations on a godly theme. Religious pluralism should be clearly seen in its full light. It is, first, *a product of an increasingly secular western society*. As officially sanctioned public discourse in western societies affirms multicultural, multi-ethnic, multi-linguistic, and multi-ideological positions, there is an inevitable overflow into the area of religious faith, producing a multifaith ideology.[1] The essence of this approach is that the multiple faces of religion should live in co-existence, harmony and mutual respect, and should be seen as equally valid. By extension, no religion should attempt to displace any other. Thus the concept of Christian mission to other faiths has become a matter of considerable controversy.

Secondly, religious pluralism is *theocentric, rather than Christocentric*. This position essentially places God at the centre of the religious world and relegates Christ to a secondary position as no more than a spokesman for one faith, just as Muhammad and the Buddha are seen as spokesmen for other faiths. By extension, any faith that portrays Christ as one among equals – Islam being the clearest example – is more likely to win the approval of pluralists on the matter of his role.

Thirdly, religious pluralism is in fact *a new religion*. It should be seen for what it is, an assimilation of multiple approaches to multiple faiths that results in a new religious product; that is, a faith in itself.

There are many cases of both Christian and Muslim writers who affirm the existence of truth in an absolute sense. While this demonstrates a shared perspective, there are fundamental differences about the identity of these overall truths. These differences, such as the different Christian and

Muslim beliefs about the crucifixion, death and resurrection of Jesus, are sometimes impossible to reconcile. Mutually exclusive claims like this make adherence to an extreme religious pluralist position untenable. Either Jesus died by crucifixion or he did not. Either Christianity or Islam is wrong on this core doctrine.

By the same token, the undeniable presence of truth found in both Christianity and Islam makes it equally untenable to assume an extreme exclusivist position. While one or other of the two must have a greater measure of truth,[2] adherents of either would agree that there is clear evidence of some truth in many key areas in the other. I would therefore wish to affirm the following statement by Anthony O'Mahony:

> . . . a fundamental tension remains between the demands of equality and reciprocity inherent in true dialogue and the legitimate claim of Christianity to be the religion of the absolute and definitive manifestation of God in Jesus Christ. If Jesus himself is only one mediator among others and not God's decisive manifestation for all men and women, then we can seriously question whether we have not already discarded the faith inherited from the apostles.[3]

There must be serious doubts about the long-term sustainability of the kind of religious pluralism which pertains in much of western society today. Christopher Bull expresses this well: 'Pluralism leads to a hopelessly impoverished view of religious doctrine. A society's values cannot remain permanently fragmented. The current brand of pluralism may prove to be more a provisional tolerance of divergent ideas than a permanent system of beliefs. It may well begin to collapse as its inner tensions pull it apart.'[4]

Lessons learnt

I shall conclude this study by summarizing some of the macro-level issues which have arisen.

Diversity and unity

We have seen how diverse is the world of Islam, thus, I hope, satisfying the calls to recognize its diversity made in numerous documents, such as the WCC Guidelines on Dialogue and the Runnymede Trust Islamophobia Report.

This diversity can be seen on many levels. Muslims are diverse in their geographical spread, being found especially in Pakistan, the Arab world, and Indonesia, as well as in substantial numbers elsewhere. Muslims manifest sectarian diversity as well, being identified as belonging to the Sunni, Shi'ite or Ahmadi groups, among others. They can be distinguished according to mystical inclination: Sufi and non-Sufi. Muslims often differ in terms of their engagement with doctrine; this can clearly be seen in rationalist versus literalist approaches, with wide-ranging ramifications. There are ideological differences relating to their response to modernity, with modernizing, traditionalist and Islamist responses being distinguishing features. We also saw how they could be distinguished according to their interaction with British society, adopting either a participatory or a separatist mindset. No doubt there are many other ways of slicing the Muslim cake.[5]

But we should not stop there. As Zaki Badawi says, 'Looking at the Muslim community in comparison with other religious communities, perhaps we have less [sic] differences than, say, the Jews or the Christians . . . in a sense, Islam is more united, for all the differences that might appear, because we have our *Shari'ah*. Though we differ in small areas, we all accept the basic principles of the Law.'[6] We might not necessarily accept that Islam is more united than Judaism or Christianity. But Badawi's overall point is correct. There is a glue that binds Muslims together into a common religious system. This glue is a compound of various factors, including regard for Muhammad as the final and greatest prophet; holding to the Qur'an and Hadith as sacred scripture (though Sunni and Shi'a have different Hadith collections); considering the Islamic *shari'a* as divine law, given by God for human guidance (though the various law schools differ in matters of detail); and recognizing the pillars of Islamic practice and the core doctrines as shared elements of the faith.

In responding as Christians, we should therefore remind ourselves that there are two angles of approach to the other faith: the human faces of Muslim people, which reflect the diversity of Islam, and the system of Islam, which provides its elements of unity. Thus engagement should be two-pronged: engaging with the people, and engaging with the system.

It is wrong to attach stereotypes deduced from the system to the human faces of its adherents, as is pointed out by the first of the Four Principles of dialogue prepared by the WCC. By the same token, in addition to engaging with the people, there is nothing wrong with engaging with, and if necessary challenging, aspects of the system. In the words of the Inter Faith Network for the UK: 'Respect for other views does not exclude critique of them. We cannot abdicate our responsibility to make some assessment of the theological or philosophical truth and the moral and spiritual value of other traditions, both for ourselves and for our society.'[7] We should be wary of those Christians who take a blinkered approach, insisting that we should focus on only one or the other of these two dimensions of Islam. It is no less blinkered only to speak approvingly about the people than only to focus on perceived defects in the system.

Participation, integration or fragmentation?

Discussion in earlier chapters engaged with a range of challenging issues, but there are clear lessons to be learnt. In considering immigration and asylum, for example, Christians should take note of the biblical injunction to be hospitable: 'Do not forget to entertain strangers, for by so doing some people have entertained angels without knowing it' (Hebrews 13:2:).

But does that assume a stranger who is willing to co-operate and potentially to integrate, rather than to shun and separate? We saw Ruth's willingness to become part of her host family, even though she came from a different people group. She told Naomi: 'Where you go I will go, and where you stay I will stay. Your people will be my people and your God my God. Where you die I will die, and there I will be buried' (Ruth 1:16–17). How does this square with the statement by Ataullah Siddiqui of the Islamic Foundation in Leicester, who says: 'Fair play demands that the "new British", who are part and parcel of British society but with a different religious and cultural expression new to the British Isles, should be given a proportionate opportunity in the public expressions of the society.'[8] A vital message is in fact shared by both quotations: the importance of participation in the host society by immigrant groups.

The lesson for host societies should therefore be to show warm hospitality to those who immigrate, and, by extension, respect the differences of the newcomers. In return, host societies can reasonably expect newcomers to adopt a participatory approach, and even to be open to the integration of their locally born descendants into the host society, rather than striving for perpetual separation and difference. This is essential in order to achieve social cohesion and for the greater common good. Integration is a matter of mindset; it does not necessarily entail changing faith,[9] but it should certainly involve a visible and constructive participation in majority society, its institutions and interests.

Recommended modes of interaction

Our examination of selected case studies points to a wide variety of approaches to Christian–Muslim interaction. The report from the 1980 Lausanne consultation in Thailand referred to three types of dialogue: discursive dialogue; dialogue on religious experience; and secular dialogue, the last of which I have preferred to identify as dialogue on social concerns. In addition to these three, we could add traditional mission (by both Christians and Muslims) as a mode of interaction; campaigns on advocacy and justice; and apologetics in the form of debate.[10]

Our examination of church policy and practice suggests that different Christian groups share certain methods of interaction but that others are avoided by specific groups. Indeed, the method chosen will be largely

Table 6 Modes of Christian–Muslim interaction

	Muslim modernizers	Muslim traditionalists	Islamists
World Council of Churches	1. Dialogue on religious experience 2. Dialogue on social concerns 3. Campaigns on advocacy and justice	1. Dialogue on religious experience 2. Dialogue on social concerns 3. Campaigns on advocacy and justice	
Christian evangelicals	1. Traditional mission 2. Campaigns on advocacy and justice 3. Dialogue on social concerns 4. Dialogue on religious experience	1. Traditional mission 2. Campaigns on advocacy and justice 3. Dialogue on social concerns 4. Dialogue on religious experience	1. Traditional mission 2. Campaigns on advocacy and justice 3. Debate/ apologetics
Catholic Church	1. Dialogue on religious experience 2. Dialogue on social concerns 3. Campaigns on advocacy and justice	1. Dialogue on religious experience 2. Dialogue on social concerns 3. Campaigns on advocacy and justice	

determined by the kinds of Christians and Muslims involved in the inter-action. This can be tabulated as in Table 6, in which the numbering system reflects the broad priority given by each Christian group to the respective mode of interaction.

Several important observations can be drawn from this table. First, the World Council of Churches, predominantly representing Protestant liberals and traditionalists, tends to engage primarily with Muslim modernizers and traditionalists, preferring to ignore radical Islamists. Secondly, the WCC prefers to engage in dialogue on religious experience and social concerns, with a secondary emphasis on campaigning for advocacy and justice, and a disavowal of apologetics and debate. Thirdly, the profile of the Catholic Church's preferences resembles that of the WCC. Discussion in previous chapters, however, showed that the Catholic leadership has frequently issued robust statements on advocacy and justice issues of a type unlikely to be heard with such force from WCC leaders. The Catholic Church, like WCC members, avoids the debate mode of interaction. Finally, Christian evangelicals, grouped under the WEA, maintain the priority of traditional mission as well as of advocacy and justice issues. Nevertheless, there is an increasing evangelical participation in dialogue on religious experience and social concerns. Furthermore, the only Christian group to be responding directly to the Muslim radical minority and its anti-Christian polemic comes from the evangelical stream, using debate, or, in the terminology of the Lausanne movement, discursive dialogue.

The wide range of modes of interaction presented here reflects the rich tapestry of both Christianity and Islam. An issue for Christian consideration is whether such diverse approaches may well be appropriate, given the diversity of Muslim communities with which Christians are interacting. This is the view I recommend.

It would be as inappropriate to engage in robust debate with congenial Muslim traditionalists as to engage in soft dialogue with radical Islamists. Christians should allow for the fact that some types of engagement, which move outside their comfort zone, may well be appropriate for some other Christians engaging with different kinds of Muslims. Those committed to dialogue should not delegitimize the efforts of the debaters, nor should the reverse occur. If such eclecticism is used by both Christians and Muslims in their mutual engagement, we can hope that greater openness will result from this expanded interaction, rather than the continuation of the wall of silence and mutual suspicion that has characterized so much Christian– Muslim interaction in the past.

APPENDIX 1: GLOSSARY

Writers quoted in this book may differ slightly in their spelling of these transliterated Arabic words and in their use of italics and initial capitals.

alim a religious scholar in Islam

caliph a successor of Muhammad (his four immediate successors are known as the Rightly Guided Caliphs); head of the *umma*

da'wa(h) Islamic missionary outreach

dhimmi non-Muslims (especially Jews and Christians) living in a Muslim state

fatwa an edict based on Islamic law

Fiqh codified laws of Islam, compiled by legislators from the Qur'an, Sunna, analogy and consensus

Hadith books containing the Sunna

haram forbidden; sacred territory, especially the holy cities of Mecca and Medina

imam a religious leader; one who leads congregational prayer

iman faith, belief

janna(h) Paradise

jihad war against an unjust regime; 'holy war'; the struggle to be devout

jihadis radical Islamists who interpret *jihad* as armed assault on everything that is, in their view, un-Islamic

kafir unbeliever, infidel

khalifa(h) caliph

Malekite school one of the four schools or systems of Sunni Islamic law that were founded in the eighth and ninth centuries AD

mu'min a believer in Allah; his righteous and obedient servant

qisas retaliation; punishment

Qur'an (Koran) The Islamic holy book, whose contents are claimed to have been revealed to Muhammad by Allah through the angel Gabriel

shahada(h) the Muslim declaration of faith: 'There is no God but Allah, and Muhammad is his messenger'

shahid martyr

shari'a the divine law of Islam

shaykh (sheikh) a wise elder; a religious leader in a community

Shi'a literally 'faction', comprising about 15% of Muslims worldwide; Shi'ites await the coming of the 'hidden Imam', who will herald the reign of divine justice

Sira(h) (Seerah) biography of Muhammad

Sufi a follower of Sufism, the mystical tradition within Islam

Sunna the traditions about the sayings and customs of Muhammad, compiled into the books of Hadith by various scholars

Sunni the majority stream of Islam, comprising around 85% of Muslims worldwide

sura(h) one of the 114 chapters of the Qur'an

SWT *subhanahu wa ta'ala*, 'Glorified be he', an expression of respect on pronouncing the name of Allah

ulama (ulema) religious scholars of Islam (plural of *alim*)

umma(h) the worldwide brotherhood of Muslims

APPENDIX 2: WCC EXPENDITURE IN 2002 BY COMPONENT

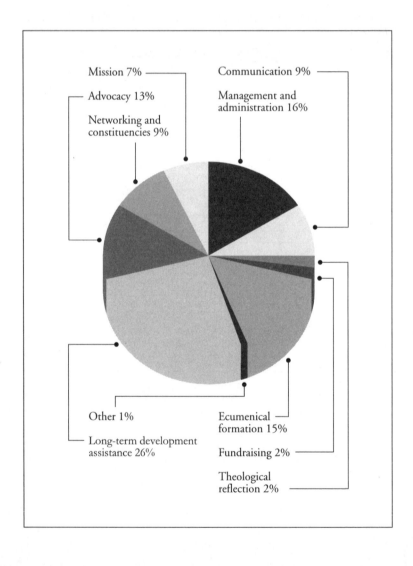

Mission 7%

Advocacy 13%

Networking and constituencies 9%

Communication 9%

Management and administration 16%

Other 1%

Long-term development assistance 26%

Ecumenical formation 15%

Fundraising 2%

Theological reflection 2%

APPENDIX 3: 'AN AGREEMENT FOR DIALOGUE BETWEEN THE ANGLICAN COMMUNION AND AL-AZHAR AL-SHARIF'[1]

We affirm the importance of building on the excellent relations between the Anglican Communion and the al-Azhar al-Sharif.

We acknowledge the brotherly relations between the Grand Sheikh of al-Azhar, Dr Mohamed Sayed Tantawy, and Dr George Carey, the Archbishop of Canterbury and the President of the Anglican Communion.

We believe that friendship which overcomes religious, ethnic and national differences is a gift of the Creator in whom we all believe.

We recognize that both sides need to accept each other in a straightforward way so as to be able to convey the message of peace to the world.

Continuing from the visit of Dr Carey to al-Azhar al-Sharif in October 1995 and the visit of Dr Tantawy, the Grand Sheikh of al-Azhar al-Sharif, to Lambeth Palace in 1997, and the return visit of Dr Carey to al-Azhar al-Sharif in November 1999,

And because of our common faith in God and our responsibility to witness against indifference to religion on the one hand and religious fanaticism on the other,

We hope that we may contribute to international efforts to achieve justice, peace, and the welfare of all humanity,

Resourced by the positive experiences in our long history as Christians and Muslims living together both in Egypt and the United Kingdom and many other parts of the world.

In consequence of this, Dr George Carey, the President of the Anglican Communion, has appointed the following members to the Interfaith Commission:

The Revd Canon Dr Christopher Lamb
The Rt Revd Mouneer Hanna Anis, Bishop in Egypt with North Africa
The Rt Revd David Smith, Bishop of Bradford, UK

The members of the Permanent Committee of al-Azhar al-Sharif for Dialogue on Monotheistic Religions are

Sheik Fawzy El Zefzaf, President
Dr Ali El Samman, Vice President
Dr Mustaffa Al Shukfah
Sheikh Abu Agour
Ambassador Nabil Badre

Representatives of both sides met on 10 and 11 September 2001 in al-Azhar and discussed the proposal for the dialogue between the Anglican Communion and al-Azhar al-Sharif with the hope of achieving the following goals:

> *To encourage* Anglicans to understand Islam and to encourage Muslims to understand the Christian faith.

> *To share* together in solving problems and conflicts that happen sometimes between Muslims and Christians in different parts of the world, and to encourage religious leaders to use their influence for the purpose of reconciliation and peace making.

> *To work together* against injustice and the abuse of human rights among different nationalities and to spread the good teaching of both Islam and Christianity.

> *To encourage* institutions on both sides to play a positive role in development.

To achieve these goals the following decisions were taken:

> *A Joint Committee will be established* from both sides composed of a Chairman and two members from each side already appointed. It may be possible in the future to add new members but each side will inform the other about its membership.

> *This Joint Committee will meet at least once a year* in Egypt and the United Kingdom alternately. Each delegation will cover its expenses for travel and accommodation and could meet more than once a year if necessary.

> *At the end of each meeting a Press Release* will be issued. The text of the communiqué must be agreed by the Joint Committee before publication. No information about papers presented to the Joint Committee will be released outside it without the agreement of both sides.

Signed by:

The Most Revd and Rt Hon. Dr George Carey
Archbishop of Canterbury

His Eminence Sheikh Mohamed Sayed Tantawy
Grand Imam of al-Azhar

The Rt Revd Mouneer Hanna Anis
Bishop in Egypt with North Africa

Sheikh Fawzy El Zefzaf
President, Permanent Committee of al-Azhar
for Dialogue with the Monotheistic Religions

The Revd Canon Dr Christopher Lamb

Dr Ali El Samman
Vice President, Permanent Committee of al-Azhar
for Dialogue with the Monotheistic Religions

APPENDIX 4: A SHARED ACT OF REFLECTION AND COMMITMENT BY THE FAITH COMMUNITIES OF THE UNITED KINGDOM

On Monday, 3rd January 2000, the Department for Culture, Media and Sport hosted a shared faith communities event in London as part of the Millennium festivities. The event, televized by the BBC, was held in the Royal Gallery in the Houses of Parliament. It was an unprecedented opportunity for members of the UK's nine major faith communities to come together to celebrate the shared values which they hoped would characterize life in the United Kingdom in the twenty-first century.

The event was not an act of worship, but a shared act of reflection and commitment involving a series of presentations by faith leaders and young people from the various communities, including readings and appropriate musical contributions. Its content was developed by the faith communities, through the Inter Faith Network for the UK, at the invitation of the Department.

An Act of Commitment

Faith community representatives:
In a world scarred by the evils of war, racism, injustice and poverty,
we offer this joint Act of Commitment as we look to our shared future.

> *All:* We commit ourselves,
> as people of many faiths,
> to work together
> for the common good,
> uniting to build a better society,
> grounded in values and ideals we share:
>
> community,
> personal integrity,
> a sense of right and wrong,
> learning, wisdom and love of truth,

care and compassion,
justice and peace,
respect for one another,
for the earth and its creatures.

We commit ourselves,
in a spirit of friendship and co-operation,
to work together
alongside all who share our values and ideals,
to help bring about a better world
now and for generations to come.

NOTES

Introduction
1 'Churchgoing', *The Times*, 10 December 2003.
2 Cf. Derek Tidball, *Who Are the Evangelicals?* (London: Marshall Pickering, 1994), pp. 11–18.
3 Ida Glaser, 'Faith and Society in the UK', *Transformation* 17.1 (January–March 2000), p. 27.
4 Cf. Ishtiaq Ahmed, *The Concept of an Islamic State: An Analysis of the Ideological Controversy in Pakistan* (London: Pinter, 1987), and *State, Nation and Ethnicity in Contemporary South Asia* (London: Pinter, 1998).
5 Paul Vallely, 'Bradford Rises Above the Ashes', *The Independent*, 14 January 1999.
6 Andrew Rippin, *Muslims: Their Religious Beliefs and Practices*, 2nd edn (London: Routledge, 2001), pp. 182–185.
7 The New Zealand scholar Douglas Pratt adds a fourth category, that of 'pragmatic secularists', and presents a useful analysis of varying manifestations of Islamism. Cf. Pratt, *Identity and Interaction: Islam and the Challenge of Interreligious Dialogue* (the Charles Strong Memorial Trust Lecture 1999, Sydney), pp. 13–21.
8 Ataullah Siddiqui, 'The Presence of "Secular" in Christian–Muslim Relations: Reflections on the Da'wah, "Mission" and "Dialogue"', in Anthony O'Mahony and Ataullah Siddiqui (eds.), *Christians and Muslims in the Commonwealth* (London: Altajir World of Islam Trust, 2001), pp. 88.
9 For a different angle on this topic, see Peter Cotterell, 'The Bible and Other Religions', in Peter Cotterell and Peter Riddell, *Christianity and Other Religions*, Occasional Paper no. 5 (London: Centre for Islamic Studies and Muslim–Christian Relations, London School of Theology, 2004).
10 Cf. Chawkat Moucarry, *Faith to Faith: Christianity and Islam in Dialogue* (Leicester: IVP, 2001), pp. 266–272.
11 The term 'people of faith' is used here to represent those people who are faithful to God's revelation, whether general or specific, leading to commitment to the message of Jesus Christ contained in the Bible. This concept of 'people of faith' will recur in reinterpreted form in subsequent chapters.

1. The how and why of changing attitudes
1 Christianity's engagement and competition with secular culture represents a crucial challenge for the church. Our primary focus on Christian–Muslim relations, however, precludes a detailed consideration of the Christian–secular nexus in this work.
2 Jacques Waardenburg, 'Between Baghdad and Birmingham: Minorities – Christian and Muslim', *Islam and Christian–Muslim Relations* 14/1 (2003), p. 12.
3 William Carey, *An Enquiry into the Obligations of Christians to use Means for the Conversion of the Heathens* (1792; London: Baptist Missionary Society, 1934), pp. 69–70.

4 J. N. D. Anderson, 'Islam', in H. A. Evan Hopkins (ed.), *The Inadequacy of Non-Christian Religion* (London: Inter-Varsity Fellowship, 1944), pp. 13–15. Note that in his later writing Anderson took a much more irenic tone, while at the same time maintaining the same level of confidence in the message of the Gospels. Cf. Anderson, *Christianity and World Religions: The Challenge of Pluralism* (Leicester: IVP, 1984).

5 Roger Hooker and Christopher Lamb, *Love the Stranger* (London: SPCK, 1986), p. 76.

6 For a liberal approach to this subject, see Paul F. Knitter, *No Other Name? A Critical Survey of Christian Attitudes Towards the World Religions* (Maryknoll, NY: Orbis, 1985), chapters 5–8.

7 Myles Harris, *Tomorrow is Another Country* (London: Civitas, 2003), p. 18.

8 <http://www.vexen.co.uk/religion/rib.html>, drawing on the <http://www.religioustolerance.org> website.

9 'Religion in Britain', <http://www.statistics.gov.uk/CCI/nugget.asp?ID=293&Pos=3&Col Rank=1&Rank=192>

10 '2001 Census Makeup of London Revealed', *London Sustainability Exchange*, 21 February 2003, <http://www.lsx.org.uk/news/_page329.aspx>, accessed November 2003.

11 The impact of the latter trend is evident in figures from the 2001 British census, when 15.5% of respondents declared themselves to have no religion.

12 Genaro C. Armas, 'Foreign-Born Population Surges in US', *Associated Press*, 6 November 2003.

13 'Immigration Reform', editorial, *The New York Times*, 3 January 2004.

14 A. Heywood, *Political Ideologies: An Introduction* (Basingstoke: Macmillan, 1998), p. 28.

15 'Orwell and Colonialism', <http://www.victorianweb.org/post/poldiscourse/orwell.html>, accessed April 2004.

16 Edward Stourton, 'How to Be a Missionary', *The Tablet*, 5 July 2003, p. 11.

17 Lamin Sanneh, *Translating the Message: The Missionary Impact on Culture* (Maryknoll, KY: Orbis, 1989), p. 4.

18 Kate Zebiri, *Muslims and Christians Face to Face* (Oxford: Oneworld , 1997), p. 30.

19 Lamin Sanneh, 'Christian Missions and the Western Guilt Complex', <http://www.asu.edu/clas/religious_studies/home/cmg.html>, accessed April 2004.

20 Lamin Sanneh, *Encountering the West* (London: Marshall Pickering, 1993), p. 179.

21 Sanneh, 'Christian Missions and the Western Guilt Complex'.

22 Susan M. Okin, 'Reply', in Joshua Cohen, Matthew Howard and Martha C. Nussbaum (eds.), *Is Multiculturalism Bad for Women?* (Princeton, NJ: Princeton University Press, 1999).

23 *A Very Light Sleeper* (London: Runnymede Trust, 1994).

24 Though the Runnymede Trust is not itself a religious body.

25 *Islamophobia: A Challenge for Us All* (London: Runnymede Trust, 1997), pp. 4ff.

26 *The Church Times*, 28 February 1997.

27 Bhikhu Parekh, 'Preface', *The Future of Multi-Ethnic Britain* (the Parekh Report) (London: Profile, 2000).

28 Ibid.

29 Examples are the *Bradford Commission Report: The Report of an Inquiry into the Wider Implications of Public Disorders in Bradford which occurred on 9, 10, and 11 June* (London: HMSO, 1995), the report on the northern riots by Lord Ouseley, *Community Pride not Prejudice: Making Diversity Work in Bradford* (Bradford Vision, 2001), and various documents produced by the Inner Cities Religious Council.

30 Yasmin Alibhai-Brown, 'Faith Communities in Public Life', lecture for the Inner Cities Religious Council, Manchester University, 26 April 2001.

31 David Lochhead, *The Dialogical Imperative: A Christian Reflection on Interfaith Encounter* (London: SCM, 1988), p. 2.

32   *Charles: The Private Man, The Public Role,* Central Television, UK, 1994.
33   Hereafter referred to as '9/11'.
34   For an analysis of the phenomenon of Islamist terrorism, its causes and manifestations in the early twenty-first century, see Peter G. Riddell and Peter Cotterell, *Islam in Conflict: Past, Present and Future* (Leicester: IVP, 2003), especially chapter 10.
35   Usamah bin Muhammad bin Laden, 'Declaration of War against the Americans Occupying the Land of the Two Holy Places', 23 August 1996, Hindukush Mountains, Khurasan, Afghanistan, <http://www.kimsoft.com/2001/binladenwar. htm>, accessed April 2004.
36   Citing Q9:36.
37   Citing Q2:193.
38   'Text of Fatwah Urging Jihad against Americans', *Al-Quds al-'Arabi,* 23 February 1998; translated text available at <http://www.ict.org.il/articles/fatwah.htm>.
39   'Straw blames lack of global action for 9/11', *Reuters,* 20 March 2004.
40   Riddell and Cotterell, *Islam in Conflict,* p. 179.
41   Usually defined as chemical, biological and nuclear weapons.
42   Riddell and Cotterell, *Islam in Conflict,* pp. 177–178.
43   See chapter 2 below for a fuller discussion of Muslim reactions to these campaigns.
44   This report by Anthony Cordesman showed that, in the period 1973–1991, US weapons exports to Iraq totalled only $5 million while the UK sold $330 millions' worth of arms to Iraq. In contrast, those countries most outspoken in their criticism of the 2003 war were in fact the chief sources of arms to Iraq: Germany sold $995 millions' worth, China $5,500 million, France $9,240 million, and Russia $31,800 million. See Andrew Hamilton, 'Supplies of Arms and Oil Revenues', *The Times,* 21 March 2003.
45   'Christian and Muslim Leaders Plea for Peace', Muslim Council of Britain press statement, 20 March 2003.
46   Osama bin Laden, speaking on 3 November 2001, <http://news.bbc.co.uk/low/ english/world/monitoring/media_reports/ newsid_1636000/1636782.stm>.
47   Amir Butler, 'Speak Up, I Won't be Offended', *A True Word,* 11 July 2003, <http:// www.atrueword.com/index.php/article/articleview/61/1/4>.
48   *The Bradford Commission Report.*
49   Lesslie Newbigin, Lamin Sanneh and Jenny Taylor, *Faith and Power: Christianity and Islam in 'Secular' Britain* (London: SPCK, 1998), pp. 89–90. For a full account of this case, see Carol Sarler's report in *The Sunday Times Magazine,* 25 August 1996.
50   Newbigin, Sanneh and Taylor, *Faith and Power,* pp. 90–92.
51   Peter Cotterell, *The Eleventh Commandment: Church and Mission Today* (Leicester: IVP, 1981), p. 102.
52   The Westophobia Report, *Anti-Western and Anti-Christian Stereotyping in British Muslim Publications* (Centre for Islamic Studies, London Bible College, 1999).
53   See also Vinoth Ramachandra, *Faiths in Conflict? Christian Integrity in a Multicultural World* (Leicester: IVP, 1999), pp. 34–37.
54   Quoted in Kaleem Muhammad Alleyne, 'Equality Before Law', *Common Sense* (Summer 1997), p. 7.
55   *Q-News,* December 1997. Not all Muslims believe this conspiracy theory. Mohamed Medjahdi, who was driving directly in front of Diana's Mercedes limousine when it crashed in a Paris tunnel in August 1997, insisted that the car had been speeding out of control, and that no other cars or people had been involved. He said in interview, 'I am absolutely convinced, clear and certain that this was a tragedy – but it was an accident . . . Any conspiracy would have had to be carried out by invisible men.' *Reuters,* 15 January 2004.
56   Ramachandra, *Faiths in Conflict?,* p. 16.
57   Islamic Forum Europe, *The Middle Path* (London, March 1994), p. 6.
58   *The Muslim News,* 29 August 1997.

59 Rashid Abdul Latif, 'The First Community in a Hostile Land', *Trends* 7/1, p. 18.

60 Personal communication, September 2003, italics added.

61 Yasmin Alibhai-Brown, 'When Muslims Behave Badly', *The Independent*, 28 January 2002.

62 Such as female circumcision (clitoridectomy), arranged marriages for minors, and wife-beating. Consider also the case of honour killings, such as that of a sixteen-year-old Kurdish girl killed by her father when he suspected her of fornication. This case aroused much media discussion in Britain in September 2003.

63 Toby Howarth provides another angle on the impact of political correctness: 'Muslims [in western Europe] have often sought actively to portray their religion in a positive light, sometimes by glossing over difficult aspects. This has been aided and reinforced by the "political correctness" of some in government, academia and the media who are actively engaged in promoting Islam.' See his 'The Church Facing Islam in Western Europe', *Transformation* 20/4 (October 200), p. 230.

64 Quoted in Tom Baldwin and Gabriel Rozenburg, 'Britain "Must Scrap Multiculturalism"', *The Times*, 3 April 2004.

65 'Asylum Seekers "Could Overwhelm UK"', *Sky News*, <http://uk.news.yahoo.com/030508/140/dzi9v.html>, citing a report by the UK Parliament's Home Affairs Select Committee.

66 'The Asylum Game', *Panorama*, BBC1, 23 July 2003.

67 'Thousands Oppose Asylum Centre', 23 February 2003, <http://www.femail. co.uk/pages/standard/article.html?in_article_id=164972&in_page_id=2>.

68 'It's Not Racist to Worry about Asylum Seekers, it's Just . . .', *The Daily Telegraph*, 16 January 2004.

69 'Asylum Statistics: 4th Quarter 2002, United Kingdom', Home Office, <http://image.guardian.co.uk/sys-files/Guardian/documents/2003/02/28/asylumq402.pdf>.

70 Melanie Phillips, 'How the West was Lost', *The Spectator*, 11 May 2002.

71 Anthony Browne, *Do We Need Mass Immigration?* (London: Civitas, 2002), p. 123.

72 Personal communication, 17 October 2003.

73 'Pair "Plotted Bin Laden Holy War"', *Sky News*, 6 February 2003.

74 David Leppard, 'Police Seize UK Suicide Bomber', *The Sunday Times*, 11 January 2004.

75 Warren Hoge, 'British Court Charges 4 Men as Terrorists; Arrests Spread', *The New York Times*, 14 January 2003.

76 Susan Bisset and Chris Hastings, 'Taliban Who Fought British Troops is Granted Asylum Here', *The Daily Telegraph*, 19 January 2003.

77 Padraic Flanagan and Cyril Dixon, 'Sickening', *Daily Express*, 31 January 2004.

78 The topic of asylum is similarly a subject of much debate in Australia, with the Australian government of John Howard taking a much firmer stance than the British government and imposing detention on all newly arriving asylum seekers. For a critical response to this policy, see Ian George, *General Synod Refugee Working Group: Statement for Federal and State Parliamentarians* (Anglican Church of Australia, November 2003), <http://www.anglican.org.au/docs/RefugeeWGreport.doc>, accessed April 2004.

79 Jason Hopps, 'Britain Introduces Tough Asylum Measures', *Reuters*, 8 January 2003.

80 'Blair Sets Tough Asylum Target', *Reuters*, 7 February 2003.

81 Press briefing: 10.30am, Tuesday 11 March 2003, asylum.

82 Dominic Casciani, 'Sharp Fall in Asylum Applications', *BBC News*, 28 August 2003.

83 Andrew Sparrow, 'Asylum Seekers With No Papers Face Prison', <http://www.news.telegraph.co.uk>, 28 October 2003.

84 'Ferry Firms Face Stowaway Fines', *10 Downing Street Weekly Newsletter*, 10 October 2003, <http://www.pm.gov.uk/output/page4566.asp>.

85 In spite of criticism of this proposal from civil-liberties groups, a MORI poll found that 80% of people surveyed supported the identity-card proposal. See 'Blunkett Wants ID Cards in Three Years', *Reuters*, 25 April 2004.

86 For the text of this Act, see <http://www.hmso.gov.uk/acts/acts2002/20020041.htm>.

87 Casciani, 'Sharp Fall in Asylum Applications'.

88 Katherine Baldwin, 'Asylum Applications Drop', *Reuters*, 24 February 2004.

89 Any criticism of Carey on this point, however, must acknowledge that he was merely articulating widely held views of his time. Commentators in the early twenty-first century speak with the benefit of hindsight; they are no less windows into their own age than was Carey.

2. Diverse Muslim approaches to British society

1 Mohammad S. Raza, *Islam in Britain: Past, Present and the Future* (Leicester: Volcano, 1991) , pp. 107ff.

2 For a discussion of the ideological orientations and influence of Khurram Murad, see Anthony McRoy, *Rushdie's Legacy: The Emergence of a Radical British Muslim Identity* (PhD dissertation, London Bible College, Brunel University, 2001), pp. 202–209.

3 Khurram Murad, *Islamic Movement in the West: Reflections on Some Issues* (Leicester: Islamic Foundation, no date), p. 7.

4 Ibid.

5 J. Nielsen, *Muslims in Western Europe* (Edinburgh: Edinburgh University Press, 1992), p. 45.

6 'Playing a Part in Society: Jenny Taylor talks to Iqbal Sacranie OBE', *Third Way*, July 2000, p. 19.

7 'Two Sides of a Different Coin? Anthony McRoy talks to Sheikh Omar Bakri Muhammad and Shagufta Yaqub', *Third Way*, March 2003, p. 18.

8 Ibid.

9 Christian Troll, 'Germany's Islamic Charter', *Encounter* 290 (December 2002), p. 6.

10 Of course, some Muslims are forced into a separate existence by circumstances such as poverty, ignorance and lack of English language. Our primary concern here is with focusing on mindset rather than on circumstances; on those who choose to participate or separate, whether or not their circumstances enable them to realize their choice.

11 Kalim Siddiqui, *The Implications of the Rushdie Affair for Muslims in Britain* (London: Muslim Institute, 1989), p. 4.

12 It should, however, be noted that, in many cases that occur within the framework of the English legal system, Islamic legal contexts have to be taken into account in making rulings where Muslims are involved. See David Pearl, 'The Application of Islamic Law in the English Courts', <http://www.soas.ac.uk/Centres/IslamicLaw/Coulson_Pearl.html>.

13 The case of Canada provides a contrast. In October 2003, an Islamic Institute of Civil Justice (Dar al-Qada) was established to act as a judicial tribunal to arbitrate in cases of civil dispute between Muslims. Under changes to the Canadian Arbitration Act, secular courts will henceforth recognize the *shari'a*-based decisions of the new Islamic Institute. 'Canada: Applying Shariah through Islamic arbitration', *World Evangelical Alliance Religious Liberty News and Analysis*, 15 December 2003.

14 Lesslie Newbigin, Lamin Sanneh and Jenny Taylor, *Faith and Power: Christianity and Islam in 'Secular' Britain* (London: SPCK, 1998), p. 114.

15 'Happy Families', BBC, 1996.

16 A. Jabeer, 'Institute Moves to Galvanise Popular Local Support', *The Muslim News*, no. 16 (30 June 1990), 1, cited in Raza, *Islam in Britain*, p. 107.

17 McRoy, *Rushdie's Legacy*, p. 226.

18 'True Submission: Zaki Badawi talks to Peter Riddell', *Third Way*, May 1996, pp. 16–19.
19 'Two Sides of a Different Coin?', p. 18.
20 'Questions and Answers', <http://www.almuhajiroun.com.pk/faq.asp>, accessed May 2003.
21 Muhammad Hisham Kabbani, 'The Muslim Experience in America is Unprecedented', *Middle East Quarterly*, June 2000.
22 Quoted in Shagufta Yaqub, 'Conversation with Abu Hamza', *Q-News*, February 1999, p. 25.
23 'Muslims in Church Schools', *British Muslims Monthly Survey* 1/11 (November 1993), p. 3, citing *Q-News*, 12 November 1993.
24 <http://www.mcb.org.uk/vs/Education.htm>, accessed July 2001.
25 *The Daily Telegraph*, 19 December 1997.
26 *The Independent*, 20 December 1997.
27 *The Times*, 30 December 1997.
28 'Interview with Abdullah Trevathan', *MCB Direct*, 20 October 2003, <http://www.mcb.org.uk/mcbdirect/feature.php?ann_id=347>.
29 <http://www.muslimschools.fsnet.co.uk/why.htm>, accessed July 2001.
30 <http://ams.eteach.com/hosted/page.asp?page=about&tabNo=2>, accessed April 2004.
31 'Interview with Abdullah Trevathan'.
32 <http://www.islamicparty.com/question/schools.htm>, accessed July 2001.
33 'Muslims in Church Schools'.
34 <http://www.mcb.org.uk/vs/Education.htm>, accessed July 2001.
35 <http://www.londonschoolofislamics.org.uk/DiscView.asp?mid=132& forum_id=1&>, accessed 22 October 2003.
36 Ibid.
37 Jonathan Birt and Philip Lewis, 'The Pattern of Islamic Reform in Britain: The Deobandis between Intra-Muslim Sectarianism and Engagement with Wider Society', in Martin van Bruinessen and Stefano Allievi (eds.), *Producing Islamic Knowledge: Transmission and Dissemination in Western Europe* (London: Routledge), forthcoming.
38 <http://www.mcb.org.uk/vs/whyvote2.ph>, accessed July 2001.
39 <http://www.votesmart.org.uk>.
40 <http://www.votesmart.org.uk/index1.php?page=mps.htm>, accessed July 2001.
41 <http://www.islamicparty.com/election/vote.htm>, accessed July 2001.
42 Quoted in Philip Lewis, 'Muslims in Europe: Managing Multiple Identities and Learning Shared Citizenship', *Political Theology* (forthcoming).
43 <http://www.obm.clara.net/publictalks/votingfatwa.htm>, accessed July 2001.
44 'Cleric Jailed for Racial Hatred Offences', *The Guardian*, 7 March 2003.
45 MCB news release, <http://www.mcb.org.uk>.
46 *The Oldham Riots: Discrimination, Deprivation and Communal Tension in the United Kingdom* (Islamic Human Rights Commission, June 2001), p. 13.
47 *Anti-Muslim Discrimination and Hostility in the United Kingdom* (Islamic Human Rights Commission, 2000).
48 <http://fearsome.net/cache-machine/230.html>; <http://www.muslimnews.co.uk/fpmb103.html>, accessed July 2001.
49 <http://www.mcb.org.uk/vs/CivilSociety.htm>, accessed July 2001.
50 Quoted in Chris Marsden, 'Britain: Oldham Riots Sparked by Deliberate Cultivation of Racism', World Socialist Web Site, 29 May 2001, <http://www.wsws.org/articles/2001/may2001/old-m29.shtml>.
51 Anthony McRoy, 'Pray for Peace in Racial Tinderbox', *The Christian Herald*, 16 June 2001, p. 1.
52 Herman Ouseley, *Community Pride not Prejudice: Making Diversity Work in Bradford* (Bradford Vision, 2001).

53   *The Oldham Riots*, p. 13.
54   Cited in McRoy, 'Pray for Peace in Racial Tinderbox'.
55   Gareth Sturdy and Anthony McRoy, 'Reasons for the Riots', *Christianity +
     Renewal*, September 2001, p. 4.
56   Anthony McRoy, 'No More Cheeks to Turn: Bradford's Christian Minority',
     Q-News 338 (December 2001), p. 11.
57   Yasmin Alibhai-Brown, 'When Muslims Behave Badly', *The Independent*, 28
     January 2002.
58   McRoy, 'No More Cheeks to Turn', p. 11.
59   'Attitudes Towards British Muslims', YouGov poll for the Islamic Society of
     Britain, 4 November 2002, <http://www.isb.org.uk/iaw/pics/
     SurveyIAW2002.pdf>.
60   'Two Sides of a Different Coin?', p. 18.
61   'Islam Awareness Week Launches a Virtual Classroom', press release, 21 October
     2003.
62   *Prince Naseem's Guide to Islam*, BBC, 2001.
63   *The Mosque*, BBC, 2001.
64   Ibid.
65   *Haj: The Journey of a Lifetime*, BBC, 2001.
66   *Prince Naseem's Guide to Islam*.
67   *Haj: The Journey of a Lifetime*.
68   *My Name is Ahmed*, BBC, 2001.
69   *Prince Naseem's Guide to Islam*.
70   *Haj: The Journey of a Lifetime*.
71   *Islam, Empire of Faith, The Messenger*, BBC, 2001.
72   *Haj: The Journey of a Lifetime*.
73   *The Mosque*.
74   For instance, the middle-aged white female convert testifying to a miraculous
     experience on Mount Arafat in *Haj: The Journey of a Lifetime*.
75   'The BBC's Western Version of Islam', Al-Muhajiroun, London, 21 August 2001.
76   BBC Radio 4, 13 September 2001.
77   'Justice with Responsibility', statement by the Muslim Council of Britain on the
     occasion of the special House of Commons debate, 14 September
     2001,<http://www.mcb.org.uk>.
78   'There Are No Muslim Terrorists', *Q-News* 336 (October 2001), p. 9.
79   <http://www.islamic-foundation.org.uk/pressrelease.html>, 12 September 2001.
80   <http://news.bbc.co.uk/low/english/uk/newsid_1654000/1654426.stm>, 14
     November 2001.
81   Ibid.
82   <http://www.thetimes.co.uk/article/0,,2001370002-2001373874,00.html>.
83   'British Muslims Urge Justice, not Vengeance', MCB news release, 19 September
     2001.
84   <http://www.churchtimes.co.uk/templates/NewsTemplate_1.asp?recid=769&
     table=news&bimage=news&issue=7234&count=1>.
85   <http://www.independent.co.uk/story.jsp?story=99442>, accessed 17 October
     2001.
86   <http://www.churchtimes.co.uk/templates/NewsTemplate_1.asp?recid= 769&
     table=news&bimage=news&issue=7234&count=1>.
87   'British Muslims Urge Prime Minister to Avert War', MCB news release, 13
     January 2003.
88   'Last Minute Plea Against Invading Iraq – Muslims Meet Blair', MCB news
     release, 5 March 2003.
89   'A Black Day in Our History', MCB news release, 20 March 2003.
90   'UK Muslims Reject Neo-conservative/Zionist Plans for Iraq', MCB news release,
     11 April 2003.

91 Q9:41.
92 Q9:36.
93 Press release, 7 November 2001, <http://www.almuhajiroun.com>.
94 <http://www.almuhajiroun.com>, accessed 15 November 2001.
95 Ibid.
96 'Two Sides of a Different Coin?', p. 18.
97 Quoted in Susan Bisset and Chris Hastings, 'Briton Trained by bin Laden Recruits in London', *The Daily Telegraph*, 23 September 2001, <http://news.telegraph.co.uk/news/main.jhtml?xml=/news/2001/09/23/nmus23.xml>.
98 <http://www.guardian.co.uk/uk_news/story/0,3604,579108,00.html>, accessed 24 October 2001.
99 Quoted in 'Hard Liners call Bin Laden 'Hero'', *BBC News*, 12 September, 2002, <http://news.bbc.co.uk/1/hi/england/2252361.stm>.
100 Quoted in 'The Enemy Within?', *Tonight*, Channel 4, 2004.
101 Quoted in 'Islamic Group's "Dynamite" Warning', *BBC News*, 31 July 2003, <http://news.bbc.co.uk/1/hi/england/london/3112255.stm>.
102 Quoted in Martin Chulov, 'Aussie Muslim Leader's Jihad Call', <news.com.au>, 19 February 2004.
103 'Q-Poll: readers survey', *Q-News*, no. 337 (November 2001), p. 9.
104 'UK Muslims "Against Afghan War"', *BBC News Online*, 14 November 2001.
105 John Elliott and Maurice Chittenden, 'British Muslim Support for Terror', *The Sunday Times*, 4 November 2001.
106 This was in spite of the fact that bin Laden deputies had acknowledged al-Qa'ida responsibility for the 9/11 attacks on several occasions during 2002.
107 'Rethink Iraq War Plans, Urges MCB', Muslim Council of Britain news release, 15 October 2002 .
108 'Q-News War Survey: We Are Not Amused', *Q-News* 349 (March–August 2003), pp. 20–21.
109 'True Submission: Zaki Badawi talks to Peter Riddell', *Third Way*, May 1996, pp. 16–19.
110 'Two Sides of a Different Coin?', p. 18.
111 *Q-News*, 7 February 1997.
112 Quoted in *There's a Mosque in my Street*, programme 2: *Islam in Britain*, directed by Peter G. Riddell (London: London Bible College, Centre for Islamic Studies and Muslim–Christian Relations, 1999).
113 Ibid.
114 'To Imams, Ulema, Chairs and Secretaries of Mosques, Islamic Organisations and Institutions', Muslim Council of Britain, 31 March 2004.
115 'The Enemy Within?'
116 Fareena Alam, 'Vision of a New Islam', *The Observer*, 4 April 2004.
117 Sahib Mustaqim Bleher, 'To Vote or Not to Vote', 1 May 2001, <http://www.islamicparty.com/election/vote.htm>, accessed July 2001.
118 *There's a Mosque in my Street*, programme 2.

3. International Islamic perspectives on globalization

1 <http://www.um.edu.my/inpuma>.
2 <http://www.bernama.com/events/ulama/index.php>.
3 Hassan bin Talal, 'Towards a World with 10,000 Cultures', *Discourse* 1 (August 2000), p. 9.
4 Fred Halliday, *Two Hours that Shook the World* (London: Saqi Books, 2002), p. 175.
5 Mazrui, 'Globalisation and the Future of Islamic Civilisation', lecture given at Westminster University, London, 3 September 2000, <http://www.alhewar.com/globalisation_and_the_future.htm>.

6   Mohammadi Ali, 'Islamic Response to Globalisation', <http://www.valt.helsinki.fi/vol/cosmopolis/papers/mohammad.html>, accessed April 2004.

7   A. S. Gammal, 'The Global Protests Against Anti-globalization, and the Media's Coverage of Them', *Crescent International,* 1–15 June 2001.

8   Rahhalah Haqq, 'Framing a 'Third Way' for the Muslim Ummah and the World', *Crescent International,* 1–15 November 2000.

9   Mahathir Bin Mohamad, 'Globalization: What it Means to Small Nations', speech at the inaugural lecture of the Prime Ministers of Malaysia Fellowship exchange programme, Kuala Lumpur, 24 July 1996, <http://www.twnside.org.sg/title/small-cn.htm>, accessed 14 November 2003.

10 Mohammadi Ali, 'Islamic Response to Globalisation'.

11 'Globalisation Must Benefit Everyone', International Consultation on Globalisation, World Evangelical Fellowship, Kuala Lumpur, 31 January–2 February 2001.

12 Mahathir, 'Globalization: What it Means to Small Nations'.

13 Ibid.

14 Quoted in 'Leaders of the Most Populous Muslim Nations Debate Response to Globalization', 27 February 2001, <http://www.khilafah.com/1421/category.php?DocumentID=1100&TagID=1#>.

15 Gammal, 'The Global Protests Against Anti-globalization, and the Media's Coverage of Them'.

16 <http://www.kompas.com/pemilu/partai/24pk.htm>, accessed December 2000.

17 These multifaith principles were clearly articulated by Indonesia's first president, Sukarno, when he said in 1945: 'The fifth principle [of the new Pancasila philosophy of state] should be to build an independent Indonesia on faith in Almighty God. It is not only the Indonesian people as a whole which should have faith in God, but each Indonesian individual should believe in his own God. Christians would worship God according to the guidance of Jesus Christ, Muslims should worship God according to the guidance of the Prophet Muhammad, Buddhists should discharge their religious duties according to their own books.' Cf. Peter Riddell, 'Islam and the Cross', *LBC Review*, March 2001, p. 6.

18 M. Anis Matta, *Membangun Peradaban Alternatif,* audiocassette (Bandung: Ummul Quro Bandung, no date).

19 Director of the Institute of Contemporary Islamic Thought, administered from Toronto and London, which describes itself as 'an international intellectual centre of the global Islamic movement. It consists of individual activists, journalists and academics in all parts of the world who share a common commitment to developing the social and political ideas of the Islamic movement, and promoting them as an alternative worldview to that of the western civilization.' <http://www.islamicthought.org/icit-intro.html>, accessed 22 November 2003.

20 Zafar Bangash, 'McDonaldization of Culture: America's Pervasive Influence Globally', *Crescent International,* 1–15 February 1998.

21 Ibid.

22 Ibid.

23 From the Jamaat-el-Islami website, <http://www.jamaat.org/world.worldorder.html>, accessed 31 May 2004.

24 Mahathir, 'Globalization: What it Means to Small Nations'.

25 'Islam and the New World Order', *Worldview,* Jamaat-e-Islami Pakistan, <http://www.jamaat.org/world/worldorder.html>.

26 Currently professor of law at Cairo University, and former Egyptian minister of information. His concern is with political globalization.

27 Quoted in Amil Khan, 'Role of Islam in the Age of Globalization', *Middle East Times,* <http://www.mafhoum.com/press/metislgl.htm>, accessed July 2001.

28 'Islam and the New World Order'.

29 Ibid.

30 Quoted in Ali, 'Islamic Response to Globalisation'.
31 Mazrui, *Globalisation and the Future of Islamic Civilisation*.
32 Mahathir, 'Speech at the Opening of World Ulama Conference, Putrajaya Marriot Hotel, Putrajaya, 10 July 2003', <http://www.bernama.com/events/ulama/rspeech. shtml?speech/ se0608_pm>.
33 Ibid.
34 M. Miasami, 'Islam and Globalization', *The Fountain* 43 (July–September 2003).
35 'Resolution of World Conference of Islamic Scholars', Kuala Lumpur, 10–12 July 2003, <http://www.bernama.com/events/ulama/rspeech.shtml?speech/ se2002_resol>.
36 Hassan bin Talal, 'Towards a World with 10,000 Cultures', p. 9.
37 'Globalisation Must Benefit Everyone'.
38 'Solidarity Against Rich States Pledged', 26 February 2001, <http://www.khilafah. com/1421/category.php?DocumentID=1094& TagID=1#>.
39 'Resolution of World Conference of Islamic Scholars'.
40 Quoted in Gamal Essam El-Din, 'The Voice of Reason', *Al-Ahram Weekly Online* 613 (21–27 November 2002).
41 Abas, 'Oil as Basic Economic Strength of the Ummah', <http://www.bernama. com/events/ulama/rpp.shtml?pp/pe1107_9>.
42 Quoted in El-Din, 'The Voice of Reason'.
43 Ibid.
44 Joni T. Borhan, 'Islamic Banking in Malaysia: Past, Present and Future', *Studia Islamika: Indonesian Journal for Islamic Studies* 10/2 (2003), pp. 31–74.
45 'Malaysia: Islamic Financial System', *Q-News*, October 2003, p. 40.
46 *Money and Banking in Malaysia* (Kuala Lumpur: Bank Negara Malaysia, 1994), cited in Matt Richards, 'Islamic Contracts of Finance in Malaysia', *Studia Islamika: Indonesian Journal for Islamic Studies* 10/1 (2003), p. 161.
47 'Malaysia: Islamic Financial System'.
48 William Pesek Jr, 'Commentary: Building an Islamic Financial Hub in Asia', *The International Herald Tribune*, 19 August 2003.
49 Haqq, 'Framing a "Third Way" for the Muslim Ummah and the World'.
50 Ibid.
51 Matta, *Membangun Peradaban Alternatif*.
52 Ali, 'Islamic Response to Globalisation'.
53 Yvonne Yazbeck Haddad, 'The Globalization of Islam: The Return of Muslims to the West', in John L. Esposito (ed.), *The Oxford History of Islam* (Oxford: Oxford University Press, 1999), pp. 601–641.
54 Cf. Peter G. Riddell, *Islam and the Malay-Indonesian World: Transmission and Responses* (London: C. Hurst & Co., 2001), chapter 13.
55 'Islam and the New World Order'.
56 Ibid.
57 'OIC in Brief', <http://www.oic-oci.org>, accessed January 2003.
58 'Resolution of World Conference of Islamic Scholars', Kuala Lumpur, 10–12 July 2003.
59 Muhammad Zuhri, 'Jalan Sufi di Zaman Globalisasi' ('The Sufi Path in the Era of Globalization'), *Salman Kau*, Rajab, 1415H, <http://www.geocities.com/Athens/ 5739/globalisasi.htm>, accessed April 2004.
60 Ibid.
61 Ibid.
62 Ibid.
63 Farish A. Noor, 'The Evolution of "Jihad" in Islamist Political Discourse: How a Plastic Concept Became Harder', essay for the Social Science Research Council, <http://www.ssrc.org/sept11/essays/noor.htm>, accessed 18 November 2003.
64 'Resolution of World Conference of Islamic Scholars'.

65 'Putrajaya Declaration on Knowledge and Morality for the Unity, Dignity and Progress of the Ummah, the 10th Session of the Islamic Summit Conference, Putrajaya, Malaysia, 11–18 October 2003', <http://www.oicsummit2003.org.my/declarations_05.php>, accessed November 2003.

4. Evolving approaches to other faiths among the churches

1 Paragraph 4.12, *Towards a Common Understanding and Vision of the World Council of Churches*, policy statement, Central Committee of the World Council of Churches, September 1997, <http://www.wcc-coe.org/wcc/who/cuv-e.html>, accessed March 2000.

2 Ataullah Siddiqui, *Christian–Muslim Dialogue in the 20th Century* (London: Macmillan, 1997), p. 30.

3 'Christian–Muslim Conversations', in *Meeting in Faith: Twenty Years of Christian–Muslim Conversations Sponsored by the World Council of Churches* (Geneva: WCC Publications, 1989).

4 Douglas Pratt, *Identity and Interaction: Islam and the Challenge of Interreligious Dialogue* (the Charles Strong Memorial Trust Lecture 1999, Sydney), p. 23.

5 These were subsequently published as *Guidelines on Dialogue with People of Living Faiths and Ideologies* (Geneva: WCC, 1979).

6 World Council of Churches Interreligious Relations, <http://www.wcc-coe.org/wcc/what/interreligious/index-e.html>, accessed March 2000.

7 *Guidelines for Interfaith Dialogue* (Ecumenical Office of the Anglican Church of Canada, Toronto, 1986).

8 *Guidelines for Interfaith Dialogue* (Office of Ecumenical and Interfaith Relations, Presbyterian Church [USA]: Louisville, KY, 1969).

9 Siddiqui, *Christian–Muslim Dialogue in the 20th Century*, p. 30.

10 Kate Zebiri, *Muslims and Christians Face to Face* (Oxford: Oneworld, 1997), pp. 35–36.

11 *Impact International* 2/7 (25 August–7 September 1972), pp. 5–6. A Catholic observer at this consultation, Msgr Michael Fitzgerald of the Pontifical Council for Interreligious Dialogue, remarked that the atmosphere was rather tense because of lack of freedom among Muslim participants. See Michael Fitzgerald, '25 Years of Christian–Muslim Dialogue: A Personal Journey,' *Encounter* 183 (March 1992).

12 The WCC Assembly meets every seven years.

13 For an excellent study of the WCC's evolving use of the terms 'evangelism', 'mission', 'witness', and 'dialogue', see Eun-ah Hur, *Evolving Terminology in Interfaith Relations: Paradigm Shifts and the World Council of Churches* (MTh dissertation, London Bible College, Brunel University, 2000).

14 By 2002, the proportion of the WCC annual budget allocated to mission was only 7%, of which a significant amount was devoted to dialogue activities. The largest allocations were directed to long-term development assistance (26%), ecumenical formation (15%) and advocacy (13%). <http://www.wcc-coe.org/wcc/who/index-e.html#3>, accessed 30 October 2003. See Appendix 2.

15 Note that such a logic-driven approach to the choice of religion ignores traditional Christian belief in the supreme work of the Spirit.

16 Cragg is undoubtedly one of the leading Christian Islamicists of the twentieth century. He has written over forty books on subjects relating to Christian–Muslim relations. For a list of his principal publications, as well as a tribute to his life's contribution, see David Thomas and Clare Amos (eds.), *A Faithful Presence: Essays for Kenneth Cragg* (London: Melisende, 2003).

17 Kenneth Cragg, *Sandals at the Mosque: Christian Presence amid Islam* (London: SCM, 1959), pp. 8–10.

18 Ibid.

19 Kenneth Cragg, *The Call of the Minaret* (Oxford: Oxford University Press, 1956).

20 Kenneth Cragg, *Common Prayer* (Oxford: Oneworld, 1999).

21 *Charles: The Private Man, The Public Role,* Central Television, UK, 1994.

22 'Keynote speech – Jonathan Dimbleby', <http://www.shef.ac.uk/city/sidf/keynote.html>, accessed December 2003.

23 Rachel Sylvester, 'Multi-faith Coronation for Charles', *The Daily Telegraph,* 10 April 2000.

24 Charles, Prince of Wales, 'Islam and the West', Sheldonian Theatre, Oxford, 27 October 1993.

25 *The Daily Telegraph,* 10 May 1997.

26 Charles, Prince of Wales, 'A Sense of the Sacred: Building Bridges Between Islam and the West', the Wilton Park Seminar, Wilton Park, West Sussex, 13 December 1996, <http://www.princeofwales.gov.uk/speeches/religion_13121996.html>. See also *Q-News* 246–247 (13–26 December 1996), pp. 12–13, and <http://www.193.36.68.132/speeches/religion_13121996.html>.

27 Catherine Bennett, 'What on Earth is Prince Charles Up To?', *The Guardian,* 18 December 1996.

28 Patrick Sookhdeo, 'Prince Charles is Wrong: Islam Does Menace the West', *The Daily Telegraph,* 19 December 1996.

29 Charles, Prince of Wales, 'An Example to all Faiths', East London Mosque, 23 November 2001, <http://www.princeofwales.gov.uk/speeches/religion_23112001.html>.

30 'A speech by His Royal Highness The Prince of Wales during his visit to The Islamic Foundation, Markfield', Leicestershire, 24 January 2003, <http://www.princeofwales.gov.uk/speeches/multiracial_24012003.htm>.

31 For a detailed review of this work, see Peter G. Riddell, 'In Search of Muhammad: A Review Essay', *Australian Religion Studies Review* 12/2 (Spring 1999), pp. 155–160.

32 Clinton Bennett, *In Search of Muhammad* (London and New York: Cassell, 1998), p. 7.

33 Ibid., p. 11.

34 Ibid., p. 71.

35 Ibid., p. 229.

36 Ibid., p. 242.

37 Ibid., p. 242.

38 E. C. Dewick, *The Gospel and Other Faiths* (London and Edinburgh: Canterbury Press, 1948), p. 122.

39 Ian Randall, *Educating Evangelicalism: The Origins, Development and Impact of London Bible College* (Carlisle: Paternoster, 2000), pp. 154–155.

40 John Stott, *Christian Mission in the Modern World* (Downers Grove, IL: IVP, 1975), p. 61.

41 Randall, *Educating Evangelicalism,* pp. 95, 135.

42 A similar trend among trainees for Anglican ordination was witnessed in Australia in the same period. *The Australian,* 1 May 2000, p. 4.

43 Martin Goldsmith and C. Wright, Anglican Evangelical Assembly Paper, 1992, quoted in Anne Cooper and Elsie Maxwell, *Ishmael My Brother,* 3rd edn (London: Monarch, 2003), p. 28.

44 Barns, Ian, 'Christianity in a Pluralist Society: A Dialogue with Lesslie Newbigin', *St Mark's Review* 158 (Winter 1994), pp. 27–37.

45 Lesslie Newbigin, *The Gospel in a Pluralist Society* (London: SPCK, 1989), pp. 182ff.

46 Lesslie Newbigin, Lamin Sanneh and Jenny Taylor, *Faith and Power: Christianity and Islam in 'Secular' Britain* (London: SPCK, 1998), p. 162.

47 For another work by Chapman that addresses hands-on questions concerned with Christian–Muslim relations, see his *Cross and Crescent* (Leicester: IVP, 1995).

48 Colin Chapman, *Islam and the West: Conflict, Co-Existence or Conversion?* (Carlisle: Paternoster, 1998), p. 7.

49 For a spirited plea for a Christian apology along the lines of the Reconciliation Walk organized by the evangelical group Youth With A Mission (YWAM), see

Colin Chapman, 'Living Through the 900th Anniversary of the First Crusade: To Apologise or not to Apologise?' *Faith to Faith Newsletter* 1 (November 1998), pp. 1–3.

50 Chapman, *Islam and the West*, pp. 49–50.

51 Ibid., p. 59.

52 For excerpts of this text in English, see Andrew Rippin and Jan Knappert (eds.), *Textual Sources for the Study of Islam* (Chicago, IL: University of Chicago Press, 1986), pp. 192–197. The full text is available online at <http://www.alhewar.comISLAMDECL.html>.

53 For the full English text of this declaration, see Masykuri Abdillah, *Responses of Indonesian Muslim Intellectuals to the Concept of Democracy (1966–1993)* (Hamburg: Abera Verlag Meyer & Co., 1997), pp. 269–273.

54 Chapman, *Islam and the West*, pp.123–124.

55 Chapman, 'Educating and Training Christians to Understand and Relate to Muslims', *Transformation* 17.1 (January–March 2000), p. 15.

56 Chapman, *Islam and the West*, p. 141.

57 Michael Nazir-Ali, *Mission and Dialogue: Proclaiming the Gospel Afresh in Every Age* (London: SPCK, 1995).

58 Cf. Bill Musk, *The Unseen Face of Islam* (Eastbourne: MARC, 1989).

59 Cf. Vivienne Stacey, *Mission Ventured: Dynamic Stories Across a Challenging World* (Leicester: IVP, 2001).

60 Patrick Sookhdeo, *A People Betrayed* (Fearn, Ross-shire: Christian Focus Publications, 2002).

61 Cf. Caroline Cox and John Marks, *The 'West', Islam and Islamism* (London: Civitas, 2003).

62 The WEA changed its name from the World Evangelical Fellowship in 2002.

63 It indirectly speaks for evangelicals throughout the world, who numbered in total around 700 million in late 2003, according to Joel Edwards, 'You Don't Have to Be a Mad Extremist to Oppose Geoffrey John', <http://www.telegraph.co.uk>, 11 July 2003.

64 'WEF Missions Commission Ministry Goals', <http://www.worldevangelical.org/default.html>, accessed March 2000.

65 'The World Evangelical Alliance Religious Liberty Commission', <http://www.worldevangelical.org/rlc.html>, accessed April 2004.

66 ' WEA RLC Scriptural Justification', <http://www.worldevangelical.org/rlcscripture.html>, accessed April 2004.

67 *The Geneva Report 2001: A Perspective on Global Religious Freedom: Challenges Facing the Christian Community*, <http://worldevangelical.org/rlc_genevareport01.htm>, accessed June 2004.

68 Ibid.

69 Ibid.

70 Lausanne movement website, <http://www.gospelcom.net/lcwe/whatis.htm>, accessed March 2000.

71 'The Manila Manifesto', <http://www.gospelcom.net/lcwe/statements/manila.html>, accessed March 200.

72 For a comprehensive record of Vatican II discussion, see Walter M. Abbott, *The Documents of Vatican II* (London and Dublin: Geoffrey Chapman, 1966).

73 *Ecclesiam suam*, encyclical of Pope Paul VI on the church, 6 August 1964, <http://www.vatican.va/holy_father/paul_vi/encyclicals/documents/ hf_p-vi_enc_06081964_ecclesiam_en.html>, accessed April 2004.

74 'Reporters Unwelcome at Vatican II Meeting', *The Tablet*, 11 March 2000.

75 Cited in Anthony O'Mahony, 'Christians and Muslim–Christian Relations: Theological Reflections', in Anthony O'Mahony and Ataullah Siddiqui (eds.), *Christians and Muslims in the Commonwealth* (London: Altajir World of Islam Trust, 2001), p. 109.

76 Michael Fitzgerald, 'From Heresy to Religion', *Priests & People* (January 2004), p. 6.
77 Second Vatican Council, declaration on religious freedom, *Dignitas humanae*, 7 December 1965, cited in *Interfaith Dialogue: The Teaching of the Catholic Church* (Committee for Other Faiths, Catholic Bishops' Conference of England and Wales, 2002), pp. 8–9.
78 Cf. Jacques Jomier, *How to Understand Islam* (London: SCM, 1989).
79 Cf. Robert Caspar, *Pour un regard chrétien sur l'Islam* (Paris: Centurion, 1990).
80 Cf. Henri Sanson, *Dialogue intérieur avec l'Islam* (Paris: Centurion, 1990).
81 O'Mahony, 'Christians and Muslim-Christian Relations', p. 110.
82 Geffré, 'Christian Uniqueness and Dialogue', *Focus* 2 (1993), pp. 101–102.
83 W. R. Burrows, *Redemption and Dialogue* (Maryknoll, NY: Orbis, 1993).
84 Fitzgerald, 'From Heresy to Religion', p. 4.
85 'Reporters Unwelcome at Vatican II Meeting'.
86 Pope John Paul II, *Crossing the Threshold of Hope* (London: Jonathan Cape, 1993), p. 93.
87 Cited in Burrows, *Redemption and Dialogue*.
88 Pontifical Council for Interreligious Dialogue and Congregation for the Evangelisation of Peoples, *Dialogue and Proclamation*, 19 May 1991, cited in *Interfaith Dialogue*, p. 15.
89 'Pope Prays for Forgiveness for Sins of Catholic Church', *CNN.com*, 12 March 2000.
90 'Pope Sorry for Sins of History', *The Australian Online*, 13 March 2000.
91 Cardinal Francis Arinze, 'Christianity and the Realities of Life Today', in Anthony O'Mahony and Michael Kirwan (eds.), *World Christianity: Politics, Theology, Dialogues* (London: Melisende, 2004), p. 19.
92 Cardinal Francis Arinze, *Religions for Peace: A Call for Solidarity to the Religions of the World* (London: Darton, Longman & Todd, 2002), p. 125.
93 Ibid., p. 126.
94 Quoted in Ira Rifkin, 'Vatican Official: Christian–Muslim Relations Must Be Reciprocal', *Religious News Service*, June 1997.
95 Quoted in ibid.
96 *Reuters*, Vatican City, 13 October 1999.
97 *CMI Newsletter*, quoting *Australian Islamic Review*, November 1999.
98 'Fr. Samir Says Islamic 'Re-conquest' is Possible Thanks to Europe's Loss of Identity', *AsiaNews.it*, 29 April 2004.

5. Methods of interfaith engagement

1 Robert Traer, 'Freedom of Religion or Belief: Hopes and Realities', The International Association for Religious Freedom, briefing for the Department of Public Information, 5 November 1998, <http:// iarfreligiousfreedom.net>, accessed April 2000. For an evangelical statement of opposition to such a practice of proselytism, see the Lausanne movement's report on the 1980 Thailand consultation at <http.www.gospelcom.net/lcwe/LOP/lop13.htm>.
2 'Interreligious Relations: List of Major Meetings: 1969–1998',<http:// www.wcc-coe.org/wcc/what/interreligious/meetings.html>, accessed March 2000.
3 For a report on this conference and the early 1993 conference in Vienna, see Jan Slomp, '"One World for All": The Vienna Dialogue Process', *Journal of Muslim Minority Affairs* 18/1 (1998), pp. 181–185.
4 Tarek Mitri, 'Christian–Muslim Relations', *Current Dialogue* 31 (December 1997), pp. 42–43.
5 For a discussion of WCC thinking and activity in these areas, see 'Interreligious Dialogue is Not an Ambulance: A Discussion on Religious Tolerance, Conflict and Peace-building', press feature, World Council of Churches, 23 May 2001.
6 Don M. McCurry (ed.), *The Gospel and Islam: A 1978 Compendium* (Monrovia, CA: Missions Advanced Research and Communication Center, 1979).

7 <http://www.gospelcom.net/lcwe/LOP/lop04.htm>.

8 <http://www.gospelcom.net/lcwe/LOP/lop13.htm>.

9 Cf. Eric J. Sharpe, 'Dialogue of Religions', in Mircea Eliade (ed.), *The Encyclopedia of Religion* 4 (New York: Macmillan, 1987), p. 347.

10 'Christian Witness to Muslims' Lausanne Occasional Paper no. 13 (Wheaton, IL: Lausanne Committee for World Evangelization, 1980, p. 23.

11 Helen Saxbee, 'Islam Talks to Get Priority', *Church Times*, 23 May 1997.

12 'Religious Leaders Unite for Bishop's Funeral', *ArabicNews.Com*, 23 October 1997.

13 'Religious Dialogue between Grand Imam and Vatican', *ArabicNews.Com*, 5 November 1997.

14 'Tantawi, Shenuda take Part in a Religious Dialogue at Vatican', *ArabicNews.Com*, 14 June 1999.

15 'Anglican Communion / Al Azhar Meeting Postponed', Anglican Communion News Service (ACNS) 3579, 17 September 2003.

16 'Al-Azhar Academy Approves Islamic–Jewish Meeting', *ArabicNews.Com*, 31 December 1997.

17 'Lawsuit Filed against Sheikh of Al Azhar and Egyptian Mufti', *ArabicNews.Com*, 21 January 1998.

18 *The Inter Faith Network for the UK 1999–2000 Annual Review* (London), pp. 17–25.

19 See Appendix 4 below.

20 Anthony O'Mahony and Ataullah Siddiqui (eds.), *Christians and Muslims in the Commonwealth* (London: Altajir World of Islam Trust, 2001).

21 Cf. *Discourse* 1 (August 2000).

22 Andrew Wingate, *Encounters in the Spirit: Muslim–Christian Meetings in Birmingham* (Geneva: WCC, 1988), p. 3.

23 Ibid., pp. 77ff.

24 'Ibn Mughaffal reported: The Messenger of Allah (may peace be upon him) ordered killing of the dogs, and then said: What about them, i.e. about other dogs? and then granted concession (to keep) the dog for hunting and the dog for (the security) of the herd, and said: When the dog licks the utensil, wash it seven times, and rub it with earth the eighth time.' See Abdul Hamid Siddiqi (trans.), *Sahih Muslim* 1/2 (Lahore: Sh. Muhammad Ashraf Publishers, reprinted 1996), no. 551.

25 Wingate, *Encounters in the Spirit*, pp. 20–22.

26 Ibid., p. 60.

27 Anne Davison, 'Encounter Youth Exchange Project between England and the Holy Land for Christians, Jews and Muslims', *Current Dialogue* 32 (December 1998).

28 Quoted in *The Jewish Chronicle*, 12 February 1999.

29 The website for this village is found at <http://nswas.com>.

30 'Youth Exchange Project', *British Muslims Monthly Survey* 7/2 (February 1999), pp. 10–11.

31 Ida Glaser, 'Faith and Society in the UK', *Transformation* 17/1 (January–March 2000), pp. 26–29.

32 *Faith to Faith Newsletter* 1 (November 1998), p. 1.

33 *Faith to Faith Newsletter* 2 (April 1999), p. 4.

34 Peter G. Riddell, 'Christians and Muslims are "Seeking the Common Good" ', *Christian Herald*, 23 October 1999, p. 3.

35 *CMI Newsletter* 1/2 (December 1997).

36 'Wa-Ghana: An Example of Christian–Muslim Dialogue in Ghana', *Pro Dialogo* 93/3 (1996), pp. 379–380.

37 Ibid.

38 'The Bible's Witness', the University of Sheffield Islamic Circle, <http://www.shef.ac.uk/~ics/quran/bible/biblewit.htm>, accessed 20 March 2004.

39 M. M. Rahmatullah Khairanvi, *Izhar-ul-Haq (Truth Revealed): Contradictions and Errors in the Biblical Text*, 2nd edn (Jeddah: World of Knowledge for Publishing

and Distribution, 1992), p. 52. This work, still widely distributed by Muslim polemicists, was originally produced in response to C. G. Pfander, *The Mizan-ul-Haqq (Balance of Truth)*, ed. W. St Clair-Tisdall (Villach: Light of Life, 1986).

40 Maurice Bucaille, *The Bible, The Qur'an and Science* (Indianapolis, IN: American Trust Publications, 1978), p. 109.

41 Anthony O'Mahony, 'Islam Face-à-Face Christianity', *The Way Supplement 104* (November 2002), p. 84.

42 Cf. Pfander, *The Mizan-ul-Haqq*. For a critique of Pfander's approach, see Colin Chapman, *Cross and Crescent* (Leicester: IVP, 1995), pp. 101–104.

43 Cf. 'Who is the True Jesus?', <http://www.faithandscience.org/ past_events.html>, accessed 30 October 2003.

44 Jay Smith, 'Courage in our Convictions: Debating Muslims: New Life for an Old Method?' *Evangelical Missions Quarterly* 31/1 (January 1998), p. 29.

45 Jay Smith, 'Is it Time to Confront?', *LBC Centre for Islamic Studies Newsletter* 12 (Winter 2003), p. 14.

46 See the critique from Christian writers in Smith, 'Courage in our Convictions'.

47 See Appendix 3 for the text of this agreement.

48 Michael Ipgrave (ed.), *The Road Ahead: A Christian–Muslim Dialogue* (London: Church House Publishing, 2002), p. 10.

49 Ibid., p. 21.

50 Ibid., p. 52.

51 Ibid., pp. 84–85.

52 Ibid., p. 100.

53 For the published proceedings of this seminar, cf. Michael Ipgrave (ed.), *Scriptures in Dialogue: Christians and Muslims Studying the Bible and the Qur'an Together* (London: Church House Publishing, 2004).

54 'Archbishop's Statement on Christian–Muslim Seminar', 10 April 2003, <http://www.archbishopofcanterbury.org/releases/030410.html>.

55 Pope John Paul II, message for World Day for Peace 2002, 8 December 2001, cited in *Interfaith Dialogue: The Teaching of the Catholic Church* (Committee for Other Faiths, Catholic Bishops' Conference of England and Wales, 2002), p. 29.

56 Bruce Johnston and P. J. Bonthrone, 'Pope Unites Religious Leaders in Pilgrimage for Peace', *The Daily Telegraph*, 25 January 2002.

57 Proceedings of the conference were published as Anthony O'Mahony, Wulstan Peterburs and Mohammad Ali Shomali (eds.), *A Catholic–Shi'a Dialogue: Studies in Theology and Spirituality* (London: Melisende, 2004).

58 Reproduced below as Appendix 4.

59 'Clergy, Academics, Take Bold Step in Interfaith Relations', media statement, Jewish–Christian–Muslim Conference of Australia, 21 April 2004.

6. Issues in Christian–Muslim relations today

1 *Al-Hayat*, 23 October 2001, cited in *Religious News Service from the Arab World*, 24–30 October 2001.

2 'Muslims Have the Right to Attack America', *The Observer*, 11 November 2001.

3 On the homogeneous-unit church, see Peter Cotterell, *Mission and Meaningless: The Good News in a World of Suffering and Disorder* (London: SPCK, 1990), pp. 168ff.

4 Primarily Christians and Jews.

5 *The Holy Qur'an* (1768), n. 6227.

6 'Two Sides of a Different Coin? Anthony McRoy talks to Sheikh Omar Bakri Muhammad and Shagufta Yaqub', *Third Way*, March 2003, p. 21.

7 Clinton Bennett, *In Search of Muhammad* (London and New York: Cassell, 1998), p. 236.

8 Several of the national Orthodox churches are members of the WCC, so our earlier discussion of that body also covers Orthodoxy to some extent.

9   Basil Cousins, 'The Russian Orthodox Church, Tartar Christians and Islam', in
    Anthony O'Mahony (ed.), *Eastern Christianity: Studies in Modern History, Religion
    and Politics* (London: Melisende, 2004), p. 339. See also Cousins, 'Russian
    Orthodoxy: Contemporary Challenges in Society, Interreligious Encounters and
    Mission', in Anthony O'Mahony and Michael Kirwan (eds.), *World Christianity:
    Politics, Theology, Dialogues* (London: Melisende, 2004), pp. 308–346.

10 <http://www.russian-orthodox-church.org.ru/ne101251.htm>, accessed 3 November
    2003.

11 Anastasios Yannoulatos, 'Byzantine and Contemporary Greek Orthodox
    Approaches to Islam', *Journal of Ecumenical Studies* 33/4 (Fall 1996), pp. 513–520.

12 Petros VII, Greek Orthodox Patriarch of Alexandria, 'Christianity and Islam in
    Dialogue', address of His Beatitude to the 12th International Meeting 'People and
    Religion', 31 August 1998, <http://www.greece.org/ gopatalex/islam.html>, accessed
    3 November 2003.

13 Ibid.

14 The Muslim minority represents 10–15% of Bulgaria's total population of around
    8 million.

15 Imad ad-Din Zengi (1087–1146).

16 M. Shahid Alam, 'Pakistan "Recognizes" Israel', <http://www.khilafah.com/home/
    category.php?DocumentID=8225& TagID=2>, accessed 7 September 2003.

17 J. Bennet, 'A New Mideast Battle: Arafat vs. Hamas', *The New York Times*, 6
    December 2001.

18 Press release, 7 November 2001, <http://www.almuhajiroun.com>.

19 For a detailed discussion of the origins of anti-western feeling in the Muslim
    world, see Peter G. Riddell and Peter Cotterell, *Islam in Conflict: Past, Present and
    Future* (Leicester: IVP, 2003), chapter 10.

20 'EU Embarrassed as Poll Labels Israel World's Biggest Threat', AFP, 3 November,
    2003, <http://story.news.yahoo.com/ news?tmpl=story&u=/afp/20031103/
    wl_mideast_afp/eu_poll_israel_031103172948>.

21 UN Security Council Resolution 1373 (2001), <http://www.un.org/News/Press/
    docs/2001/sc7158.doc.htm>, accessed April 2003.

22 '"Negotiate with Bin Laden": Mowlam', *The Guardian*, 8 April 2004.

23 Matthew 5:39. See also Luke 6:29.

24 Matthew 21:12. See also Mark 11:15 and John 2:15. Admittedly, these passages
    record the use of force against objects and animals, not against people. But it
    could be argued that the biblical sanctioning of force, even under restricted
    conditions, opens up the possibility of its use under broader circumstances, on
    condition that the pursuit of justice be the overriding motivation.

25 An earlier version of the discussion in this section appeared as 'Why Not All
    Muslims Support the Radicals', *Church Times*, 3 January 2003, p. 11.

26 Hedieh Mirahmadi, 'Jihadi Tomb Raiders', *National Review Online*, 13 December
    2002.

27 For an analysis of such comments, see Riddell and Cotterell, *Islam in Conflict*,
    chapter 10.

28 See also Vinoth Ramachandra, *Faiths in Conflict? Christian Integrity in a
    Multicultural World* (Leicester: IVP, 1999), pp. 30–34.

29 Cf. the work of the Barnabas Fund, <http://www.barnabasfund.org>, Christian
    Solidarity Worldwide, <http://www.csw.org.uk>, and Middle East Concern,
    <http://www.idop.org/mec.html>.

30 Kate Zebiri, *Muslims and Christians Face to Face* (Oxford: Oneworld, 1997), p. 29.

31 Quoted in *Egypt's Converts* (Loughborough: Middle East Concern, 1995), p. 3.

32 Bukhari 9/83, no. 17. Cf. Muhammad Muhsin Khan (trans.), *The Translation of the
    Meanings of Sahih Al-Bukhari* 9 (Medina: Dar Ahya us-Sunnah al Nabawiya, 1971),
    pp. 10–11.

33 <http://www.iiu.edu.my/deed/lawbase/risalah_maliki/, 37.19 Crimes Against

Islam. Cf. Ibn Abi Zayd al-Qayrawani, 'Abd Allah ibn 'Abd al-Rahman, *Al-Risala* (London: Ta-Ha, 1999)

34 <http://www.iiu.edu.my/deed/lawbase/risalah_maliki>, 32.11 Effects of Change of Religion.

35 *Pakistan: Use and Abuse of the Blasphemy Laws*, ASA 33/08/94 (London: Amnesty International, 1994).

36 Hassan Abdullah Al-Turabi, 'Opinion on Apostasy Stirs a Heated Debate in Islamic Juristic Circles', *The Diplomat* 2 (Muharram 1417 / June 1996), p. 39.

37 Anil Netto, 'Malaysia: PAS Winning Few Hearts So Far', *Asia Times Online*, 6 March 2004.

38 *Reciprocity and Beyond: A Muslim Response to the European Churches' Document on Islam* (Leicester: Islamic Foundation, 1997), pp. 21–23.

39 Michael Ipgrave (ed.), *The Road Ahead: A Christian–Muslim Dialogue* (London: Church House Publishing, 2002), p. 107.

40 Ibid.

41 *Reciprocity and Beyond*, pp. 4–5. The tone of this statement is reiterated in Ataullah Siddiqui, 'Issues in Co-existence and Dialogue: Muslims and Christians in Britain', in Jacques Waardenburg, *Muslim–Christian Perceptions of Dialogue Today* (Leuven: Peeters, 2000), pp. 194–195.

42 Cardinal Francis Arinze, *Religions for Peace: A Call for Solidarity to the Religions of the World* (London: Darton, Longman & Todd, 2002), p. 134.

43 Jonathan Petre, 'Carey's Scathing Assault on Islam', <http://smh.com.au>, 27 March 2004.

44 Yannoulatos, 'Byzantine and Contemporary Greek Orthodox Approaches to Islam', pp. 525.

45 Samuel P. Huntington, *The Clash of Civilizations and the Remaking of World Order* (New York: Simon & Schuster, 1996).

46 Giles Fraser, 'Evangelicals Have Become This Century's Witch Burners', *The Guardian*, 14 July 2003.

47 Such guidelines exist in many areas of Britain. A complaint often heard from Christians, however, is that minority immigrant communities find it far easier to gain approval for building projects than do white majority communities, because local councils are reluctant to attract accusations of racism by refusing applications from the minority groups.

48 Sophie Arie, 'Muslim Wins Italian Court Ban on Crucifixes in Classroom', *The Guardian*, 27 October 27 2003.

49 'Storm Over Italy Crucifix Ruling', *BBC News Online*, 26 October 2003.

50 <http://www.bbc.co.uk/religion>, accessed 3 November 2003. The religions allocated space are Baha'i, Buddhism, Christianity, Hinduism, Islam, Judaism, Mormonism, Paganism, Sikhism; space is also allocated to atheism.

51 Howarth, '9/11: A Call to Integrity in Mission , *CMS Annual Sermon 2002* (London: Church Mission Society, 2002), p. 5.

52 David Pawson, *The Challenge of Islam to Christians* (London: Hodder & Stoughton, 2003).

53 Peter Hitchens, 'Will Britain Convert to Islam?', *The Mail on Sunday*, 2 November 2003, <http://www.femail.com/pages/standard/article.html?in_page_id=2& in_article_id=201325>, accessed 23 November 2003.

54 Dani Garavelli, 'The Attraction of the Veil', *The Times*, 10 March 2002.

55 Himself a convert to Islam.

56 Yahya Birt, 'Lies! Damn Lies! Statistics and Conversions', *Q-News*, October 2003, p. 20.

57 Ibid.

58 Ibid.

59 For a detailed discussion of this issue, see Myles Harris, *Tomorrow is Another Country* (London: Civitas, 2003).

60   Howarth, '9/11: A Call to Integrity in Mission', p. 5.
61   Arinze, *Religions for Peace*, p. 125.
62   Ataullah Siddiqui, 'The Presence of "Secular" in Christian–Muslim Relations: Reflections on the Da'wah, "Mission" and "Dialogue"', in Anthony O'Mahony and Ataullah Siddiqui (eds.), *Christians and Muslims in the Commonwealth* (London: Altajir World of Islam Trust, 2001), p. 88.
63   Douglas Pratt, 'Christian–Muslim Encounter: From Diatribe to Dialogue',' *Australian Religion Studies Review* 7/1 (Autumn 1994), p. 13.
64   Mohamed Talbi, 'Islamo–Christian Encounter Today: Some Principles', *MECC Perspectives* 4/5 (July–August 1985), p. 10.
65   Claude Geffré, 'Christian Uniqueness and Dialogue', *Focus* 2 (1993), pp. 101–113; cf. Anthony O'Mahony, 'Christians and Muslim–Christian Relations: Theological Reflections', in O'Mahony and Siddiqui (eds.), *Christians and Muslims in the Commonwealth*, p. 97.
66   Michael Barnes, *Religions in Conversation* (London: SPCK, 1989), p. 4.
67   Leonard Swidler, 'Interreligious and Interideological Dialogue: The Matrix for All Systematic Reflection Today', in *Toward a Universal Theology of Religion* (Maryknoll, NY: Orbis, 1987), pp. 14–16.
68   Personal communication, 26 March 2003.
69   Pope John Paul II, apostolic letter on preparation for the jubilee year 2000, *Tertio millennio adveniente*, 10 November 1994, cited in *Interfaith Dialogue: The Teaching of the Catholic Church* (Committee for Other Faiths, Catholic Bishops' Conference of England and Wales, 2000), p. 25.
70   In Ipgrave (ed.), *The Road Ahead*, p. 15.
71   Ibid., p. 120.
72   Mark O'Keefe, 'Has The United States Become Judeo-Christian-Islamic?' *Newhouse News Service*, 14 February 2003, <http://www.newhouse.com/archive/okeefe051503.html>.
73   Ibid.
74   <http://www.aqsa.org.uk/bookreviews/islamism.html>, accessed 4 November 2003.
75   Caroline Cox and John Marks, *The 'West', Islam and Islamism* (London: Civitas, 2003).
76   Scot had fled from Pakistan when accused of blasphemy, a criminal offence under Pakistan legal codes.
77   Piers Akerman, 'When Legal Absurdity is Watched World-wide', *The Daily Telegraph*, 4 March 2004.
78   Complaint no. A392/2002, Victorian Civil and Administrative Tribunal, 13 March 2003.
79   Akerman, 'When Legal Absurdity is Watched World-wide'.
80   Amir Butler, 'Speak Up, I Won't Be Offended', *A True Word*, 11 July 2003, <http://www.atrueword.com/index.php/article/ articleview/61/1/4>.
81   Ibid.
82   Ipgrave (ed.), *The Road Ahead*, pp. 26–37.
83   David A. Kerr, 'Christian–Muslim Relations: Lessons from History', in Ipgrave (ed.), *The Road Ahead*, pp. 25.
84   Of course, historians face great challenges in pursuing these goals, and can never report and interpret the totality of past events. See Karl Popper, *The Open Society and its Enemies* 2: *The High Tide of Prophecy: Hegel, Marx and the Aftermath*, 4th edn (London: Routledge & Kegan Paul, 1962), chapter 13.
85   'Transcript of Osama bin Laden videotape', <http://www.cnn.com/2001/US/12/13/tape.transcript>.
86   See Colin Chapman, 'Going Soft on Islam?', *Vox Evangelica* 19 (1989), pp. 15–18.
87   2 Peter 1:5–7.
88   This does not mean, however, that Christians must believe that other faiths necessarily satisfy their quest.

89 Mike O'Brien, 'The Threat of the Modern Kharijites', speech at the conference 'Militant Islam in Asia: The Challenges', Royal United Service Institute for Defence Studies, London, 21 November 2002.

90 In fact, many scholars argue that the opposite is the case in the Islamic scriptures, with the earlier Meccan chapters lending themselves to a message of peace and the later Medinan chapters developing the notion of military *jihad*. See Kenneth Cragg, *The Call of the Minaret* (Oxford: Oxford University Press, 1956), pp. 72ff.

91 For a more detailed discussion of this issue, see Riddell and Cotterell, *Islam in Conflict*, pp. 205ff.

92 'Islam and the Textbooks', <http://www.historytextbooks.org/islam.htm>, accessed April 2003.

93 Michelle Dardashti, 'Survey: Saudi Arabian Textbooks Filled with Hatred of West, Jews', <http://www.jta.org/page_view_story.asp?intarticleid=12426& intcategoryid=3>, accessed April 2004.

94 Peter Hicks, *Truth: Could it Be True?* (Carlisle: Solway, 1996), p. 107.

95 Bruce Kaye, 'Many Aspects of Pluralism', *St Mark's Review* 171 (Spring 1997), p. 5.

96 J. R. Middleton and B. J. Walsh, *Truth is Stranger than it Used to Be: Biblical Faith in a Postmodern Age* (London: SPCK, 1995), p. 25.

97 Seyyed Hossein Nasr, *Knowledge and the Sacred* (New York: Crossroad, 1981), p. 66.

98 Michael Green, *The Truth of God Incarnate* (London: Hodder & Stoughton, 1977), p. 9.

99 *The Sunday Times,* 30 November 1997.

100 Hicks, *Truth: Could it Be True?* pp. 91–93.

101 Nasr, *Knowledge and the Sacred*, p. 68.

102 Peter Cotterell, *Mission and Meaningless: The Good News in a World of Suffering and Disorder* (London: SPCK, 1990), p. 34.

103 Ibid., p. 33.

104 Harold A. Netland, *Dissonant Voices: Religious Pluralism and the Question of Truth* (Leicester: Apollos, 1991), p. 112.

105 Cotterell, *Mission and Meaningless*, p. 35.

106 Seyyed Hossein Nasr, *Islamic Life and Thought Islamic Life and Thought* (London: Allen & Unwin, 1981), p. 209.

107 Talbi, 'Islamo–Christian Encounter Today', p. 9.

Conclusion

1 It should be noted that religious pluralism is not simply a recent development, but has deep roots. The current positive response to it in the West is, however, contextually driven to a large degree. Cf. Michael Barnes, *Religions in Conversation* (London: SPCK, 1989), p. 12.

2 That being Christianity, in my view. The mutually exclusive claims about the roles of Jesus Christ and Muhammad in Christianity and Islam respectively entail that one faith is wrong about certain of its fundamental tenets. Hence, to suggest that both faiths contained an equal measure of truth would be simplistic.

3 Anthony O'Mahony, 'Christianity, Interreligious Dialogue and Muslim–Christian Relations', in Anthony O'Mahony and Michael Kirwan (eds.), *World Christianity: Politics, Theology, Dialogues* (London: Melisende, 2004), p. 78.

4 Christopher Bull, 'Pluralism', unpublished manuscript.

5 See also Vinoth Ramachandra, *Faiths in Conflict? Christian Integrity in a Multicultural World* (Leicester: IVP, 1999), pp. 21–22.

6 'True Submission: Zaki Badawi Talks to Peter Riddell', interview, *Third Way*, May 1996, p. 16.

7 *Mission, Dialogue and Inter Religious Encounter: A Consultative Document* (London: The Inter Faith Network for the UK, 1993), p. 9.

8 Ataullah Siddiqui, 'Issues in Co-existence and Dialogue: Muslims and Christians in Britain', in Jacques Waardenburg, *Muslim–Christian Perceptions of Dialogue Today* (Leuven: Peeters, 2000), p. 192.
9 But neither should that be ruled out. Here Islamic doctrine on apostasy represents a challenge that cries out for Muslim reformist engagement.
10 'The silent dialogue of prayer' is also suggested; see Claude Geffré, 'Christian Uniqueness and Dialogue', *Focus* 2 (1993), p. 111.

Appendix 3: 'An Agreement for Dialogue . . . '
1 Available from the Anglican Network for Interfaith Concerns, <http://www.anglicannifcon.org/Dialogue.htm>, accessed 22 June 2004. Used by permission.

SELECT BIBLIOGRAPHY

Newspaper articles cited in the text are not listed here; details are given in the Notes.

Books, journal articles and public lectures

A Very Light Sleeper (London: Runnymede Trust, 1994)

Abas, Datuk Ishak Iman, *Oil as Basic Economic Strength of the Ummah: Its Prudent Management for the Benefit of the Ummah*, paper presented at the World Conference of Islamic Scholars, Putrajaya, 10–12 July 2003

Abbott, Walter M., *The Documents of Vatican II* (London and Dublin: Geoffrey Chapman, 1966)

Abdillah, Masykuri, *Responses of Indonesian Muslim Intellectuals to the Concept of Democracy (1966–1993)* (Hamburg: Abera Verlag Meyer & Co., 1997)

Ahmed, Ishtiaq, *State, Nation and Ethnicity in Contemporary South Asia* (London: Pinter, 1998)

— *The Concept of an Islamic State: An Analysis of the Ideological Controversy in Pakistan* (London: Pinter, 1987)

Ali, Abdullah Yusuf, *The Meaning of the Holy Qur'an*, new edition (Beltsville, MD: Amana Publications, 1989)

Alibhai-Brown, Yasmin, 'Faith Communities in Public Life', lecture for the Inner Cities Religious Council, Manchester University, 26 April 2001

Anderson, J. N. D., *Christianity and World Religions: The Challenge of Pluralism* (Leicester: IVP, 1984)

— 'Islam', in H. A. Evan Hopkins (ed.), *The Inadequacy of Non-Christian Religion* (London: Inter-Varsity Fellowship, 1944), pp. 7–15

— *Islam in the Modern World: A Christian Perspective* (Leicester: Apollos, 1990)

Anti-Muslim Discrimination and Hostility in the United Kingdom, 2000 (Islamic Human Rights Commission, 2000)

Arinze, Cardinal Francis, 'Christianity and the Realities of Life Today', in Anthony O'Mahony and Michael Kirwan (eds.), *World Christianity: Politics, Theology, Dialogues* (London: Melisende, 2004), pp. 19–26

— *Religions for Peace: A Call for Solidarity to the Religions of the World* (London: Darton, Longman & Todd, 2002)

Ayoub, Mahmoud, 'Towards an Islamic Christology', *The Muslim World* 70 (1980), pp. 91–121

Barnes, Michael, *Religions in Conversation* (London: SPCK, 1989)

Barns, Ian, 'Christianity in a Pluralist Society: A Dialogue with Lesslie Newbigin', *St Mark's Review* 158 (Winter 1994), pp. 27–37

Basetti-Sani, Giulio, *The Koran in the Light of Christ* (Chicago, IL: Franciscan Herald Press, 1977)

Bell, Richard, *The Origin of Islam in Its Christian Environment* (London: Frank Cass, 1926, reprinted 1968)

Bennett, Clinton, *In Search of Muhammad* (London and New York: Cassell, 1998)

Birt, Jonathan, and Lewis, Philip, 'The Pattern of Islamic Reform in Britain: The Deobandis between Intra-Muslim Sectarianism and Engagement with Wider Society', in Martin van Bruinessen and Stefano Allievi (eds.), *Producing Islamic Knowledge: Transmission and Dissemination in Western Europe* (London: Routledge, forthcoming)

Borhan, Joni T., 'Islamic Banking in Malaysia: Past, Present and Future', *Studia Islamika: Indonesian Journal for Islamic Studies* 10/2 (2003), pp. 31–74

Bouma, Gary D., *Mosques and Muslim Settlement in Australia* (Canberra: AGPS, 1994)

Bradford Commission Report: The Report of an Inquiry into the Wider Implications of Public Disorders in Bradford which occurred on 9, 10, and 11 June (London: HMSO, 1995)

Brown, Stuart, *The Nearest in Affection: Towards a Christian Understanding of Islam* (Geneva: WCC, 1994)

Browne, Anthony, *Do We Need Mass Immigration?* (London: Civitas, 2002)

Bucaille, Maurice, *The Bible, The Qur'an and Science* (Indianapolis, IN: American Trust Publications, 1978)

Burrows, W. R., *Redemption and Dialogue* (Maryknoll, NY: Orbis, 1993)

Carey, George, 'The Challenges Facing Christian–Muslim Dialogue', *Islam and Christian–Muslim Relations* 7/1 (1996), pp. 95–101

Carey, William, *An Enquiry into the Obligations of Christians to use Means for the Conversion of the Heathens* (1792; London: Baptist Missionary Society, 1934)

Cash, W. W., *Christendom and Islam* (London: SCM , 1937)

Caspar, Robert, *Pour un regard chrétien sur l'Islam* (Paris: Centurion, 1990)

Chapman, Colin, *Cross and Crescent* (Leicester: IVP, 1995)

— 'Educating and Training Christians to Understand and Relate to Muslims', *Transformation* 17.1 (January–March 2000), pp. 15–17

— 'Going Soft on Islam?', *Vox Evangelica* 19 (1989), pp. 7–31

— *Islam and the West: Conflict, Co-Existence or Conversion?* (Carlisle: Paternoster, 1998)

— 'Living Through the 900th Anniversary of the First Crusade: To Apologise or not to Apologise?' *Faith to Faith Newsletter* 1 (November 1998), pp. 1–3

Charles, Prince of Wales, 'A Sense of the Sacred: Building Bridges Between Islam and the West', the Wilton Park Seminar, Wilton Park, West Sussex, 13 December 1996

— 'A speech by His Royal Highness The Prince of Wales during his visit to The Islamic Foundation, Markfield', Leicestershire, 24 January 2003

— 'An Example to all Faiths', East London Mosque, 23 November 2001

— 'Islam and the West', *Islam and Christian Muslim Relations* 5/1 (1994), pp. 67–74

'Christian Witness to Muslims', Lausanne Occasional Paper no. 13 (Wheaton, IL: Lausanne Committee for World Evangelization, 1980)

Cohn-Sherbok, Dan (ed.), *The Salman Rushdie Controversy in Interreligious Perspective* (Lampeter: Edwin Mellen, 1990)

Consultation Document, London: Commission on the Future of Multi-Ethnic Britain (Runnymede Trust, 1998)

Cooper, Anne, and Maxwell, Elsie, *Ishmael My Brother*, 3rd edn (London: Monarch, 2003)

Cotterell, F. P., 'The Bible and Other Religions', in Peter Cotterell and Peter Riddell, *Christianity and Other Religions*, Occasional Paper no. 5 (London: Centre for Islamic Studies and Muslim–Christian Relations, London School of Theology, 2004), pp. 3–9

— *Mission and Meaningless: The Good News in a World of Suffering and Disorder* (London: SPCK, 1990)

— 'The Christology of Islam', in H. H. Rowdon (ed.), *Christ the Lord* (Leicester: IVP, 1982), pp. 282–298

— 'The Gospel of Barnabas', *Vox Evangelica* 10 (1977), pp. 43–47

— *The Eleventh Commandment: Church and Mission Today* (Leicester: IVP, 1981)

Cousins, Basil, 'Russian Orthodoxy: Contemporary Challenges in Society, Interreligious Encounters and Mission', in Anthony O'Mahony and Michael Kirwan (eds.), *World Christianity: Politics, Theology, Dialogues* (London: Melisende, 2004), pp. 308–346

— 'The Russian Orthodox Church, Tartar Christians and Islam', in Anthony O'Mahony (ed.), *Eastern Christianity: Studies in Modern History, Religion and Politics* (London: Melisende, 2004), pp. 338–371

Cox, Caroline and Marks, John, *The 'West', Islam and Islamism* (London: Civitas, 2003)

Cragg, Kenneth, *Common Prayer* (Oxford: Oneworld, 1999)

— *Jesus and the Muslim* (London: Allen & Unwin, 1985)

— *Sandals at the Mosque: Christian Presence amid Islam* (London: SCM, 1959)

— *The Call of the Minaret* (Oxford: Oxford University Press, 1956)

— 'The Riddle of Man and the Silence of God: A Christian Perception of Muslim Response', *International Bulletin of Missionary Research*, October 1993, pp. 160–163

Davison, Anne, 'Encounter Youth Exchange Project between England and the Holy Land for Christians, Jews and Muslims', *Current Dialogue* 32 (December 1998)

De Chergé, Ch., 'Dialogue intermonastique et Islam', *Pro Dialogo* 93 (1996), pp. 313–317

Denffer, Ahmad von, *Christians in the Qur'an and the Sunnah*, 2nd edn (Leicester: Islamic Foundation, 1979, 1987)

Dewick, E. C., *The Gospel and Other Faiths* (London and Edinburgh: Canterbury Press, 1948)

Egypt's Converts (Loughborough: Middle East Concern, 1995)

Egypt's Endangered Christians (Washington, DC: Center for Religious Freedom, Freedom House, 1999)

Ellsworth, C. W., 'Islam and the Trinity', *Areopagus* 5.3 (Pentecost 1992), pp. 31–35

Esposito, John L., *Islam: The Straight Path*, 2nd edn (New York and Oxford: Oxford University Press, 1991)

Fitzgerald, Laurence, *The Justice God Wants: Islam and Human Rights* (Melbourne: Collins Dove, 1993)

Fitzgerald, Michael, '25 Years of Christian–Muslim Dialogue: A Personal Journey,' *Encounter* 183 (March 1992)

— 'From Heresy to Religion', *Priests & People* (January 2004), pp. 3–8

Geaves, Ron, 'Britain', in D. Westerlund and I. Svanberg (eds.), *Islam Outside the Arab World* (Richmond: Curzon, 1999), pp. 357–378

— *Sectarian Influences within Islam in Britain, with Reference to the Concepts of 'Ummah' and 'Community'* (Leeds: Department of Theology and Religious Studies, University of Leeds, 1996)

Geffré, Claude, 'Christian Uniqueness and Dialogue', *Focus* 2 (1993), pp. 101–113

Geneva Report 2001: A Perspective on Global Religious Freedom: Challenges Facing the Christian Community, a report delivered to the United Nations in Geneva, World Evangelical Fellowship

George, Ian, *General Synod Refugee Working Group: Statement for Federal and State Parliamentarians* (Anglican Church of Australia, November 2003)

Gibb, H. A. R., *Modern Trends in Islam* (Chicago, IL: University of Chicago Press, 1947)

Glaser, Ida, 'Beyond the Dialogue v Evangelism Dichotomy', *Faith to Faith Newsletter* (2 April 1999), pp. 1–2

— 'Faith and Society in the UK', *Transformation* 17.1 (January–March 2000), pp. 26–29

Glen Eyrie Report: Muslim Evangelization: Report of the North American Conference on Muslim Evangelization, October 15–21, 1978, Lausanne Occasional Papers no. 4, Lausanne Committee for World Evangelization

Goldsmith, Martin, *Islam and Christian Witness* (London: Hodder & Stoughton, 1982)

Gorman, Ulf, *Towards a New Understanding of Conversion* (Lund: Teologiska Institutionen, 1999)

Green, Michael, *The Truth of God Incarnate* (London: Hodder & Stoughton, 1977)

Guidelines for Interfaith Dialogue (Ecumenical Office of the Anglican Church of Canada, Toronto, 1986)

Guidelines for Interfaith Dialogue (Office of Ecumenical and Interfaith Relations, Presbyterian Church [USA]: Louisville, KY, 1969)

Guidelines on Dialogue with People of Living Faiths and Ideologies (Geneva: WCC, 1979)

Habib, Gabriel, 'Muslim–Christian Dialogue in the Middle East', *MECC Newsreport* 7/7–10 (July–October 1994), pp. 20–27

Haddad, Yvonne Yazbeck, 'The Globalization of Islam: The Return of Muslims to the West', in John L. Esposito (ed.), *The Oxford History of Islam* (Oxford: Oxford University Press, 1999), pp. 601–641

Halliday, Fred, *Two Hours that Shook the World* (London: Saqi Books, 2002)

Harris, Myles, *Tomorrow is Another Country* (London: Civitas, 2003)

Haslam, David, *Race for the Millennium* (London: Church House Publishing, 1996)

Hassan bin Talal, 'Towards a World with 10,000 Cultures', *Discourse* 1 (August 2000), pp. 9–11

Hassan, Riaz, 'Muslim Relations in Australian Society', in Syed Z. Abedin and Ziauddin Sardar (eds.), *Muslim Minorities in the West* (London: Grey Seal, 1995), pp. 117–133

Hefner, Robert W. (ed.), *Conversion to Christianity: Historical and Anthropological Perspectives on a Great Transformation* (Berkeley and Los Angeles, CA, and Oxford: University of California Press, 1993)

Heywood, A., *Political Ideologies: An Introduction* (Basingstoke: Macmillan, 1998)

Hicks, Peter, *Truth: Could it Be True?* (Carlisle: Solway, 1996)

Hooker, Roger, and Lamb, Christopher, *Love the Stranger* (London: SPCK, 1986)

Howarth, Toby, '9/11: A Call to Integrity in Mission', *CMS Annual Sermon 2002* (London: Church Mission Society, 2002)

— 'The Church Facing Islam in Western Europe', *Transformation* 20/4 (October 200), pp. 229–231

Huntington, Samuel P., *The Clash of Civilizations and the Remaking of World Order* (New York: Simon & Schuster, 1996)

Hur, Eun-ah, *Evolving Terminology in Interfaith Relations: Paradigm Shifts and the World Council of Churches* (MTh dissertation, London Bible College, Brunel University, 2000)

Husband, C., 'The Political Context of Muslim Communities' Participation in British Society', in B. Lewis and D. Schnapper (eds.), *Muslims in Europe* (London: Pinter, 1994), pp. 79–97

Ibn Abi Zayd al-Qayrawani, 'Abd Allah ibn 'Abd al-Rahman, *Al-Risala* (London: Ta-Ha, 1999)

In Good Faith: The Four Principles of Interfaith Dialogue: A Brief Guide for the Churches (London: CCBI, 1991)

Inter Faith Network for the UK, 1999–2000 Annual Review (London)

Interfaith Dialogue: The Teaching of the Catholic Church (Committee for Other Faiths, Catholic Bishops' Conference of England and Wales, 2002)

Ipgrave, Michael (ed.), *Scriptures in Dialogue: Christians and Muslims Studying the Bible and the Qur'an Together* (London: Church House Publishing, 2004)

— (ed.), *The Road Ahead: A Christian–Muslim Dialogue* (London: Church House Publishing, 2002)

Islamophobia: A Challenge for Us All (London: Runnymede Trust, 1997)

Jacobson, J., *Islam in Transition: Religion and Identity among British Pakistani Youth* (London: Routledge, 1998)

John Paul II, Pope, *Crossing the Threshold of Hope* (London: Jonathan Cape, 1993)

Johns, Anthony H., 'In Search of Common Ground: The Qur'an as Literature?', *Islam and Christian–Muslim Relations* 4/3 (December 1993), pp. 191–209

— 'Muslim Communities in Australia: An Opportunity for Inter-Faith Conciliation', *Hamdard Islamicus* xx/3 (July–September 1997), pp. 7–22

Jomier, Jacques, *How to Understand Islam* (London: SCM, 1989)

Kabbani, Muhammad Hisham, 'The Muslim Experience in America is Unprecedented', *Middle East Quarterly*, June 2000

Kateregga, Badru D., and Shenk, David W., *Islam and Christianity: A Muslim and Christian in Dialogue* (Grand Rapids, MI: Eerdmans, 1980)

Kaye, Bruce, 'Many Aspects of Pluralism', *St Mark's Review* 171 (Spring 1997), pp. 2–5

Kenny, Joseph, OP, *Views on Christian–Muslim Relations* (Lagos: Dominican Publications, 1999)

Kerr, David A., 'Christian–Muslim Relations: Lessons from History', in Michael Ipgrave (ed.), *The Road Ahead: A Christian—Muslim Dialogue* (London: Church House Publishing, 2002), pp. 26–37

— 'The Challenge of Islamic Fundamentalism for Christians', *International Bulletin of Missionary Research* 17/4 (October 1993), pp. 169–172

Khairanvi, M. M., Rahmatullah, *Izhar-ul-Haq (Truth Revealed): Contradictions and Errors in the Biblical Text*, 2nd edn (Jeddah: World of Knowledge for Publishing and Distribution, 1992)

Khan, Muhammad Muhsin (trans.), *The Translation of the Meanings of Sahih Al-Bukhari* (Medina: Dar Ahya us-Sunnah al Nabawiya, 1971)

Khodr, M. Georges, 'Christians in their Relationship with Islam – Spiritual Perspectives', *MECC Perspectives* 4/5 (July–August 1985), pp. 20–22

Kimball, Charles, *Striving Together: A Way Forward in Christian–Muslim Relations* (Maryknoll, NY: Orbis, 1991)

Knitter, Paul F., *No Other Name? A Critical Survey of Christian Attitudes Towards the World Religions* (Maryknoll, NY: Orbis, 1985)

Kuitse, Roelf S., 'Christology in the Qur'an', *Missiology: An International Review* 20/3 (July 1992), pp. 355–369

Kung, Hans, and Moltmann, J. (eds.) *Islam: A Challenge for Christianity* (London: SCM, 1994)

Lamb, Winifred, 'Intellectual Eros: A Model for Inter-Faith Dialogue', *Australian Religion Studies Review* 7/1 (Autumn 1994), pp. 2–7

Lester, Toby, 'What is the Koran?', *Atlantic Monthly* (January 1999), pp. 43–56

Lewis, Bernard, *The Jews of Islam* (London: Routledge & Kegan Paul, 1984)

Lewis, Philip, 'Christian–Muslim Relations in Britain', in Anthony O'Mahony and Ataullah Siddiqui (eds.), *Christians and Muslims in the Commonwealth* (London: Altajir World of Islam Trust, 2001), pp. 182–197

— 'Muslims in Europe: Managing Multiple Identities and Learning Shared Citizenship', *Political Theology* (forthcoming)

— *Islamic Britain: Religion, Politics and Identity among British Muslims: Bradford in the 1990s* (London: I. B. Tauris, 1994)

— *The Functions, Education and Influence of the 'Ulama in Bradford's Muslim Communities* (Leeds: University of Leeds, Department of Theology and Religious Studies, 1996)

Lochhead, David, *The Dialogical Imperative: A Christian Reflection on Interfaith Encounter* (London: SCM, 1988)

McCurry, Don M. (ed.), *The Gospel and Islam: A 1978 Compendium* (Monrovia, CA: Missions Advanced Research and Communication Center, 1979)

McRoy, Anthony, *Rushdie's Legacy: The Emergence of a Radical British Muslim Identity* (PhD dissertation, London Bible College, Brunel University, 2001)

Mahathir Bin Mohamad, 'Globalization: What it Means to Small Nations', speech at the Inaugural Lecture of the Prime Ministers of Malaysia Fellowship Exchange Programme, Kuala Lumpur, 24 July 1996

— 'Speech at the Opening of the World *Ulama* Conference, Putrajaya Marriot Hotel, Putrajaya, 10 July 2003', <http://www.bernama.com/events/ulama/rspeech.shtml?speech/se0608_pm>

Masood, Steven, *The Bible and the Qur'an* (Carlisle: OM Publishing, 2001)

Mazrui, Ali, 'Globalization and the Future of Islamic Civilization', lecture given at Westminster University, London, 3 September 2000

Meeting in Faith: Twenty Years of Christian–Muslim Conversations Sponsored by the World Council of Churches (Geneva: WCC Publications, 1989)

Middleton, J. R., and Walsh, B. J., *Truth is Stranger than it Used to Be: Biblical Faith in a Postmodern Age* (London: SPCK, 1995)

Miller, William, *A Christian's Response to Islam* (Bromley, Kent: STL Books, 1986)

Mission, Dialogue and Inter Religious Encounter: A Consultative Document (London: The Inter Faith Network for the UK, 1993)

Mitri, Tarek, 'Christian–Muslim Relations', *Current Dialogue* 31 (December 1997), pp. 43–44.

Mohammed, Ovey N., *Muslim–Christian Relations: Past, Present and Future* (Maryknoll, NY: Orbis, 1999)

Moucarry, Chawkat, *Faith to Faith: Christianity and Islam in Dialogue* (Leicester: IVP, 2001)

— *The Search for Forgiveness* (Leicester: IVP, 2004)

Murad, Khurram, *Islamic Movement in the West: Reflections on Some Issues* (Leicester: Islamic Foundation, no date)

Musk, Bill, *The Unseen Face of Islam* (Eastbourne: MARC, 1989)

Nasr, Seyyed Hossein, *Islamic Life and Thought* (London: Allen & Unwin, 1981)

— *Knowledge and the Sacred* (New York: Crossroad, 1981)

Nazir-Ali, Michael, *Frontiers in Muslim–Christian Encounter* (Oxford: Regnum, 1987)

— *Islam: A Christian Perspective* (Exeter: Paternoster, 1983)

— *Mission and Dialogue: Proclaiming the Gospel Afresh in Every Age* (London: SPCK, 1995)

Netland, Harold A., *Dissonant Voices: Religious Pluralism and the Question of Truth* (Leicester: Apollos, 1991)

Newbigin, Lesslie, *The Gospel in a Pluralist Society* (London: SPCK, 1989)

Newbigin, Lesslie, Sanneh, Lamin, and Taylor, Jenny, *Faith and Power: Christianity and Islam in 'Secular' Britain* (London: SPCK, 1998)

Nielsen, J., *Muslims in Western Europe* (Edinburgh: Edinburgh University Press, 1992)

— *Towards a European Islam* (Basingstoke: Macmillan, in association with the Centre for Research in Ethnic Relations, University of Warwick, 1999)

O'Brien, Mike, 'The Threat of the Modern Kharijites', speech at the conference 'Militant Islam in Asia: The Challenges', Royal United Service Institute for Defence Studies, London, 21 November 2002

Okin, Susan M., 'Reply', in Joshua Cohen, Matthew Howard and Martha C. Nussbaum (eds.), *Is Multiculturalism Bad for Women?* (Princeton, NJ: Princeton University Press, 1999), pp. 115–132

Oldham Riots, The: Discrimination, Deprivation and Communal Tension in the United Kingdom (Islamic Human Rights Commission, June 2001)

O'Mahony, Anthony, 'Christianity, Interreligious Dialogue and Muslim–Christian Relations', in Anthony O'Mahony and Michael Kirwan (eds.), *World Christianity: Politics, Theology, Dialogues* (London: Melisende, 2004, pp. 63–92)

— 'Christians and Muslim–Christian Relations: Theological Reflections', in Anthony O'Mahony and Ataullah Siddiqui (eds.), *Christians and Muslims in the Commonwealth* (London: Altajir World of Islam Trust, 2001), pp. 90–128

— 'Islam Face-à-Face Christianity', *The Way Supplement 104* (November 2002), pp. 75–85

O'Mahony, Anthony, Peterburs, Wulstan, and Shomali, Mohammad Ali (eds.), *A Catholic–Shi'a Dialogue: Studies in Theology and Spirituality* (London: Melisende, 2004)

O'Mahony, Anthony, and Siddiqui, Ataullah (eds.), *Christians and Muslims in the Commonwealth* (London, Altajir World of Islam Trust, 2001)

Ouseley, Herman, *Community Pride not Prejudice: Making Diversity Work in Bradford* (Bradford Vision, 2001)

Pakistan: Use and Abuse of the Blasphemy Laws, ASA 33/08/94 (London: Amnesty International, 1994)

Parekh, Bhikhu, *The Future of Multi-Ethnic Britain* (the Parekh Report) (London: Profile, 2000)

Parshall, Phil, *Bridges to Islam: A Christian Perspective on Folk Islam* (Grand Rapids, MI: Baker, 1983)

Paul VI, Pope, *Ecclesiam suam*, 6 August 1964

Pawson, David, *The Challenge of Islam to Christians* (London: Hodder & Stoughton, 2003)

Pearl, David, 'The Application of Islamic Law in the English Courts', the 1995 Noel Coulson Memorial Lecture, London: Centre of Islamic and Middle Eastern Law, School of Oriental and African Studies

Peters, Ruud, 'Islamic Law and Human Rights: A Contribution to an Ongoing Debate', *Islam and Christian–Muslim Relations* 10/1 (1999), pp. 5–14

Petros VII, Patriarch of Alexandria, 'Christianity and Islam in Dialogue', address of His Beatitude to the 12th International Meeting 'People and Religion', 31 August 1998

Pfander, C. G., *The Mizan-ul-Haqq (Balance of Truth)*, ed. W. St Clair-Tisdall (Villach: Light of Life, 1986)

Pollitt, Herbert J., *The Inter-faith Movement: The New Age Enters the Church* (Edinburgh: Banner of Truth, 1996)

Popper, Karl, *The Open Society and its Enemies 2: The High Tide of Prophecy: Hegel, Marx and the Aftermath*, 4th edn (London: Routledge & Kegan Paul, 1962)

Pratt, Douglas, 'Christian–Muslim Encounter: From Diatribe to Dialogue',' *Australian Religion Studies Review* 7/1 (Autumn 1994), pp. 8–15

— *Identity and Interaction: Islam and the Challenge of Interreligious Dialogue* (the Charles Strong Memorial Trust Lecture 1999, Sydney)

— 'Phenomenology and Dialogue: A Methodological Consideration', *Islam and Christian–Muslim Relations* 5/1 (1994), pp. 5–13

Race, Alan, *Interfaith Encounter: The Twin Tracks of Theology and Dialogue* (London: SCM, 2001)

Ramachandra, Vinoth, *Faiths in Conflict? Christian Integrity in a Multicultural World* (Leicester: IVP, 1999)

Randall, Ian, *Educating Evangelicalism: The Origins, Development and Impact of London Bible College* (Carlisle: Paternoster, 2000)

Rath, J., Pennix, R,, Groenendijk, K., and Meyer, A., *Western Europe and its Islam* (Leiden: Brill, 2001)

Raza, Mohammad S., *Islam in Britain: Past, Present and the Future* (Leicester: Volcano, 1991)

Reciprocity and Beyond: A Muslim Response to the European Churches' Document on Islam (Leicester: Islamic Foundation, 1997)

Richards, Matt, 'Islamic Contracts of Finance in Malaysia', *Studia Islamika: Indonesian Journal for Islamic Studies* 10/1 (2003), pp. 161–200

Riddell, Peter G., 'In Search of Muhammad: A Review Essay', *Australian Religion Studies Review* 12/2 (Spring 1999), pp. 155–160

— *Islam and the Malay-Indonesian World: Transmission and Responses* (London: C. Hurst & Co., 2001)

Riddell, Peter G., and Cotterell, Peter, *Islam in Conflict: Past, Present and Future* (Leicester: IVP, 2003)

Rippin, Andrew, *Muslims: Their Religious Beliefs and Practices*, 2nd edn (London: Routledge, 2001)

Rippin, Andrew, and Knappert, Jan (eds.), *Textual Sources for the Study of Islam* (Chicago, IL: University of Chicago Press, 1986)

Saifi, Naseem, *Presenting Islam to the Christians* (Rabwah, Pakistan: Tabshir, 1973)

Sanneh, Lamin, 'Can a House Divided Stand? Reflections on Christian–Muslim Encounter in the West', *International Bulletin of Missionary Research* (October 1993), pp. 164–168
— *Encountering the West* (London: Marshall Pickering, 1993)
— *Translating the Message: The Missionary Impact on Culture* (Maryknoll, KY: Orbis, 1989)
Sanson, Henri, *Dialogue intérieur avec l'Islam* (Paris: Centurion, 1990)
Scattolin, G., 'Spirituality in Interreligious Dialogue: Challenge and Promise', *Encounter* 274 (April 2001)
Sharpe, Eric J., 'Dialogue of Religions', in Mircea Eliade (ed.), *The Encyclopedia of Religion* 4 (New York: Macmillan, 1987), pp. 344–348
Shenk, David W., 'Muslims and Christians: Finding Doors Through the Walls', *Mission Focus* 1 (1993), pp. 39–44
Siddiqi, Abdul Hamid (trans.), *Sahih Muslim,* 4 volumes (Lahore: Sh. Muhammad Ashraf Publishers, reprinted 1996)
Siddiqui, Ataullah, *Christian–Muslim Dialogue in the 20th Century* (London: Macmillan, 1997)
— 'Issues in Co-existence and Dialogue: Muslims and Christians in Britain', in Jacques Waardenburg, *Muslim–Christian Perceptions of Dialogue Today* (Leuven: Peeters, 2000), pp. 194–195
— 'The Presence of "Secular" in Christian–Muslim Relations: Reflections on the Da'wah, "Mission" and "Dialogue"', in Anthony O'Mahony and Ataullah Siddiqui (eds.), *Christians and Muslims in the Commonwealth* (London: Altajir World of Islam Trust, 2001), pp. 67–89
Siddiqui, Kalim, *The Implications of the Rushdie Affair for Muslims in Britain* (London: Muslim Institute, 1989)
Slomp, Jan, '"One World for All": The Vienna Dialogue Process', *Journal of Muslim Minority Affairs* 18/1 (1998), pp. 181–185
Smith, Jay, 'Courage in our Convictions, Debating Muslims: New Life for an Old Method?' *Evangelical Missions Quarterly* 31/1 (January 1998), pp. 28–35
Sookhdeo, Patrick, *A People Betrayed* (Fearn, Ross-shire: Christian Focus Publications, 2002)
St Clair-Tisdall, W., 'The Sources of Islam', in Ibn Warraq (ed.), *The Origins of the Koran: Classic Essays on Islam's Holy Book* (Amherst, NY: Prometheus, 1998), pp. 227–292
Stacey, Vivienne, *Mission Ventured: Dynamic Stories Across a Challenging World* (Leicester: IVP, 2001)
Stott, John, *Christian Mission in the Modern World* (Downers Grove, IL: IVP, 1975)
Straw, Jack, 'The United Kingdom and the Muslim World', speech in Jakarta, 9 January 2003
Sweetman, J. W., *Islam and Christian Theology,* 3 volumes (London: Lutterworth, 1945)
Swidler, Leonard, *Toward a Universal Theology of Religion* (Maryknoll, NY: Orbis, 1987)
Talbi, Mohamed, 'Islamo–Christian Encounter Today, Some Principles', *MECC Perspectives* 4/5 (July–August 2001), pp. 7–11
Thailand Report on Muslims, Report of the Consultation on World Evangelization, mini-consultation on reaching Muslims, held in Pattaya, Thailand, 16–27 June 1980, Lausanne Occasional Papers no. 13, Lausanne Committee for World Evangelization
Thomas, David, and Amos, Clare (eds.), *A Faithful Presence: Essays for Kenneth Cragg* (London: Melisende, 2003)
Tibawi, A. L., 'Christians under Muhammad and his first two Caliphs', *Islamic Quarterly* 6/1–2 (1961), pp. 30–46
Tidball, Derek J., *Who Are the Evangelicals?* (London: Marshall Pickering, 1994)
Towards a Common Understanding and Vision of the World Council of Churches, policy statement, Central Committee of the World Council of Churches, September 1997
Troll, Christian, 'Germany's Islamic Charter', *Encounter* 290 (December 2002)
Turabi, Hassan Abdullah Al-, 'Opinion on Apostasy Stirs a Heated Debate in Islamic Juristic Circles', *The Diplomat* 2 (Muharram 1417 / June 1996), pp. 38–39

Vertovec, S., 'Muslims, the State, and the Public Sphere in Britain', in G. Nonneman, T. Niblock and B. Szajkowski, *Muslim Communities in the New Europe* (Reading: Ithaca, 199), pp. 169–186
'Wa-Ghana: An Example of Christian–Muslim Dialogue in Ghana', *Pro Dialogo* 93/3 (1996), pp. 379–380
Waardenburg, Jacques, 'Between Baghdad and Birmingham: Minorities – Christian and Muslim', *Islam and Christian–Muslim Relations* 14/1 (2003), pp. 3–22
— (ed.), *Islam and Christianity: Mutual Perceptions since the Mid-20th Century* (Leuven: Peeters, 1998)
— (ed.), *Muslim–Christian Perceptions of Dialogue Today: Experiences and Expectations* (Leuven: Peeters, 2000)
Waddy, Charis, 'The People of the Book: A New Chapter in Co-operation', *Islamic Quarterly* 23/4 (1979), pp. 195–203
Watt, W., Montgomery, *Islam and Christianity Today: A Contribution to Dialogue* (London: Routledge and Kegan Paul, 1983)
Westophobia Report: Anti-Western and Anti-Christian Stereotyping in British Muslim Publications (Centre for Islamic Studies, London Bible College, 1999)
Williams, I. G., 'Fundamentalist Movements within British Islam', in C. Partridge (ed.), *Fundamentalisms* (Carlisle: Paternoster, 2001), pp. 75–92
Wingate, Andrew, *Encounters in the Spirit: Muslim–Christian Meetings in Birmingham* (Geneva: WCC, 1988)
Woodberry, J. Dudley (ed.), *Muslims and Christians on the Emmaus Road* (Monrovia, CA: MARC, 1989)
Yannoulatos, Anastasios, 'Byzantine and Contemporary Greek Orthodox Approaches to Islam', *Journal of Ecumenical Studies* 33/4 (Fall 1996), pp. 512–527
Zebiri, Kate, *Muslims and Christians Face to Face* (Oxford: Oneworld, 1997)

Audiovisual resources

Anis Matta, M., *Membangun Peradaban Alternatif*, audiocassette (Bandung: Ummul Quro Bandung, no date)
Are All Religions the Same?, Anglican TV (Australia), 1994
Charles: The Private Man, The Public Role, Central Television, UK, 1994
Haj: The Journey of a Lifetime, BBC, 2001
'Happy Families', *East*, BBC, 1996
Islam, Empire of Faith, The Messenger, BBC, 2001
My Name is Ahmed, BBC, 2001
Prince Naseem's Guide to Islam, BBC, 2001
'The Asylum Game', *Panorama*, BBC, 2003
'The Enemy Within?', *Tonight*, Channel 4, 2004
The Mosque, BBC, 2001
There's a Mosque in my Street, programme 2: *Islam in Britain*, (London: London Bible College, Centre for Islamic Studies and Muslim–Christian Relations, 1999)

INDEX